GALLAGHER

GALLAGHER
P.J. HARRISON

SPHERE

SPHERE

First published in 2025 by Sphere

1 3 5 7 9 10 8 6 4 2

Copyright © PJ Harrison 2025

The moral right of the author has been asserted.

All rights reserved.
No part of this publication may be reproduced, stored in a retrieval system, or transmitted, in any form, or by any means, without the prior permission in writing of the publisher, nor be otherwise circulated in any form of binding or cover other than that in which it is published and without a similar condition including this condition being imposed on the subsequent purchaser.

A CIP catalogue record for this book is available from the British Library.

Hardback ISBN 978-1-4087-2387-6
Trade paperback ISBN 978-1-4087-2388-3

Typeset in Sabon by M Rules
Printed and bound in Great Britain by Clays Ltd, Elcograf S.p.A.

Papers used by Sphere are from well-managed forests and other responsible sources.

Sphere
An imprint of
Little, Brown Book Group
Carmelite House
50 Victoria Embankment
London EC4Y 0DZ

The authorised representative
in the EEA is
Hachette Ireland
8 Castlecourt Centre
Dublin 15, D15 XTP3, Ireland
(email: info@hbgi.ie)

An Hachette UK Company
www.hachette.co.uk

www.littlebrown.co.uk

Contents

Foreword	1
Introduction	3
The Past is Prelude: Oasis 1992–2009	15
1 Waiting for the Rapture – Liam, 2009	21
2 The Death of You and Me – Noel, 2009	37
3 The Roller – Liam, 2010–11	47
4 Flying High – Noel, 2010–11	65
5 Second Bite of the Apple – Liam, 2012–14	83
6 You Know We Can't Go Back – Noel, 2012–14	99
7 For What It's Worth – Liam, 2015–17	113
8 Keep On Reaching – Noel, 2015–17	129
9 Why Me? – Liam, 2018–19	141
10 This is the Place – Noel, 2018–19	149
11 One of Us, 2019	159

12	Bring it on Down – Noel and Liam, 1972–93	167
13	Supersonic – Noel and Liam, 1994–6	187
14	Some Might Say – Noel and Liam, 1997	201
15	Fade In-Out – Noel and Liam, 1997–2009	211
16	Too Good for Giving Up – Liam, 2020–1	233
17	Back the Way We Came – Noel, 2020–1	243
18	Just Another Rainbow – Liam, 2022–4	251
19	Trying to Find a World That's Been and Gone – Noel, 2022–4	259
20	Hello – Noel and Liam, 2024	273
	Acknowledgements	293
	Endnotes	295

Foreword

So, I first met PJ at Vancouver Airport. I'd gone out there with Mickey Rourke, the car, not the actor, and he had written to me.[*] I believe it was about my book or something similar to my book. He wrote a very good letter. He writes and does a very good everything. I invited him. And there I was at Vancouver Airport when PJ came sailing through. I think I had brought him to go on a film scam. I have to look that up in the dictionary ... yes, 'film scam', page 47B.[†] The film scam didn't work out, but *we* did ... Well, the people were below us. It was like, you know, pitching for a Richard Attenborough B movie when you come in all Daniel Craig and A. And we just hit it off. And that's what one does with PJ. And that's the great thing to remember about him, as he comes now into your

---

[*] Some help with the Loogisms ...
Mickey Rourke was the name of Andrew's lovely black town car, so named after he took a shine to a similar set of wheels from one of Rourke's films. It was adorned by personalised plates reading 'OLD PRO'.
[†] It wasn't an actual scam.

life: just be a conduit. Just be open. You will hit it off. And he will be good for you. Just let him.

Andrew Loog Oldham

Introduction

27.08.24

The six digits that pulsed on the big screens immediately after Blossoms' Wythenshawe Park headline set confirmed that the seemingly impossible was happening. The date, framed in Brian Cannon's iconic early Decca-style Oasis logo, told the whole music world that the guns had indeed 'fallen silent' and a sibling truce had been struck. Fans, like myself, from all over the world set time aside for the impending ticket scramble come 8 a.m. on 27 August – almost fifteen years to the day since another sign had flashed on another set of big screens, telling a French festival crowd that Oasis had cancelled their performance. After Noel and Liam seemingly did each other's heads in for good. Rocking-horse droppings were easier to come by than reunion tour tickets when Ticketmaster clicked the big dynamic pricing button at 8 a.m. that day. It had seemed like the chance of Oasis ever playing together again had passed. For a long time, Liam had lobbied for it before going cold. Then Noel had opened the door slightly, caveated by a big enough bag of cash. But neither was on the same page at the same time. Shocker. When it did happen it happened fast and with an impressive level of secrecy.

This book was originally conceived as a dual biography of both Liam and Noel's respective solo careers. It's an aspect of their lives that I found fascinating and felt was underappreciated. The public image of them remains hard boiled in the lager-drinking, V-sign-waving mould of nineties tabloid headlines. Their artistic evaluations remain lazy, built on the back of early mentions of T. Rex and the Beatles. Oasis, and the Gallaghers, deserve a fresh perspective. As it happened, the band announced their reunion just as I was working on it. That seismically altered context now frames this as the story of the brothers' journey from breakup to reunion. It's written by a fan who lived an *Almost Famous*-esque experience. I went from a teenager queuing at record shops to buy their CD singles to going on the road with Oasis and even spending time in the studio with them as they recorded *Dig Out Your Soul*. It was an extraordinary experience and a gift for the teenage self.

Above all, this is a book about family and what it is to wear the name Gallagher. It shows them as individuals, both within and without the context of brotherhood. They have both achieved huge success as solo stars in the years since Oasis broke up and have both had various personal challenges to contend with during that time. The Liam and Noel we see today are significantly developed from those who bolted from the traps in the heat of *Definitely*

Maybe. That said, their dynamic remains arrested. Their disharmony, stuck in adolescence, has fascinated music fans for decades. Why is it these two don't get on? How does the trauma of their childhood still drive the volatile chemistry at the heart of Oasis, and how does it shape their personal lives? Hopefully we can get close to the heart of these questions. I hope any journalists who read this book keep those aspects in mind when covering the band in the future and apply appropriate humanity to their descriptions.

I'll start by saying I have a huge amount of respect for any self-made individual who has excelled at the top of a highly competitive field. Especially if they're from a northern council estate. And especially if they're from a difficult home. For those unfamiliar with Britain's geographic and class divide, the easiest way to explain it is to say *Game of Thrones* isn't entirely pulled from its author's imagination, with its portrayal of those in the south as wealthy sophisticates, while those in the freezing north are simple and brutish, and those beyond the wall (i.e. Hadrian's Wall) are red-haired wildlings. This is essentially how the country is sometimes viewed by some of its more advantaged populous.

I grew up in the same class and geographical space as the Gallaghers. I saw very close up just how hard life can be for some children and wives when the home is not a sanctuary. Media portrayals of these two men are almost always lacking in empathy when it comes to this aspect. Often their incredible achievements are obscured by naked classism in the British media. Noel and Liam Gallagher are the most uniquely successful and fascinating siblings in the history of British music. They transcended the art form and cast a monobrowed shadow over the British cultural landscape for decades. Two lads from a Moss Side-adjacent council estate who shook the world, Noel and Liam occupy two digits on the single hand required to count the number of former British band members who have succeeded as solo acts at this level. It's an extraordinary accomplishment from uniquely different siblings.

As for my experience, Oasis changed my life. The first time I heard them, it felt like someone had fired a starting gun in my brain and real life had begun. I was crammed into the back of a school minibus staring into the pitch-black night through the condensation-coated window as we headed to a biology residential in soggy Wales, just a few miles from Monnow Valley, where *Definitely Maybe* had been recorded. One of the lads at the front of the bus had insisted on playing his new tape. He clunked the play button, and it rattled from the bus's tinny speakers: Noel's siren of a guitar clearing the approach for the supersonic vocal flyby of Liam's opening line of 'Rock 'n' Roll Star'. The dozen or so captive teen minds being driven to that educational black site all stopped what they weren't doing and tuned in. Liam's snarling Lydon-meets-Lennon delivery of a line about his dreams being real in his head landed just right for this committed daydreamer with a northern chip on his shoulder. The droning promise of a weekend poking at Welsh wildlife didn't seem so bad now that we had this. This wasn't just music – it was a declaration. Nothing was ever the same for me after that. In the eighteen months that followed, they became the biggest band on the planet and defined nineties culture.

The third Oasis album dropped on school results day. I sacked off the trip to my school and discovery of my grades, and headed to HMV to get my hands on the third Oasis album the moment it was released. The record's title, *Be Here Now* (an album I later had the surreal experience of defending to its writer), was a mandate. I knew exam results paled in significance to rock 'n' roll. The anticipation and excitement had swelled to a generation-defining phenomenon. National news outlets dispatched outside-broadcast crews to document the moment the first copies were bought. I grabbed that LP like it was a ticket to the future and gorged on the songs and the accompanying artwork. It was more than simply music; it was the cresting wave of the 'Cool Britannia' tsunami that had swelled over the previous few years and swept away me and millions of others.

A month or so later, I saw my first Oasis concert at Sheffield Arena and, a month after that, my second at Manchester G-Mex. The hours spent freezing my arse off in line to secure a place on the barrier, right in front of Noel, were worth it. It was pure adrenaline, free-based through the ears. I was hooked as they played one decade-defining anthem after another. Loudly ... very loudly. My ears rang well into the next week. I treasured the temporary tinnitus. I'd earned those high-frequency rings. The last resonance of the guitar chords, smashed through Noel's stacked Marshall cabs, stuck with me for days. They were aural battle scars. I began to scramble together money from my part-time jobs and bought a Squier Stratocaster. It wasn't a good guitar by any stretch nor my preferred style (an Epiphone Sheraton, of course), but it's all I could afford, and it meant I could play these life-affirming songs myself, so it was good enough.

The impact Oasis had on people my age, especially in the northwest of England, was profound. Their music instilled a sense of belief and possibility. For the minutes those songs played, we had the feeling we could achieve anything. The representation my particular class had seen of itself in the media until then had been largely as criminal or thick. Seeing lads from where I was from, who looked and dressed like me and my mates, suddenly opened the world up, and it even became cool to be an Umbro-clad northern lad. It was a collective refuge for optimism. From now on, anything was possible.

Years later, in my twenties, after following the path floodlit by my Mancunian musical epiphany, I started my own record label as a joint venture with Sony Music. As part of the same division as Oasis's label, Creation, no less. Oasis became fans of some of the bands I signed, and I had the incredible opportunity to tour with the Gallaghers across the UK and the US on a few occasions. I got to experience their energy first-hand from the side of the stage, played football on empty pitches before the stadium doors opened, chatted at catering and hung out in their dressing room after shows.

As the years moved on, I became friendly with several of the band and their circle, socialising from time to time. On one occasion, a mate and I dropped by the

LA recording studio where they were recording *Dig Out Your Soul*. I sat in the live room, and we all (minus Liam who was AWOL) chatted while the producer, Dave Sardy, compiled tracks in the control room. Noel lined up a sequence of YouTube videos that had tickled him. We watched one after another on his laptop until we literally cried with laughter. Among those he was enjoying that particular week were videos featuring an Iraqi soldier who fell over each time the rifle he was firing kicked back, and the 'Santana Shreds' video, which is a masterpiece of comic overdubbing.

These experiences further galvanised my enthusiasm for the Gallagher brothers and deepened my understanding of them as people. By chance, I attended their last-ever show. When I heard of the breakup a few days later, I couldn't help but recall something Liam had said the last time I'd seen him. I've always suspected Liam of being shy or perhaps suffering a degree of stage fright before his big shows. He tends to keep himself to himself more than Noel and the others, saying warm hellos while never stopping for conversation. The younger Gallagher brother is a man who both literally and figuratively grabs people by the balls ... I remember when we were in the England dressing room at Wembley Stadium, post-show. Liam has arguably the world's most identifiable gait, and it was now swaggering towards me, feet at ten and two. He stopped, clutched my crotch, looked me in the eye and with a half-smile, said 'All right?'

For a while now, 'All right' had been the only word Liam and I had ever exchanged. We'd had entire conversations on a daily basis with just 'All right?' Certain words in the northern lexicon are incredibly versatile, and 'all right' is up there with 'mate' for usefulness.

'Let's have that fuckin' drink then,' he continued as he gestured to the fully loaded fridge.

During that drink and those subsequent, Liam began to express his boredom at playing 'the same shows', as he put it. He didn't share my wonderment at the fact we were sitting on the same seats where Wayne Rooney, David Beckham and the rest of the Three Lions sat to prepare for a home international. But why would he? This wasn't his first dance. He had a long and chequered history with this particular stadium and, anyway, he's Irish at heart. He expressed it with his customary articulate directness: 'It's the same fuckin' show every night. It's boring, man.'

I'd argued that playing Wembley Stadium to tens of thousands of fans isn't that boring, but he was stuck in his thought. He gazed into the middle distance. The horizon of his hinterland was a distant destination to that of mine. A month later, he wouldn't have to worry about the tedium of playing Wembley Stadium or any Oasis shows ever again. They had broken up. This time for good. Or so we thought . . .

Hard to believe it has been over a decade and a half since Noel and Liam's volatile chemistry imploded Oasis. The now estranged brothers have charted their own paths, becoming two distinct solo artists. The music of Liam and Noel Gallagher continues to resonate with me on a visceral level, each brother offering something unique that speaks to different aspects of my life, and the lives of millions around the world. Noel's music is a tapestry of uplifting introspection. His lyrics project emotions, offering solace without ever being too direct. With Noel Gallagher's High Flying Birds, he's ventured into new sonic territories – electronica, orchestration, anything that sparks his creative curiosity. He retains a sense of vulnerability wrapped in lyrical opacity. His evolution as a solo artist, marked by his willingness to experiment, had long been hinted at during his time in Oasis, but the gravity of the band and its sound always kept him in the rock 'n' roll orbit. It's not always what Oasis fans want, but Noel's journey is his own, and he's stayed true to his vision, even in the face of criticism or commercial pressures.

Noel has a generational gift for melody, and solo success came swiftly – his debut album was a commercial and critical triumph. But as his music drifted away from the classic Oasis sound, some fans dropped off. Noel didn't care. He was exploring new frontiers, pushing the boundaries of what he could create. His music became more introspective, a reflection of a solitary artist carving out his own path.

The commercial and critical trajectories of their solo careers further underscore their individual significance. Noel experienced immediate success with his debut solo album. The acclaim for his initial work was a testament to his established reputation and his ability to innovate within the rock genre. However, as Noel's music moved away from the quintessential Oasis sound towards more expansive sonic territories, there was a gradual decline in live sales and radio exposure. This shift, while artistically fulfilling for Noel, highlighted the challenges of balancing personal artistic growth with audience expectations.

Liam, on the other hand, has seen an enormous resurgence in relevance and commercial success as a solo artist. His albums have topped charts, and his live performances have drawn massive crowds, reaffirming his enduring appeal. Liam's ability to channel the spirit of Oasis while injecting his own personality into his music has landed strongly with existing fans and a new generation. The swagger and bravado are pure, uncut type-A masculinity. He is an almost entirely unreconstructed megastar. Liam's presence is a celebration of confidence and defiance – a kid from nothing who acts like he owns everything. It is as bulletproof a stage persona as they come. His ability to connect with audiences purely through standing centre stage and occasionally shaking a tambourine is a unique frequency of magnetism in an industry defined by charisma. He has navigated his solo career by trusting the elemental nature that defined him during the Oasis years, while also showing an underrated development as a songwriter. His solo efforts, particularly, reflect a maturation in his writing and a willingness to collaborate with other musicians. His voice remains unlike any other. Liam Gallagher doesn't sing notes so much as buzzsaw through them. If you stand within earshot of one of Liam's stage monitors when he sings, it's like a jet plane taking off. His performances, with their raw energy and uniquely undulating swagger, are the essence of what made Oasis a phenomenon.

The legacy of Oasis had loomed large over both Noel and Liam. They are two men for ever measured against the eternal yardsticks of history and brotherhood, but both have managed to carve out distinct and vastly successful solo careers – a genuine rarity among history's great rock bands. Together they created something bigger than the sum of its parts and now they prepare to show the world once more the innate ability Oasis has to connect with audiences on a tribal level. Their concerts are more than just musical performances – they are communal celebrations of a shared cultural heritage and continue to inspire new generations. Their paths from single-parent, council-estate lads to global rock icons attest their perseverance and artistic integrity as much as talent. When an artist is relentlessly authentic, it allows people to believe in them and to believe in their work. And the Gallaghers believe in each other once more.

So here we are. The brothers are back together and preparing to share a stage for this first time since one of them threw a plum at the other in a Parisian dressing room back in 2009.

The Past is Prelude: Oasis 1992–2009

This book assumes the reader is coming to it as a fairly knowledgeable fan of the band and their history. If you're new to the Oasis phenomenon and less familiar with the history of the band, this section will serve as a little map to help you navigate the forward path. There's a good chunk of Oasis history in the pages ahead but this will see you right if you need a cheatsheet. Feel free to flick forward to the main event if you know your Oasistory.

Oasis covered a lot of ground in their seventeen years of noise and confusion. We'll jog through the story, starting in Manchester, 1992, when Noel joined Liam's band, the Rain, and Oasis properly began.

The original lineup consisted of Liam Gallagher on vocals, Paul 'Bonehead' Arthurs on guitar, Paul 'Guigsy' McGuigan on bass and Tony McCarroll on drums. Liam's older brother, Noel Gallagher, sat in with them in a rehearsal at Manchester's Boardwalk practice space and joined soon after. Noel brought his songwriting prowess and guitar skills to the band along with a degree of experience in the industry after touring the world as a member of fellow Mancunians Inspiral Carpets' road crew. Noel insisted on becoming the former Rain's only songwriter, and after playing them songs like 'Live Forever' that seemed a pretty good idea to all involved.

Oasis's debut album, *Definitely Maybe*, released in 1994, was an instant classic, becoming the fastest-selling debut album in UK history at the time. The album's raw energy and anthemic tracks like 'Supersonic' and 'Live Forever' captured the spirit of the era and catapulted Oasis to stardom.

The band's success continued with their second album, *(What's the Story) Morning Glory?*, released in 1995. The album included iconic mega-hits like 'Wonderwall' and 'Don't Look Back in Anger', cementing Oasis's place as one of the biggest bands in the world. *(What's the Story) Morning Glory?* remains the best-selling album recorded in the 1990s in the UK.

In 1995, Tony McCarroll was reportedly sacked from his own band by Noel, who felt that his drumming skills were not up to par with the band's growing ambitions. McCarroll later sued the band and received a settlement. He had been given a rough ride by the band, effectively being forced out, even being buried alive by the other band members in the 'Live Forever' music video.

McCarroll was replaced by Alan White, who became Oasis's longest-serving drummer, staying with the band until 2004. White's drumming style was more technically proficient than McCarroll's, and he was able to handle the complex rhythms of the band's later material. However, White was also known for his laid-back personality, which sometimes clashed with the more intense Gallagher brothers.

Oasis's meteoric rise to fame was accompanied by the brothers' infamous rivalry, which often spilled over into public spats and physical altercations. Despite the tensions, the band continued to produce hit albums and sell out massive concerts, including two legendary shows at Knebworth House in 1996, which were attended by over 250,000 fans.

In that same year, Liam Gallagher quit the band's American tour citing a pressing need to house hunt, leaving Noel to front the shows himself and arguably costing Oasis the chance to truly crack America. Liam returned to the band a few weeks later. Noel also quit the band on several occasions, most notably in 2000 after a fight with Liam during a concert in Spain. Noel later said that he was 'sick' of the band and that he needed to 'get away' from Liam. He floated the idea of pulling a Brian Wilson and leaving the band to tour without him while he focused on studio work. Guitarist Matt Deighton stood in for the remaining shows. However, Noel soon returned to Oasis.

The band's third album, *Be Here Now*, released in 1997, was a commercial success. In contemporary reviews it was also a critical hit, but over time reviews were rewritten and, viewed outside of its time period, even Noel became dismissive of the record. The album's wall-of-sound production and excessive length signalled a plateau in the band's creative force.

In 1999, McGuigan and Arthurs left the band, citing exhaustion (Guigsy) and creative differences (Bonehead). They were replaced by Gem Archer of Heavy Stereo on guitar and Andy Bell of Ride on bass. The new lineup released Oasis's fourth album, *Standing on the Shoulder of Giants*, in 2000.

When Alan White left in 2004, Oasis brought in Zak Starkey, the son of Ringo Starr and drummer in the Who. Starkey enhanced the band's more rock-driven tracks. Despite the enormous fame of his father he was a very low-key presence, often being able to walk through the front door of the arena an hour before stage time with barely a turned head. He was also relatively expensive to employ and travel with, and after Zak declined to leave the Who, the band turned to Chris Sharrock, who was known for his versatility and experience.

Oasis continued to tour and release albums throughout the 2000s. Critics never received the subsequent LPs with the same gusto as their early work but the band continued to be a behemoth of the touring world, monobrowed Godzillas glam stomping through the world's football stadia. The band's final album, *Dig Out Your Soul*, was released in 2008.

In 2009, Noel Gallagher announced his departure from the band after a backstage fight with Liam at a festival in Paris. The implosion brought one of the most successful, influential and controversial bands in British music history – as well as the relationship between the brothers Gallagher – to what appeared to be a permanent end.

1

Waiting for the Rapture – Liam, 2009

22 August: A Field in England

Fist raised. A defiant silhouette cuts through the blazing lights. Liam Gallagher's unmistakable, sweeping cadence breezes through the haze, a force of nature ready to meet the roaring and adoring crowd. As his big brother, Noel, loops the strap of his beautiful red Gibson over his head, his name rings out in bisyllabic terrace chant ... Liam, Liam, Liam. Oasis are about to smash through the 114th of 118 scheduled mega-gigs on their latest, year-long, tour. They're booked to headline England's dual-site V Festival, starting tonight in Staffordshire, before moving on to the Chelmsford location tomorrow.

The summer air, thick with anticipation and the aroma of stale fags, urine and a thousand spilled lagers, crackles with a primal static before turning eighty thousand people into one rolling mass when a single snare drum detonates the band's walk-on music, 'Fuckin' in the Bushes'. The snarling, swaggering, unapologetically brash intro rips through the night. It's a call to arms, a behavioural double dare for a festival crowd, and those gathered in this Staffordshire field respond as one.

Liam thrives on this, the connection with the crowd, the symbiotic relationship between performer and audience, the shared energy that surges back and forth, forming a tangible current that cracks through the air. As the sampled voices of peeved Isle of Wight residents and helter-skelteresque guitars fade from the speakers, he sneers four simple, monosyllabic words that ignite the tinderbox crowd. 'Rock 'n' Roll Star.'

That famously flat, almost nasal Mancunian accent, untouched by decades spent in north London's leafy suburbs, cuts through the roar like a razor blade. It's a statement of intent, a declaration of war on the mundane, the ordinary, the predictable.

This song from Oasis's debut album, released almost fifteen years earlier, has served as a manifesto for Liam, a blueprint for his life. He doesn't just sing the lyrics; he lives and breathes them. They are a design for life. His vocal tonight is an exorcism of rock 'n' roll's belligerent spirit. It is hope and ambition, bottled. As it rips through the masses, their voices join his and lift it into the twilight sky and beyond. He's not just singing to them; he's singing with them and for them. Tonight everyone is a Rock 'n' Roll Star. That's the point of Oasis. They deliver an uplifting, communal experience that makes the present euphoric and a better future seem possible.

Liam slowly scans the sea of faces rolling in front of him. It stretches beyond the neon fairground rides until the horizon is a hazy tide of limbs and faces, all moving as one. He offers a subtle nod, the raised chin and cocksure pout of a champion prizefighter concluding his ring walk, and then a glance to his left.

There he is. Noel. The anchoring presence in Liam's life since he came screaming into this world. The stoic, guitar-strumming yin to Liam's volatile, tambourine-swinging yang. His cherry guitar gleams under the lights. Two second-generation immigrant brothers from a broken council-estate home who joined their heroes at rock 'n' roll's big table. The music tonight is a visceral, primal force. It's not just heard; it's felt, deep in the bones, in the gut and in the soul. Liam, draped in one of his own Pretty Green olive parkas, stands loose and defiant – a sartorial middle finger to the world – exuding the effortless cool and era-defining swagger that has made him a legend. He is a rock 'n' roll icon for the ages. A man of few words on stage, fewer still that are actually intelligible to a swaying, beer-soaked crowd, but he doesn't need elaborate pronouncements or witty stage banter. His very presence is a statement, a performance in itself. He prowls the stage, his movements economical yet charged. It's a captivating sight, this display of controlled chaos.

The crowd's response grows into a lyrical roar, and a seismic push towards the barriers carries them nearer to their heroes. Liam is on top of the world, revelling in the riotous connection. He stands motionless between songs, eyeballing desperately adoring face after face, watching it all unfold. He thrives on the communal mayhem. It's a feeling that is amplified when he has his brother alongside him.

It's impossible truly to deconstruct what makes a star, to pinpoint that elusive, intangible quality that separates the truly great from the merely good. But charisma, that magnetic, almost mystical aura, is the essential component. Some exude it through elaborate stage shows, through frenetic movement and choreographed dance routines. Or through witty, crowd-whipping anecdotes. Liam's radiates through stillness. It's fucking fascinating. He is a captivating contradiction. He stands almost motionless, and yet, all eyes are glued to him. Right hand clasping left wrist behind his back. Knees bent, locked in a semi-crouch. Throat raised towards the microphone in a larynx-shredding posture that would make any singing tutor clutch their pearls. Pure instinct. The occasional backward bounce, a coiled spring releasing tension, before jabbing back in, leaning in to unleash the physical assault of the next note, the next snarled lyric, the next guttural roar. There's a raw, primal energy to him and a magnetism that draws the pupil and holds it captive. He's a study in contrasts, a masterclass in the art of less being more.

There is a primal humanity in the Liam Gallagher experience. His voice, as powerful as ever, perhaps even more so with the added grit of age and experience, retains its untamed quality. Those signature, dive-bombing pitch shifts, those soaring, anthemic choruses, cut across the night air, sending shivers down the spines of the assembled masses. His presence on stage is utterly magnetic, every movement, every gesture, every glance imbued with meaning, a testament to his enduring charisma, his unwavering self-belief, his punk spirit, distilled over decades in the spotlight. He feeds on the energy of the crowd, absorbs it, amplifies it and gives it back tenfold, a human amplifier of pure rock 'n' roll energy. As he powers through the songs, the crowd is with him every step of the way. They sing along to every word, every chorus, their voices blending with his in a visceral, communal roar. This isn't just a concert; it's a shared experience, a collective outpouring of emotion.

The might of Oasis surges through the festival grounds, fuelled by Noel Gallagher-penned classics that have moved a generation. As the night draws to a close, the stage lights sweep across the crowd, throwing a net over the ocean of faces, a vast, undulating tapestry. The last song Oasis play is a cover of the Beatles' 'I Am the Walrus'. It had been their usual cover since the very start of the band and right through their golden run. It was an acknowledgement of the Fab Four's lasting influence on Oasis and something of a confirmation of the critical view that they never managed to escape that sound. It had been retired in favour of the Who's 'My Generation' during the second half of the band's career. A quirk of the band's journey had seen Zak Starkey, who was partially taught the kit by Keith Moon and who was a touring member of the Who, driving the rhythm with his great caveman rock style. Zak's absence from Oasis's final stretch probably made it easier for the band to revisit the song his father Ringo had originally recorded. It has only recently been revived in their set.

Noel, a lover of feedback folded through his extensive pedal board, allows the drone to spill from his semi-acoustic guitar as he gives a cursory softened clap to the crowd before leaving the stage. Unlike the aforementioned Fab Four, Oasis have never troubled with the showbiz bow, even when they bow out for good.

Liam, meanwhile, prowls to the front of the gigantic stage, his ears ringing with the deafening roar of thousands of impassioned voices, a sound that seems to resonate with him on a spiritual level. The adulation missing from so much of his early life now delivered to him en masse by a chorus of thousands. He crouches down, a predator surveying its domain, and looks out, taking it all in, absorbing the energy. This is his kingdom. He is rock's apex roller. The chin-out heavyweight champion of the world who has risen from nothing to take the belt.

But this triumphant return, this apparently perfect moment, is tinged with a bittersweet irony, a subtle undercurrent of melancholy. The seeds of destruction are already sown, buried deep within the band's DNA, like a dormant volcano waiting to erupt, and the fateful explosion will occur less than a week later in Paris.

Cracks, hairline fractures at first, have destabilised the band from the very beginning. Liam himself, in a moment of rare self-awareness, has compared Oasis to a high-performance sports car, a finely tuned machine capable of breathtaking speed and exhilarating performance, but also prone to spinning out of control, to crashing and burning in spectacular fashion. The volatile, often explosive relationship between Liam and Noel – the very thing that makes Oasis so compelling, so unique, so great; the palpable friction that drives the public's endless fascination with the band – will finally cause it to crash, to careen off the road and burst into flames. The answer to the ever-looming question of whether they will break up, a question that has hung over the band like the sword of Damocles since their inception, will soon have an emphatically definitive answer.

Even in this moment of triumph in a Staffordshire field where once a year tens of thousands of music lovers come together for V Festival's northern leg, the fault lines that run through the band are shifting. The tension between Liam and Noel is a living, breathing entity, a constant, malevolent presence that lurks in the shadows, threatening to consume them both.

The following night, the tectonic plates of brotherly love increase in magnitude on the rock 'n' roll Richter scale. Oasis abandon the Chelmsford V set due to Liam having developed 'viral laryngitis' in the past twelve hours or so. Rumours of a growing fissure begin to move among those in the industry. On 24 August 2009, tensions between Noel and Liam escalate further following an article by Gordon Smart in the *Sun*'s 'Bizarre' gossip column. The piece speculates about the band's future, suggesting that their upcoming performance in Milan could be their last. Liam Gallagher has long harboured resentment towards Noel's association with media figures, often referring to them sneeringly as Noel's 'pals in the media'. He feels that Noel has been using the papers to cast him as the primary source of the band's internal issues. Liam's disdain for Gordon Smart is especially pronounced, viewing him as emblematic of the external influences he distrusts. To be fair to Liam, having been subjected to long-term invasive press coverage, he is loath to see anybody from any paper in his dressing room, let alone the tabloids for which the phrase 'gutter press' would be an insult to sewers. 'I was seeing the *Sun* around all the time. I was thinking, "What the fuck is this about?" That caused a lot of fucking aggro, in Paris and in the build-up to Paris. I was going, "What you fucking doing having them here?" I knew that if I stepped out of line they were going to write a story about me. Or write a story about my other brother [Paul], saying he's on benefits. That was going down. Yet the geezer who was writing it was in the corner of my fucking dressing room getting pissed on my ticket. And Noel, was like, "He's my mate." Oh, he's your mate now, is he? And Noel knows how I am. I don't have any of that.'

Liam's 'us against them' mentality is deeply rooted in his working-class upbringing in Manchester. He believes that the band's strength lies in its unity and is wary of any external influences that might disrupt their cohesion. Noel's growing friendships outside the band, particularly with media personalities, are seen by Liam as threats to this unity. Noel's friendship with Smart extends beyond professional interactions. They are increasingly close friends. This closeness has only deepened Liam's sense of exclusion and possessiveness over his brother's attention. He struggles with the idea that Noel is sharing aspects of his life with outsiders, perceiving it as a betrayal of their fraternal bond. And Noel's choice of the *Sun* as a platform is particularly jarring to Oasis fans.

The publication of Smart's article on that August day acts as a catalyst, bringing underlying tensions to the surface. Paranoia is a corrosive force. Its gnaws relentlessly at the mind and magnifies insecurities. Added to that, Liam's enthusiasm for drugs and alcohol has done little to dull the edges of an already heightened sense of suspicion.

The story predictably sparks Liam's emotions. It is the trifecta of Liam buttons required to induce paranoia-driven anger: a media pal of Noel's suggesting the band is nearing its end and Liam is the reason. Noel understands Liam's psychology. He knows the stimulus and the response. As Oasis's former tour manager Maggie Mouzakitis will perfectly phrase it in the 2016 *Oasis: Supersonic* documentary, 'Liam has a lot of buttons, and Noel has a lot of fingers.' In fact, years earlier Noel told *Spin* magazine, 'I've kind of learnt that instead of arguing stuff out with [Liam] and ending up in a fight, I work on his psychology and he's completely freaked out by me now. He's actually frightened to death of me.' In the north, we call this 'working the head'. This pattern of provocation and reaction have driven their entire relationship since childhood.

Heading into Oasis's headline appearance at the Rock en Seine festival in Paris that weekend, Liam is primed for explosion. His insecurity around Noel isn't just emotional – it is existential, tied to his very identity as the defining rock star of his generation.

Paris, 28 August 2009. The City of Light. The final, fatal blow. A backstage argument, yet another in a long and storied history of backstage blowouts, fuelled by decades of pent-up frustration, unresolved conflicts and deep-seated emotional baggage, erupts into a full-blown, no-holds-barred confrontation. The inevitable is upon them. A moment that will for ever be etched in the annals of rock 'n' roll history.

It is meant to be just another show, another landmark performance in their latest tour, a seemingly endless trek through the world's megadomes. Another night of musical transcendence for the band. Another night of joyous, communal release for the waiting Parisian crowd. Instead, it becomes the night when everything falls apart, the night the music dies. The fraying butterfly stitches of brotherly love finally become an open scar of sibling resentment.

Backstage, in the cramped, poorly lit confines of the dressing room, the air is thick with fraternal tension. Liam and Noel are at each other's throats, locked in yet another vicious verbal sparring match. Years of simmering rivalry, of petty jealousies, of creative differences, of mounting frustrations, have reached a boiling point, a critical mass. It starts, as these things often do, with something small, utterly insignificant in the grand scheme of things. A misplaced word, a misinterpreted glance, a perceived slight. The rest of the band, seasoned veterans of the Gallagher wars, had witnessed far worse confrontations between the two, far more explosive arguments. But something about this one just takes grip. This one feels different, heavier, more ominous. Maybe it's the accumulated friction and fatigue that come with spending far too much time with a loved one, the inevitable wear and tear of a relationship under constant strain. Maybe it's simply time, the natural end of a cycle. Precision-strike insults, honed over years of practice, echo through the dressing room, accusations fly back and forth like poisoned arrows, and then, the inevitable: argy-bargy, a physical altercation, a brief but violent scuffle. Liam, in a fit of pique, throws a plum at Noel, a bizarre, almost comical act of aggression. Noel, according to Liam, smashes one of Liam's guitars, a deliberate, calculated act of revenge. And Liam, never one to back down from a physical fight, according to Noel, retaliates in kind, smashing one of his own guitars in a brilliant moment of blind Spinal Tappery, mistakenly believing it to be Noel's.

Noel, his patience finally, irrevocably exhausted, storms out of the dressing room with internalised rage worn across his face. The dressing room falls into a painful silence, punctuated only by the growing, expectant hum of the festival crowd outside who remain blissfully unaware of the drama unfolding backstage. Waiting for a show that will never come.

Liam stands there, seething, still hurling insults at his

brother's retreat, but not quite believing what is happening, not fully comprehending the enormity of the situation. Noel has quit the band several times before, most notably during their first, chaotic US tour, but he's always returned. The gravitational pull of Oasis has been too great for him to escape its orbit, but not this time. This time's different. It's final. Noel gets into the back of his Mercedes people carrier, his silhouette barely visible through the tinted windows, a ghost in his own life, and the vehicle pulls silently away, disappearing into the Parisian night.

Moments later, the news filters back to Liam: Noel has sent out a press release, a cold, formal announcement, confirming what has just transpired. Oasis, the band that had defined him, is no more. He cites, among other things, Liam's ongoing violence towards him as a key factor in his decision.

The reaction is immediate and overwhelming. A global outpouring of shock, disbelief and grief. Devastated fans are left to mourn the loss of a band that has soundtracked their lives and given voice to their hopes, dreams and frustrations. The media goes into a feeding frenzy, dissecting every detail of the split. Commentators offer their own interpretations as Liam tries to make sense of the wreckage and conceive of a world without Oasis.

For Liam, the split is a betrayal of the highest order, a devastating abandonment that collapses his entire adult identity and his place in the world. Oasis is not just a band; it is the dominant landmark in Liam's inner navigation, the fixed point around which his entire life has revolved. Who is Liam Gallagher if not the frontman of

Oasis? The brain-rattling realisation that it is actually over, that this time there is no going back, hits him like a Ricky Hatton right-hander, a knockout punch that leaves him reeling, disoriented and lost.

In the days that follow, Liam will be a maelstrom of raw, unfiltered feelings. Anger, betrayal, grief, confusion, resentment, regret – he cycles through them all, sometimes within the space of a single sentence. He lashes out at Noel in the press, in interviews, on social media, calling him a coward and a sellout. He struggles to comprehend how his own brother could have done this to him, to the band, to the fans. But beneath the anger and bravado, there's a deep, abiding sense of loss, a profound sadness. Oasis was his raison d'être. And now it's gone, along with his big brother.

Yet, amid the wreckage of the immediate disorienting aftermath, a spark of defiance flickers. Liam Gallagher is not one to be defeated. He's an instinct scrapper. He's been knocked down before but he always gets back up. And he will again. He has to.

At the Rock en Seine backstage village, Liam and the remaining members of Oasis – Andy, Gem and Chris – are swiftly zipped to their hotel as the announcement is made to a royally pissed-off Parisian crowd. They'd assembled in the French capital expecting a night of anthemic sing-alongs and raucous rock 'n' roll, but instead receive the news that their heroes' star has imploded.

As is often the case during a sudden, unexpected breakup, the band members do the only thing they can think of doing: they go to the hotel bar and drink heavily, attempting to numb the pain and escape the harsh reality of what has just happened. In a state of drunken despair, sparked by the reactive rebound of a life-changing breakup, they decide they couldn't just give up. They have to move forward. They have to find a way to keep going. Fuck Noel. Fuck the media. Fuck everybody.

On the rebound, a new band is formed on the spot that night and begins to take shape in the way that only boozed-up plans, hatched in the early hours of the morning, can. It is a way to keep the dream alive and salvage something from the wreckage, and give the metaphorical middle finger to Noel en route. There and then, Beady Eye is formed.

In interviews, Liam would later reflect on this period as one of determination and unwavering grit. Beady Eye's formation was a bold, defiant step. Their debut album, *Different Gear, Still Speeding*, released in February 2011, was a statement of intent, a declaration of independence from Noel. It showcased a band reborn and eager to prove themselves all over again. While the shadow of Oasis inevitably loomed, Beady Eye's music had its own distinct flavour. It marked the first time Liam had ever given voice to an album of words not written by his brother, a significant departure. He was determined to pick up where he left off by sheer force of will, driven by a burning desire to prove his doubters wrong.

He hadn't known at the time but the final note of that

V Festival performance the weekend earlier would serve as Oasis's epitaph. One last moment of glory swallowed by the night, but its echo still reverberates through music history.

2

The Death of You and Me – Noel, 2009

Noel Gallagher sits in the backseat of the Mercedes people carrier, the darkened streets of Parisian suburbs flashing by as it speeds away from the Rock en Seine festival. His phone buzzes incessantly with messages and calls, but he ignores them. He knows he has just put a tiger among the pigeons. He later says, 'I didn't feel a sense of relief because I knew there was a shitstorm coming. And there was going to be a lot of nonsense talked about it ... One of the biggest bands ever imploded, finally.'

His management arranges a statement from Noel on the official Oasis website that will confirm what fans have long feared: Oasis is over.

'It's with some sadness and great relief to tell you that I quit Oasis tonight. People will write and say what they like, but I simply could not go on working with Liam a day longer. Apologies to all the people who bought tickets for the shows in Paris, Konstanz, and Milan.'

Tellingly it is not a statement from the band and Liam

was not consulted about the wording. Noel follows it up a few days later after being encouraged to give his disbelieving fans a sense of closure. His *Tales From Nowhere* blog is updated with the following explanation: 'The details are not important and of too great a number to list. But I feel you have the right to know that the level of verbal and violent intimidation towards me, my family, friends, and comrades has become intolerable. And the lack of support and understanding from my management and bandmates has left me with no other option than to get me cape and seek pastures new.'

Speaking to *Ultimate Guitar* magazine, Noel will later claim: 'I didn't write it. I was in such a fury, and I was in a really stressful time, and being the way that I am was prepared to walk away and say nothing. And my management was saying, "You cannot say nothing to your fans." And I was like, "There's nothing to say, it's done . . ." And I got on a flight, went to the south of France, and then Sara [MacDonald] and the kids came over. And by the time they'd got there, they said, "Well, can you sign off on this?" And I was like, "Yeah, yeah." But someone in my office wrote it.'

If Noel's recollection is accurate it would be extraordinary for Oasis's long-time management company, Ignition, to single out Liam as the primary reason for the band's demise and also include itself and the rest of the band as culprits.

Wherever they have come from, the words of the statement appear stark and final on screen, the culmination of years of simmering tensions and explosive conflicts that began almost the moment Noel's baby brother arrived all those years ago. Noel will later vividly describe the vibe in those final days as 'heavy'. He had taken his ball home a few times before in moments of intense pressure or following particularly vicious rows, most notably during the band's first US tour when their momentum was derailed by an accidental smattering of crystal meth, but this time is different. This is the end, and everyone can feel it. There has been an inevitability about it. The sibling friction that had driven Oasis to the heights of stardom would always be its undoing. For Noel Gallagher, there is no going back.

The evening of 28 August 2009 had started like so many others on the tour. But as the night drew on, the backstage atmosphere at Rock en Seine became charged. It wasn't the usual pre-gig buzz, the nervous energy that came with facing a sea of expectant faces. This was something else, something far more toxic, the culmination a relationship pushed to its breaking point over years. Tension was par for the course at this point, although it had been exacerbated in the past week by the cancellation of the second night of their V Festival headline engagement due to viral laryngitis, if you ask Liam, or Liam's boozing, if you ask Noel. (Noel would later retract this due to impending legal action from his little brother.) Noel and Liam had been travelling separately since an argument at an airport earlier in the tour and had barely spoken to each other in the intervening period. And then there was that article by Gordon Smart, adding further weight to proceedings.

The final blow-up had erupted with the suddenness and ferocity of a summer storm. Years of wind-ups, jealousy and bottled-up grievances had reached a boiling point. 'He started it, as usual,' Noel would recall in an interview with *Q* magazine, a trace of weariness in his voice. 'He came in, mouthing off about something or other, and I just snapped. It was like a volcano going off.' The plum was thrown, shouting turned to shoving, shoving to punches, guitars were smashed. According to some reports, Liam didn't just accidentally smash one of his own guitars, but wielded one of Noel's beautiful red Gibsons 'like an axe'. The band's own former Special Boat Service bodyguards intervened, a stark illustration of how volatile the situation had become, and Noel, seething with rage and frustration, stormed out.

Details of the argument remain somewhat apocryphal, filtered through the lenses of memory and differing perspectives, coloured by years of retelling and speculation, but in reality, it wasn't any one thing. It was the culmination of a lifetime of resentments, wind-ups and growing apart, as is often the case with these things; the spark that ignited the inferno was likely insignificant in the grand scheme of things, a mere pretext for a much larger, more deeply rooted conflict. Whatever the catalyst, years of frustration, rivalry and a deep-seated personality clash now poured out in a torrent of bitter accusations and recriminations. In that moment, Noel thought, 'I'm out. I'm done with this.'

The atmosphere backstage was a maelstrom of raw emotion and stunned silence. Band members, crew and onlookers stood frozen, caught in the crossfire of the Gallagher brothers' explosive feud, their faces reflecting a mixture of shock and disbelief. This was not the first time they had witnessed such a scene, such a vitriolic display of fraternal animosity. Throughout Oasis's tumultuous history, arguments, fights and even temporary departures had come and gone, almost a routine part of the band's existence. But this time felt different. There was a finality to it, a sense that a line had been irrevocably crossed, a point of no return.

After Noel climbed into the waiting people carrier and exhaled deeply in the tinted-window sanctuary of the car, away from Liam, away from everything, the driver navigated through the festival's artist area, past frantic promoters, disbelieving event staff, and towards the exit gate. Noel glanced out the window at the thousands of fans who had come to see Oasis, people for whom his songs meant so much, who would soon learn that not only was their evening ruined but the band they loved was no more – there's something inexplicably emotional about knowing you have seen an artist you love perform for the last time. It was over. The tyranny of the Oasis brand, the suffocating weight of expectation, the constant, grinding friction with his brother – it was all finally over.

For years, Noel had felt like a prisoner to the Oasis sound he had created and, more pertinently, to the increasing tension between him and his little brother. The band's success had been monumental; their music defined an era, a generation. But with that success came expectations and constraints. Noel, the primary songwriter, the architect of the Oasis sound, was bound to a formula that had brought them fame but stifled his artistic growth. Oasis fans and, in particular, the biggest Oasis fan of all, Liam, wouldn't accept the artistic change Noel longed for. Which left him feeling 'trapped' by the band's legacy.

In interviews, Noel had often hinted at his frustrations. He told *Rolling Stone* he was quite independent as a person, his words carrying a weight of unspoken meaning. He expressed that he needed to do things his own way, but that with Oasis, that wasn't possible. He'd held thoughts of a solo career since Oasis's second album, a chance to explore new musical landscapes without the baggage of the band, without the constant need to cater to a specific sound, a specific audience. There was always a curiosity, both in Noel and among fans, about what he could achieve on his own, unfettered by the constraints of Oasis. That night in Paris, chaotic and painful as it was, finally delivered that possibility, ripping the bandage off a long-festering wound.

For Noel, the decision to walk away wasn't a spur-of-the-moment act of anger, a knee-jerk reaction to yet another fight. Noel saw with cold, hard clarity: he could no longer continue down this path. Staying in Oasis simply cost too much. As he later explained in numerous interviews, the constant triggering of the fight-or-flight impulse and heightened cortisol levels, the emotional exhaustion, and the sense of being trapped in an unsustainable dynamic had taken their toll, eroded his passion for the band, and poisoned his relationship with his brother. 'It wasn't a decision I took lightly,' he said in a

2011 interview with *NME*, his voice heavy with a mixture of regret and relief. 'But I got to the point where I couldn't spend another minute in that band.' The final argument with Liam was merely the straw that broke the camel's back, the catalyst that pushed him to a decision he had likely been contemplating for months, if not years. The constant bickering, once a source of amusement for the press, fodder for the band's bad-boy image, had become a debilitating weight, a soul-destroying burden. The sheer exhaustion, the utter weariness of it all, was palpable in his tone.

The last year of Oasis, in particular, had taken a lot out of Noel. He'd always found Oasis tours 'a struggle' but this was especially exhausting. Noel had spent a long section of the run in severe pain, following an on-stage attack during the band's headline performance at the V Festival in Toronto, Canada, the preceding August. A bellend by the name of Danny Sullivan pushed Noel from the 15-foot-high stage as he played a guitar solo. Noel broke three ribs and endured months of pain. It takes a lot to get Noel to pull out of a show on physical grounds. He's played on after being punched in the face and even performed following root-canal surgery that same day at a show in Staten Island. He was still reliant on painkillers by the time the band arrived for the UK leg of the tour that autumn. Doing anything with thee broken ribs is hard, let alone singing. He's a tough cookie. During the subsequent trial, Noel described 'the sudden impact and shock as feeling as if I had been hit by a bus' and claimed he was in pain for eight months and would 'never really recover'. Sullivan pleaded guilty to causing bodily harm and was sentenced to twelve months' house arrest. The knock-on effect of this led to changes in long-time security personnel, and every individual with permission to stand at the side of the stage at Oasis shows from then on was issued a black button-up overshirt with the band's logo on front and back. It didn't exactly help add tranquillity to the Oasis mix.

The immediate aftermath of leaving the band was a strange mix of relief and sorrow, liberation and loss. As Noel walked away from the chaos, shouting and splintered guitars, a wave of liberation washed over him, a sense of freedom he hadn't felt in years. He was free from the constant tension, the endless drama, the suffocating weight of being in a band with his brother, a band that had become as much a burden as a blessing. For the first time in nearly two decades, he was no longer bound by the expectations and limitations of Oasis, by the need to maintain a certain image, to adhere to a certain sound. He could finally breathe, could be himself, whatever that might mean. In a 2012 interview with the *Independent*, Noel described that moment as a huge relief. He'd made increasingly pointed references to Oasis and Liam getting too much in the press over the past few months, making comments like 'life would be easier without Oasis'. Despite Noel's later assertions that the band might have continued had they completed their remaining tour dates, it was like he was verbalising in public his desire to leave the band as part of some emotional processing as he worked up to the act itself.

He called Sara from the back seat of the car. He knew, as quoted in *NME*, he 'couldn't go back to England because the press had descended on my house and my missus was there with my kids. So we had to kind of spirit her out in the middle of the night and they came to join me in France somewhere. And then when we eventually got back to England, of course all fucking hell broke loose.' One seemingly final chapter in the Oasis psychodrama. As far as Noel was concerned this was the last in a very long line of arguments he would ever have with his baby brother.

3

The Roller – Liam, 2010–11

As Liam rolled into 2010 he cut a slightly different figure to the imperious rock star the world had come to lionise. The familiar swagger was there, but something had shifted. It was like watching a great box-to-box midfielder whose legs were going. The implosion of Oasis the previous summer had left a gaping hole in the British music scene. And it had left Liam Gallagher divorced from the role that had defined him for nearly two decades. His voice, the instrument of a generation, a gloriously ragged snarl that could incite riots and reduce grown men to tears, was suddenly speaking for a new band. Of sorts. They looked an awful lot like Oasis, save one obvious exception: Noel. There was an unavoidable and daunting question, a question that echoed through the music world and reverberated in the hearts of millions of fans: could Liam Gallagher succeed away from the brilliant, dominating creative force of his big brother?

In fairness, the real question was: could his bandmates

now step up as writers and match the generational quality possessed by Noel? Liam could still sing and he could still be Liam Gallagher. But as a group, could they find the shells for this shotgun? Being the *frontman* means being just that: it may not have been Liam's name above the door but it was his face and his voice that the world would judge against his previous band's undefeated record.

The answer, as it often did with Liam, arrived with a mix of defiant bravado and a resolute refusal to back down. In early 2010, amidst a flurry of media speculation, driven by the insatiable appetite for Gallagher-related drama, Liam announced his intention to form a new band. This wouldn't be a solo project. He felt that to be the domain of the cunt. Instead, it would be a fresh start for all the members, a bold leap into the unknown, built on the foundations of his past and fortified by the gang mentality he'd craved ever since the early days with Oasis Mk 1. The band, he revealed, with a characteristic lack of fanfare, would include former Oasis members Gem Archer on guitar, Andy Bell also on guitar, having returned to his preferred instrument after years playing the bass in Oasis, which had to be a fairly tedious experience for a guitarist as nuanced as Bell, and the superb Chris Sharrock on drums, a percussionist so good that Liam didn't mind him having been behind the kit for Robbie Williams.

The decision to continue with his former Oasis bandmates was on one level both pragmatic and symbolic, but had been actioned purely as a reflex following the shock trauma of another perceived abandonment by a big male figure in Liam's life, following his father's absence when he was a child. In the immediate aftermath, he viewed them as his brothers-in-arms, and they gave the comfort of continuity and familiarity during a time of disorienting upheaval. There was a pre-existing chemistry, a shared history, a musical shorthand that could be refined to create something new. The remaining members had already begun working on new material just weeks after Oasis's split and, in the case of Gem and Andy, had years of songs in the tank which were deemed unsuitable for Oasis. The new band was a testament to their shared desire to move forward and a great opportunity for them to step up as writers.

Noel wasn't the only one Liam felt had betrayed him. In Liam's view, Oasis's long-term manager, Marcus Russell, had crossed the Gallagher rubicon, never to be forgiven. Marcus, a warm and amiable man with a voice and appearance not completely dissimilar to his Welsh countryman, Neil Kinnock, had sided with the elder Gallagher. Noel and Marcus had always been more closely aligned. In fact, Liam went on to express regret at not having 'filled them both in' for what he understood to have been their orchestration of events. There was a sense among insiders that Marcus had grown tired of Liam and, to be fair, you could imagine that managing Liam Gallagher can be really hard work. Artists are often sceptical when it comes to how much money their managers deserve, and when a manager leaves an act it can be received with a sense of betrayal and ingratitude. Regardless of the personalities involved, the business tends to go with the money. The songwriter makes more of that than the singer. So, despite Noel's direct criticism of his management, whom he accused of providing 'a total lack of support' in his public statement upon exiting Oasis, he stayed with Marcus and his company, Ignition. Noel, being the pragmatist he is, had commented to musician friends in the past, when they came to him for career advice, how expensive it could be to change management. Noel and Ignition stood aside, contemplated their strategy, and let Liam's emotion-driven engine sprint onwards like Road Runner watching Wile E. Coyote rocket-skate off the end of a cliff. To be fair, at the time, the entire music industry had fancied Noel to go on to continued megastardom, and nobody was quite sure what Liam would do without his brother's songs.

Symbolically, the formation of Beady Eye was a powerful statement of intent, a defiant roar into the void left by Oasis. It was a declaration that Liam was not going to fade into obscurity, a washed-up has-been trading on past glories. Nor was he going to come crawling back to his brother, cap in hand, begging for a reconciliation. The name Beady Eye was chosen quickly, almost randomly, to avoid being labelled 'The Liam Gallagher Band', a common trope in indie music (and one soon to be embraced, more or less, by Noel and his High Flying Birds) when someone leaves a well-known band but doesn't really want to go solo. Liam, never one for overthinking things, wanted a name that was simple, direct, and didn't tie the band to any particular genre or scene. People could read something into it in relation to his big brother's distant observation, but that would happen regardless.

In a 2011 interview with the *Quietus*, Liam explained that they didn't want to go down the route of using their own names, wanting to keep things simple, to let the music speak for itself. The name was sharp, intriguing and, perhaps most importantly, it didn't carry the baggage of the past. It wasn't trying to be Oasis. It was something new. Something, perhaps, a little bit strange.

Early rehearsals were a liberating experience, a breath of fresh air after the stifling atmosphere of late-period Oasis. Freed from the creative constraints and power dynamics of Oasis, a band where Noel had been the undisputed leader, the band members found a new sense of camaraderie and equity. Gem and Andy were both accomplished songwriters who had contributed to Oasis's later albums with songs tailored to the band's sonic brand, and both had been the lead songwriters in their respective bands, Hurricane No. 1 and Ride, but being the main writer of Liam Gallagher's band was a different level. They were now given more space, more freedom to express their musical ideas, to contribute to the songwriting process. Liam, too, was encouraged to participate, to put his own stamp on the music, something he had done sporadically in Oasis and on occasion outside of it (notably with the Seahorses' 'Love Me and Leave Me'), but rarely was it anything more than an interesting moment on a record, peaking with 'Songbird', the Oasis single he wrote about his wife, Nicole Appleton, a woman so well suited to him he didn't mind her having previously been Robbie

Williams's partner. In fact, that probably put Liam 1–0 up on the toxic masculinity scoreboard when it came to the world's lamest rivalry featuring him and the former Take That singer.

Nicole became Liam's second wife (Patsy Kensit being the first) on Valentine's Day in 2008. They wed at the low-key, rock-star registry office of choice, the Old Marylebone Town Hall in London. Paul McCartney and a certain Noel Gallagher had previously committed their hearts for ever and ever in the same halls. Nicole and Liam's romance had begun in 2000 and a year later they welcomed their first (and Liam's second) son, Gene. Nicole, or Nic to her friends, is a lovely woman and one who met Liam on his level. A global pop star during her time in All Saints, she was one of the few people who could understand the experience of being in a band with their sibling, and she was a woman after his own heart when it came to having a laugh down the pub. She became one of the lads. Nic and Liam would spend Sundays in the pub beer gardens of Hampstead with her sister Natalie and their various mates.

Liam had been immediately drawn to the pretty Canadian pop star when they first met in France. 'I fancied Nicole when I first saw her. Then when we hung out I thought, "You're fun". She was like a mate. We could get pissed together. Nic likes a drink. She likes the pub. Nic's like a little fucking scally bird. She doesn't walk around in Gucci every fucking minute of the day. At the end of the day they all stink and fart when you're next to them in bed.' The lyrical romance of 'Songbird' had yet to reach Liam's conversational mode. They say love is based on matched values and the pub featured highly for Liam at this time. Liam's allusion to Nicole's aversion to Gucci was a dig at ex-wife Patsy Kensit. (We'll speak about Patsy later.) It's worth noting that Liam himself had modelled for Versace and had a wardrobe bursting with Burberry and every other vogue label of the day.

Nicole loved him and was loyal and empathetic. She and her sister, Nat, are very upbeat individuals. Nicole considered herself skilled in the art of homemaking. She would cook and look after her man-child, but then go out and party toe-to-toe. She had the ability to pull herself together really quickly the next day and not let the good times impact her life.

But by the time Liam entered his Beady Eye period in 2010, the life of rock-star wife had strained Nicole. The good nature of Liam's songbird had been increasingly put upon by his erratic behaviour. She'd subscribed to the flawed conceit that the misbehaviour of the rock-star husband is the dark backing to the mirror's soul, which allows their talent to reflect life. Nicole did her best to ignore reports of Liam's occasional 'lost weekends' (a Lennonism euphemising a man abdicating real life for a bit) when he'd disappear off for a few days here and there. But there's a line for everybody. Liam swaggered past that line for Nicole when she was informed an on–off affair he'd had with American journalist, Liza Ghorbani, had produced a child, Gemma, in January 2013. She'd seen this movie before, having been supportive of another daughter Liam had conceived outside of his previous marriage to Patsy

Kensit. Nicole had been warm and encouraging to Molly while Liam continued to refuse to publicly recognise her. Now, she was crushed and humiliated. The songbird's wings had been melted by Liam's red giant.

Liza met Liam, unbelievably, while writing an article titled 'A Night Out with Liam Gallagher' for the *New York Times* in 2010. Struck by his appearance, Liza wrote that 'Gallagher looked as if he'd just stepped off Carnaby Street in London circa 1969', after meeting him at the bar of New York's Ritz Carlton. According to the *New York Post*, 'they continued the affair for around three months after Gemma's birth when she told him she was suing him in NY family court for $3M'. The *Post* claimed Liam wrote to Liza confirming Gemma was his child saying, 'she's beautiful because she has rock star genes', the baby's inherent beauty attributable solely to daddy's essence. You'd imagine it wasn't quite the acknowledgement Liza had hoped for but legally it held up just fine.

It's probably fair to say Liam can be impulsive. And for impulsive people the devil can enter when they put themselves in proximity to temptation and opportunity. A pretty woman. A hotel bar. Unfortunately for Nicole's heart, there probably wasn't much more to the equation than that.

Liam's nervous system alternates between fight or flight. Fight tends to engage during physical or verbal challenges but flight is very much the order of the day when it comes to emotional crises. Needing escape, he popped off to Spain where he was joined by Debbie Gwyther, who was then part of his management team. So Nicole was contending with not one but two names to feel displaced by. We'll leave that there for now.

One thing Beady Eye wasn't built to sustain was another alimony settlement and another child support settlement. The band was a refuge emotionally but there was now an added commercial and financial pressure for Liam when it came to his work.

The Beady Eye dynamic was markedly different from the often-fraught atmosphere of Oasis rehearsals, which sometimes went ahead without Liam. There were no simmering resentments but instead a shared sense of purpose, a collective desire to prove that they were more than the sum of their parts; it was a spirited fight for their music careers. Liam described them as being 'like a breath of fresh air'. He emphasised the collaborative nature of the process, saying, 'We're all writing, we're all contributing. It's a proper band, not just one geezer calling the shots.' This newfound sense of democracy was a welcome change for all involved. Gem Archer also echoed this sentiment, describing the process as more relaxed and the band as all pulling in the same direction; a statement made in reference to the tension between the two brothers rather than any slight on Noel. After all, one of the qualities that makes Gem a great band member is his inherent diplomacy.

The formation of Beady Eye was met with a mixture of anticipation and scepticism from the public and the media, a blend of excitement and doubt. In the post-*Be Here Now* years, Oasis had become a bit passé in critical circles and there was an underlying desire to pour cold water on the new venture. The music press, rarely averse to an obvious narrative framing, painted it as the first salvo in a battle of the bands between Beady Eye and Noel's yet-to-be-announced solo project, a sibling rivalry played out on a public stage.

There was a pervasive sense that Liam had something to prove. He was no longer just the frontman of one of the biggest bands in the world, the charismatic singer with the instantly recognisable voice. He was the leader of a new, untested group, carrying a weight of expectation and entering the market as a new act whose cultural relevance was open to question. The pressure to succeed was immense, not just from a critical perspective but a pressing financial burden carried by Liam's rock 'n' roll lifestyle. Liam, whose fight-or-flight switch always clicks to dukes-up when questioned publicly, used it as fuel. It was motivation to prove the doubters wrong. It was very much an 'us against them' mentality. In interviews, he was bullish about Beady Eye's prospects, brimming with confidence, dismissing comparisons to Oasis and insisting that his new band would stand or fall on its own merits. It was a confident stance but pertinently also an accurate one.

Beady Eye commenced recording their debut album, *Different Gear, Still Speeding*, at the legendary RAK Studios in London in the summer of 2010. RAK is a heritage studio that had hosted sessions for iconic artists such as Pink Floyd and the Who, and the band hoped to create an album that could hold its own in the pantheon of great rock 'n' roll records.

At the desk during the recording process was producer Steve Lillywhite, a veteran of the music industry and a safe pair of hands to help bring this project to realisation. A sonic architect who had worked with legendary acts such as U2, the Rolling Stones and Peter Gabriel, Lillywhite brought with him a wealth of experience, a keen ear for sonic detail and a reputation for crafting commercially successful albums, records that sounded both timeless and contemporary. In an interview with *Music Radar* in 2011, Lillywhite described the recording process with Beady Eye as very collaborative and praised the band's work ethic and creative energy. He was clearly impressed by their commitment and their willingness to experiment. 'They were open to trying new things,' he said, 'which is always exciting for a producer.'

The sessions were intense but productive, a whirlwind of creativity and hard work. The band members, eager to establish their new identity, to make their mark, threw themselves into the recording process with a renewed sense of purpose, a hunger to create something special. They experimented with different sounds, different instruments and different approaches to songwriting, pushing themselves beyond their comfort zones.

Musically, Beady Eye aimed to create an album that was both familiar and fresh, that nodded to their influences while also forging a new path. They drew inspiration from their shared love of 1960s rock 'n' roll, particularly the more obvious corners inhabited by the Beatles and the

Rolling Stones. It represented a return towards the basics of rock 'n' roll, something Liam had adopted as a mantra for life. There were echoes of the raw energy of early Oasis but also hints of psychedelia and blues, which represented a marginal shift in their collective sonic palette. The goal was to make a record with a bit of a twist. One that was exciting, that made you want to dance and jump around. Liam had become practised in the art of hyperbolic album promotion as a consequence of trying to excite Oasis fans in every album cycle post-*Morning Glory*. He also genuinely believed he had created such a record.

Liam's involvement in the songwriting process was much more significant, more hands-on, than it had been in Oasis, where he was only an occasional contributor, even during the latter years of the band when Noel started to make space for other members to contribute. While Gem and Andy took the lead on many of the Beady Eye tracks, Liam contributed lyrics and melodies to several songs, including the musical-influence-on-the-sleeve 'Beatles and Stones' and 'For Anyone', a more introspective song that offered a glimpse into his more vulnerable side. Liam's increased songwriting involvement suggested a newfound creative confidence. It was a formative step in his slow march towards becoming a 'proper' songwriter.

However, Liam's primary focus remained on his vocals, which have always been his greatest asset. That and being a genuine rock star. Maybe not in that order. He was determined to prove that he was more than just a charismatic frontman, a pretty face with great hair and one of the world's most identifiable voices. He definitely, definitely, wanted people to remember those aspects but he was slowly starting to blossom as a writer, too. He retained the familiar sneer of his Oasis days – why wouldn't you when you have one of rock's greatest and most unique vocal styles – that blend of Johnny Rotten and solo-era John Lennon, which stands out on its own in the musical terrain? Prior to Rotten, nobody had ever sung like that. It's a brilliantly bizarre style from which Liam borrowed idiosyncrasies and added the raw but gentle melody of Lennon's vocal style to make something entirely his own. But on tracks such as 'Bring the Light', the album's lead single, he adopted a more playful, bluesy tone with a slightly theatrical delivery reminiscent of late-Beatles Macca. On 'The Roller', he delivered a gritted approximation of John Lennon's vocal to complement Gem's 'Instant Karma' melody and arrangement.

Come November 2010, Beady Eye showed fans a bit of ankle, releasing 'Bring the Light' as a free download on their website. The track, a rollicking, piano-driven boogie-woogie number that owed as much to Jerry Lee Lewis as it did to the Beatles, was a departure from the sound of Oasis. It was raw, energetic and catchy. The reaction from fans and critics was mixed. Some praised the song's energy, its infectious groove and Liam's confident vocals, while others found it too derivative. Both criticisms applied to Liam throughout his career. But either way, it had set the tone for something different from Oasis.

Throughout the recording process and the lead up to

the album's release, Liam remained a figure of intense media scrutiny, a magnet for controversy and speculation. Every move, every interview, every public appearance was analysed and dissected, and often compared to his older brother. A life experience enjoyed by very few younger siblings. He has always been a gift to the tabloids, a guaranteed source of headlines, a rock 'n' roll star who always delivers good copy. Liam's public persona is a deceptively complex mix of bravado, vulnerability and defiance, and he needed it as much as ever during this period of transition. It's a carefully constructed parka-shaped armour that allows the core aspects of his inherent personality to be amplified in a manner that protects the private self. Publicly, he was still the same gobby rock star who had captivated audiences for years. But privately, there was also a developing sense of maturity and self-awareness that had arrested somewhat during the height of Oasis's fame, when the band had been swept up in a whirlwind of excess and adulation, and when every naughty or destructive action had been hugely rewarded with attention and wealth. In fact, it formed the basis of Creation Records' entire PR strategy for Oasis during the first two album cycles and worked a treat.

In interviews, Liam was keen to champion his new band, and spoke passionately about the new music, the collaborative dynamic within the band, and his eagerness to get back on the road and connect with fans. He was determined to prove that Beady Eye was not simply a side project or a vanity exercise, a way to fill the void left by Oasis. It was a serious endeavour, a band with its own unique identity and its own artistic vision, a band that deserved to be taken seriously.

The journalistic necessity of asking personal questions that would be a mega faux pas in an ordinary social context inevitably led to repeated enquiries about Noel and their breakup, about the possibility of a brotherly reunion. The questions would hang in the air like an unanswered prayer for the duration of Liam and Noel's estrangement. As with a football manager being asked on live TV if he'd likely lose his job in the immediate aftermath of a good pasting, repeatedly being asked by total strangers about whether your brother hates you has to be traumatic. Liam, for the most part, handled these questions with a mixture of humour and impatience. It was a source of genuine trauma. It's hard to process and heal when the scab is constantly picked. His practised deflection technique satisfied the press's immediate need for a quote but only provided the most temporary respite.

Of course, he couldn't resist the occasional dig at his brother, a precision barb that betrayed the lingering bitterness. It's part of what makes both brothers compelling. They just cannot resist sticking the boot in when there's a camera rolling. It's a toxified version of the tough-love language of northern men, where the calibrated insult is a sincere form of love or appreciation. Liam would often make disparaging remarks about Noel's solo work, dismissing it as 'dad rock' or 'boring', his words dripping with disdain and launched with the sole purpose of grabbing a drop of attention from Noel. But Noel knew his power lay in not giving Liam what he wanted. Classic brother stuff. Liam's comments were a perfect fit for virility on the increasingly omnipresent social media platforms. They fuelled the narrative of the ongoing Gallagher feud, a Mancunian kitchen-sinker worthy of a *Corrie* special.

The media battles were not limited to snide putdowns. In the summer of 2011, a legal dispute bubbled between the two brothers, a clash that threatened to escalate into full-blown lawfare. Noel, during the grandiose press conference that gave flight to the High Flying Birds, claimed that Liam had pulled out of Oasis's second performance at the 2009 V Festival due to having been on the lash rather than the officially cited viral laryngitis. He may have had laryngitis. He may have had a big night. Neither of those things are mutually exclusive. But all the same it was a serious accusation, one that questioned Liam's professionalism and his commitment to Oasis's fans, and it potentially opened him up to legal action and claims from insurers. In the same conference, Noel also claimed that the argument in Paris, the final, fatal blow-up, was largely about Liam wanting to advertise his clothing brand, Pretty Green, in the Oasis tour programme, and Noel had told him, in his sometimes spectacularly undiplomatic manner, that he'd need to pay commercial rates.

Liam vehemently denied these allegations, his anger palpable. He accused Noel of lying, of deliberately trying to damage his reputation. He promptly filed a libel lawsuit against his brother, demanding a public apology and a retraction of the damaging statements. The incident became one more in the increasingly bitter and seemingly endless saga of the brothers Gallagher.

4

Flying High – Noel, 2010–11

Unlike his brother Liam, who immediately channelled his energy and frustration into forming Beady Eye with the remaining members of Oasis, Noel retreated. He returned to London, to his family, and largely kept his face from the glare of the spotlight. This was a period of necessary recalibration. Time to step back, breathe, decompress and rediscover himself outside the all-consuming entity that was Oasis. Leaving the band, and especially leaving Liam, was about reasserting a sense of control in his life. Right now, playing the guitar and writing songs were at the centre of this healing process. As a boy, the violent environment of his family home led Noel to retreat to his bedroom and his guitar. When there's no place to go, you make your world so small you can only turn inwards for escape. He could escape in the music. He could control the guitar.

He needed time to recover from the breakup of the band, and a chance to regroup and plan his next move.

It wasn't just Noel who had moved on from his guitar band. Guitar-based groups were becoming an endangered species in the charts, with very few new British rock bands achieving success even close to the scale of Oasis's. There was a genuine risk of irrelevance for Noel moving forward.

In the immediate aftermath of the breakup, the music world held its breath, waiting for Noel's next move. The press speculated about solo projects and even supergroups. But Noel remained uncharacteristically quiet. He granted very few interviews, and when he did, his answers were brief, measured and devoid of detail on plans for new music.

This period of silence was crucial for Noel. It allowed him to decompress and process the events that had led to the band's demise, and to get back to the basics of songwriting without the pressure of public expectation. He spent time with his then-girlfriend, Sara MacDonald, and their two-year-old son, Donovan. Noel met Sara back in June 2000, at Space Nightclub in Ibiza, where he had a house. At the time Orange actively marketed to young customers through experiential music activations and Sara worked as a public relations officer for the network. Noel was still married to Meg Mathews and his first child, Anaïs, had been born only six months earlier. Although he refuted Meg's allegations of infidelity when they divorced a year later, he did subsequently describe his first meeting with Sara as being 'love at first sight'. Elaborating during his chat with British *Vogue* in 2020, he described the emotional significance of the moment. After asking for Sara's number, he kept 'the card like it was a fucking religious artefact'. Noel adored her. He'd play up to her in child-like ways at times, seeking her approval. As a seasoned industry member, she knew how to be around talent and not to let admiration for their work spill into the personal realm. Whether it was playing his latest song for her or play boxing with her as she stood motionless, waiting for him to stop while withholding any sign of amusement, it was a cup he could never quite fill.

Born in Edinburgh in 1971, Sara is four years Noel's junior. Attractive and tall, she cuts an elegant figure with long brown hair that cascades over the shoulder of whichever chic outfit she has selected that day. She presents well but became something of a divisive figure among Oasis fans, members of Oasis's team and the Gallagher family itself. The latter isn't all that unusual for a Gallagher partner. The trope of the rock-star wife being an agent of division is as tired as it is unfair, especially in the case of perceived original sinner, Yoko Ono, and is best avoided. In the case of Oasis, the band broke up for two reasons and two reasons only, namely Liam Gallagher and Noel Gallagher. That said, Noel's devotion to Sara led to tensions with management, with Liam and eventually with Anaïs, who initially got on really well with Sara in childhood but friction quickly drifted in over the course of their relationship.

Noel, otherwise proficient in the use of four-letter words, only really began to use the L-word in his lyrics after meeting Sara. Before then his songs of the heart were more obtuse. But during the course of their relationship he began to tap into his inner McCartney, penning songs such as 'She Is Love' which spoke directly of his affection for Sara.

The couple's second son, Sonny, came in October 2010. It was a joyful event that further grounded Noel in family life. He later described to the *Guardian* that having a new baby during this time was a welcome distraction, a source of joy and stability, helping him focus on the present rather than dwelling on the past.

In the few interviews he did grant, Noel offered glimpses into his state of mind. He spoke of the constant tension and conflict that had plagued the latter years of Oasis. He said that it was a relief to walk away from Oasis, and that the decision had been a long time coming. He described the atmosphere within the band as 'toxic' and 'unbearable', a poisonous environment that had stifled his creativity. The constant fighting had become 'soul-destroying'. When Liam threw a guitar across the dressing room in Paris, it wasn't just an outburst – it was the culmination of years of unresolved pain. Noel, tired of the volatility, walked out without another word. 'It was over before it was over,' he later said, describing the quiet finality.

However, Noel also acknowledged the sadness that accompanied the end of Oasis. It was a band that had achieved unimaginable success, a band that had given him a platform to share his songs with the world. To walk away from that was not easy, even if it was necessary. He confessed to *Q* magazine in 2012 that he still felt 'a pang of regret' about the way things had ended, particularly the impact it had on the fans.

Sara MacDonald's marriage to Noel marked a shift from the Liam-driven chaos of Oasis to the calm sense of control he craved. She was protective, pragmatic and unafraid to challenge him and those around him. She provided something Liam and Oasis never could: emotional safety. But where Noel found comfort in Sara's unwavering support, Liam saw her influence as a threat. Publicly calling her 'the Yoko Ono of Oasis', Liam's remarks cut deeply; they weren't aimed solely at Sara, but were also a reflection of his unresolved anger towards Noel's need for emotional distance.

This public clash was yet another marker of how their feud had moved into deeply personal territory. The Gallagher brothers, once inseparable, had finally reached a point where words, and even music, could no longer bridge the gap.

While Noel maintained a public silence about his musical plans, he was privately engaged in a period of intense creative activity. He had a vast treasure trove of unused material to draw from, songs and ideas that had been written over the years, including some which dated back to Oasis's earliest days but had never found a place on an album. Others were more recent compositions that had been sidelined due to creative differences with Liam, or simply because they didn't fit the Oasis landscape. Noel began revisiting these old ideas, reworking them, breathing new life into forgotten melodies and lyrics. He also started writing new material inspired by his newfound freedom and his desire to explore new terrain. He experimented with different sounds, instruments and approaches to songwriting, pushing himself beyond his comfort zone. It was a liberating experience and a creative rebirth. He could follow his instincts and create without having to justify his choices to anyone. With the composition of his debut solo album he finally received elusive musical praise from Sara. She had thus far remained beyond the charms of Noel's musical output, but gave a 'not bad' to Noel's piano-driven, dance-music-inspired 'AKA ... What a Life!'. He later reflected on this period in an interview with *Esquire* in 2015, describing it as 'like starting with a blank canvas'.

Noel rekindled his production collaboration with Dave Sardy, who'd produced Oasis's final albums, *Don't Believe the Truth* and *Dig Out Your Soul*, and had developed a strong working relationship with Noel. They shared a musical sensibility and, crucially, a work ethic. Like a lot of LA-based producers, Sardy prefers to keep more regulated hours, as does Noel. A big, warm American, Sardy is a calm and commanding presence behind the desk.

In late 2010 and early 2011, Noel travelled to Los Angeles to begin work with Sardy on the new album. The sessions were crucial in shaping the future of Noel's debut solo album, providing the sonic foundation for his new musical identity. They were not afraid to take risks, to push the boundaries of what was expected of Noel Gallagher, but retained enough familiarity for the songs to land with existing fans. *Billboard* reported on these early sessions, highlighting the collaborative nature of the project and the excitement surrounding Noel's new direction. His backlog of songs played a significant role in the development of his solo material. Tracks such as 'Everybody's on the Run', 'Dream On' and '(I Wanna Live in a Dream in My) Record Machine' had never found a place on Oasis's albums. Now Noel was able to revisit these songs and reimagine them in a new context and in his own voice. In an interview with *NME* in 2011, Noel explained that some of the songs had been hanging around for years and that he was excited to finally give them a proper home. Their delayed employment was a testament to the prolific nature of his early writing career.

On 6 July 2011, members of the media gather in the softly lit auditorium of Notting Hill's Electric Cinema, their faces illuminated by the blue light of mobile phone screens. They have been invited to a rock-star press conference, a bit of a throwback for the music business but perfectly matched to today's speaker. The setting is intimate and stylish, a far cry from Noel's last musical engagement and the chaos of Paris. Noel breezes on to the small stage in front of the lush red velvet safety curtain. Wearing a black leather trucker jacket with grey jeans and a white shirt, he looks completely at ease as he takes his seat behind the small table with its pair of microphones and a glass of water. Leaning forward on the small wooden table he looks almost presidential. It suits the Chief.

It is his first major public appearance since the demise of Oasis. Unlike Beady Eye's on-the-fly planning, the staging of Noel's return has been meticulously planned, a clear indication that he intends to control his own narrative. He is there to unveil his grand plan for Noel Gallagher, the solo star. He's happy and in complete control.

Noel announces the formation of Noel Gallagher's High Flying Birds and its eponymous debut album. It's a band name that nods to seventies rock bands that incorporated the name of the leader, like Paul McCartney & Wings, and those with a sense of unconventional optimism, like the Flying Burrito Brothers. The band's name had come during a moment of dishwashing-based inspiration. While listening to the radio he'd created a portmanteau of rock 'n' roll heritage, Noel Gallagher's High Flying Birds, for both the band and the album, inspired by the Jefferson Airplane track 'High Flying Bird' as well as the band name 'Peter Green's Fleetwood Mac', before they became known as simply Fleetwood Mac. He describes the solo vehicle's sound as 'cosmic pop', a blend of familiar and new elements, and reveals that he will be releasing not one but two new records, the second of which will be a double LP of experimental wig-out music in collaboration with very leftfield producers for Noel, the Amorphous Androgynous.

This project, intended to be a companion piece to his main release, promises to push Gallagher into new sonic territory, signalling his willingness to break free from conventional expectations. He'd come across the production duo while on a flight to Los Angeles, where he spotted an advertisement for *A Monstrous Psychedelic Bubble Exploding in Your Mind*, a compilation album curated by Amorphous Androgynous. Intrigued by their eclectic, genre-defying sound, he reached out to them. Amorphous Androgynous, comprised of Garry Cobain and Brian Dougans – also known as the Future Sound of London – were known for their sprawling, experimental compositions that fused elements of psychedelia, electronica and avant-garde production. Their prior connection to Oasis came through a remix of 'Falling Down', the final single from *Dig Out Your Soul*, which reimagined the track as a twenty-two-minute, hypnotic journey, replacing Gallagher's vocals with those of Alisha Sufit from the seventies psych-folk band Magic Carpet. Inspired, Gallagher enlisted them to create an album that was expected to be wildly different from anything he had done before. Recording sessions took place at Paul Weller's studio, running parallel to *Noel Gallagher's High Flying Birds*. However, the process quickly proved to be an intense and unconventional experience. Cobain pushed Gallagher beyond his comfort zone, often instructing him to play a single guitar riff for hours at a time: 'I almost called it off on the first day when Gaz made me play the same guitar line for 5 hours and 10 minutes ... on the 27th take we nearly came to blows.'

Expanding on how junior the pair saw him in the dynamic, Noel said, 'If I suggested something [Garry] would say: "I'm not really into other people's ideas." There was a healthy disrespect for my songwriting. I'd play him something and he'd say, "It's good, but wouldn't it be great if we got a bunch of African tribesmen to play it through an electric kettle – on acid?"'

The sessions were driven by a method of deconstructing

and reassembling music – Gallagher would record ideas, which Dougans would then manipulate, using fragments from one track to build another. The atmosphere was tense, with Cobain exerting firm creative control and continuing to prevent Gallagher from speaking directly to Dougans.

Despite the initial excitement, by mid-2012 Noel began expressing doubts about the project. He admitted in interviews that while the sessions had produced some fascinating material, the final product failed to meet his quality standards. The lack of structure, the experimental nature of the compositions and fundamental creative differences led to frustration. He hinted at the difficulty of shaping the recordings into a cohesive album and ultimately shelved the project indefinitely.

Although the Amorphous Androgynous album never saw the light of day, its influence lingered in Gallagher's subsequent work. The experience broadened his musical horizons, and elements of the experimentation carried over into his later album, *Who Built the Moon?*, which embraced a more adventurous, psychedelic sound. The project remains a fascinating 'what if' in Gallagher's career – a bold but ultimately unrealised attempt at reinvention. It did, however, provide immediate results when it came to the optics of who Noel Gallagher the solo artist would be.

When he drops this little easter egg at the press conference, journalists and fans alike buzz with the possibility of what Noel's *Revolver* could sound like.

He also addresses the inevitable questions about Oasis,

reiterating that the band is over and that he has no plans to revisit that chapter of his life. 'Oasis is done,' he states firmly. 'There's nothing left to say on it. It was a great band, we had some great times, but it's over.'

One of the most significant moments of the event comes when Noel addresses the libel lawsuit that Liam has filed against him. In a rare act of public contrition, Noel apologises for his earlier comments about Liam's absence from the 2009 V Festival. He clarifies that Liam had indeed been suffering from laryngitis and that his previous statement had been inaccurate. Noel has perhaps realised it would be substantially cheaper to hold his hands up. He also clarifies his comments about Pretty Green, stating that he had no issue with Liam's business ventures, that he respects his brother's entrepreneurial spirit. Liam, in turn, drops the lawsuit, declaring that he is 'glad to put an end to this nonsense', that he wants to move on and to focus on his new band, on his new music. The legal battle is a fleeting skirmish in the ongoing war. Acknowledgement and apology from Noel represents a bigger settlement for both Noel and Liam than any financial compensation.

This apology is a shrewd move, and shows a growing willingness to take responsibility for his words.

By the spring of 2011, Noel had a clear vision for his debut post-Oasis album. The *High Flying Birds* recording sessions took place primarily in London at State of the Ark Studios and Abbey Road Studios, with additional work done in Los Angeles with Dave Sardy. Noel brought back long-time Oasis keyboardist Mike Rowe. On drums was Jeremy Stacey, known for his work with the Lemon Trees and Sheryl Crow, with his brother Paul 'Strangeboy' Stacey on guitar. Strangeboy was another long-time Noel collaborator. Noel would often send works in progress to guitarist mates inviting them to suggest guitar parts before generally deciding his own were better. One mate who did make it into the studio was Miles Kane, best known for his work with Alex Turner in the Last Shadow Puppets, who played on one of the songs but, unfortunately for Miles, Dave Sardy felt it failed adequately to 'kiss the sky', according to Noel.

Jeremy and Mike joined the live band, accompanied by Tim Smith on guitar and Russell Pritchard of the Zutons on bass. Pritchard's involvement came about serendipitously. Noel initially contacted him to enquire about the availability of a drummer friend of Russ's. However, during their conversation, Pritchard learned that Noel was also seeking a bassist and promptly secured the role for himself, solidifying his place in the High Flying Birds lineup where he has remained as the only ever present besides Noel. Besides being a fantastic bassist with a good voice for backing vocal duties, Russ is a dependable and affable man who shares social values and interests with his boss. He grew into the role, vacated by Gem, of both band member and friend.

Noel also brought in the Crouch End Festival Chorus, who had previously played with Oasis for a show at the Roundhouse, Camden, in 2008. They were rounded out by an all-female string section called the Wired Strings to add orchestral textures to several tracks, further expanding the sonic palette beyond the familiar guitar-driven sound of Oasis. In contrast to the stripped-down, raw energy of early Oasis, the High Flying Birds embraced a fuller, more elaborate sound, both visually and musically.

The album's sound was a deliberate departure from the later work of Oasis, although it still retained elements of Noel's signature songwriting style. There were echoes of the anthemic, guitar-driven rock that had made Oasis famous, but there were also new elements, textures, influences. There were hints of psychedelia, folk, jazz, even bossa nova. The arrangements were more complex, more layered, more ambitious than anything he had done with Oasis. In an interview with the *Quietus* in 2011, Noel described the album as 'a mix of everything I've ever loved'.

One of the most striking aspects of *Noel Gallagher's High Flying Birds* was its use of non-Oasis instrumentation. Tracks like 'The Death of You and Me' featured prominent brass sections, adding a new dimension to Noel's sound. This was a conscious decision, a way of moving beyond the guitar-heavy sound of his previous group. Noel explained his decision to use brass in an interview with *Music Radar*, saying that he wanted the album to feel grand and that he was inspired by the arrangements of classic soul records.

The live rehearsals were not without their challenges. Noel was pushing himself creatively and vocally, as well as working with a new band. It took time for them to gel and to develop the kind of intuitive understanding that comes from years of playing together. He later reflected on this period as one of the most enjoyable of his career, telling *Rolling Stone* that he felt 'a sense of freedom' he hadn't experienced since the early days of Oasis.

The seventeenth of October 2011 marked the official release of *Noel Gallagher's High Flying Birds*. The album was met with widespread critical acclaim and commercial success, cementing Noel's status as a major solo artist. It debuted at number one on the UK albums chart, selling over 120,000 copies in its first week. It eventually went double platinum. Critics praised the album's mature sound, its intricate arrangements, its sophisticated production and its strong songwriting. They noted the influence of classic rock, psychedelia and even jazz, but they also recognised Noel's unique melodic sensibility. *Rolling Stone* lauded the album for its 'melodic richness and sonic depth', while *Pitchfork* praised Noel's 'songwriting prowess'. The *Independent* called it a 'stunning return to form'.

The album's success was supported by the release of singles, including 'The Death of You and Me', 'AKA ... What a Life!' and 'If I Had a Gun ...' These tracks received significant radio airplay, establishing Noel's image as a solo artist. Albeit one whose appeal resonated loudest among the world's dads.

On 9 September 2011, 'AKA ... What a Life!' became the second single from Noel's debut album. The supporting promo video hasn't aged brilliantly. It followed on from the video for the debut single, 'The Death of You And Me', and starred goth pirate turned conspiracy spiritualist, Russell Brand. In the video, a waitress enters a gypsy caravan where she's greeted by a man named, no joke, The Dark (Brand). The Dark is sat atop a throne, flanked by burning torches. An edgy touch in a wooden wagon. He says he can see the waitress has many questions. He then instructs two nieces to restrain the waitress and forces her to drink a potion. Eventually Noel appears and rescues the girl.

Noel and Russell met following one of Brand's stand-up shows in 2005; they hit it off and became close. Noel frequently appeared on Brand's Radio X show where he also developed a strong bond with Brand's sidekick, Matt Morgan. In fact, they became good enough friends for Russell to be best man at Noel's wedding to Sara the same year that the 'AKA ... What a Life!' video was released. Brand is probably the closest Oasis got to having their own Magic Alex. Liam loathed him and Matt.

Noel was one of the very few high-profile names still close enough to Brand to attend his wedding to Laura Gallacher in 2017, but they do not seem so close in recent times. He remains close to Matt Morgan.

With the album topping the charts, Noel embarked on a tour with his new band. They kicked off in Dublin on 23 October 2011, just days after the album's release. It was a moment of truth for Noel, a test of his new material and his new band. He was no longer just a songwriter and guitarist; he was now a frontman, a band leader.

The setlists were carefully curated, balancing the excitement of the new material with the familiarity of a selection of Oasis classics that Noel had written and sung lead vocals on. Songs such as 'Don't Look Back in Anger', 'The Importance of Being Idle' and 'Half the World Away' were met with rapturous applause. He explained this approach in an interview with *NME*, stating that while he was proud of the Oasis songs, he wanted the focus to be firmly on the new material, on showcasing the sound and identity of Noel Gallagher's High Flying Birds.

The tour continued throughout the UK and Europe, with Noel Gallagher's High Flying Birds playing to sold-out crowds in major cities. They also performed on the festival circuit, further expanding their fanbase and solidifying their reputation as a formidable live act. Speaking to *Ultimate Guitar* magazine, Noel explained how the writing and recording process had been a more comfortable experience than the initial live shows. Despite being unsure of how the record would be received by Oasis fans, the shows became too big too quickly for his liking. He felt he needed to earn his stripes.

Huge bands have a tendency to romanticise the simplicity of starting out. It's easy to understand when viewed through the rearview mirror of enormous success because they know the story has a happy ending. In reality, starting small and working up is a real slog and not something most people want to do twice, but it allows bands to feel they have earned their success. Even the very best sometimes catch a dose of imposter syndrome and Noel was starting to show symptoms. It was indicative that, underneath all the finger pointing and shithousing, Noel genuinely valued what his younger brother brings to the table when it comes to live performance. 'I was kind of looking around thinking, "OK, this is massive." And people like Liam can pull off that kind of thing because of the charisma, whatever that thing is that they have. They can do it. And I didn't enjoy the gig, and I hated the aftershow. Just everything about it was like a rotten night. Funnily enough, the gig was filmed for a DVD as well.'

In contrast to Liam's more boisterous and publicly confrontational approach, Noel's journey was characterised by a quiet resilience. He weathered the storm of the Oasis breakup with dignity, refusing to be drawn too far into a public slanging match with his brother.

At the heart of his renaissance was his unwavering belief in the power of songwriting. He had always been a craftsman, a meticulous creator of melodies and lyrics. In the aftermath of Oasis, he doubled down on this aspect of his artistry. He poured his energy into writing and recording, trusting that the quality of his songs would ultimately speak for itself. His dedication to his craft and his ability to connect with audiences through his music were the cornerstones of his solo success. Here lies another distinct difference between the two brothers. Liam is by spirit and trade a rock star. Noel is a writer. Totally different professions and personality types that happen to converge in the studio and on the road. And totally different experiences for the paying punter. Noel has always believed in the power of song.

The journey had been far from easy but, by the end of 2011, Noel had successfully navigated one of the most challenging periods of his career and emerged from the shadow of Oasis stronger, more confident and more creatively fulfilled. He had established himself as a solo artist, a band leader, and a songwriter of enduring power and relevance. The success of *Noel Gallagher's High Flying Birds* and the subsequent tour were not just a personal triumph for Noel; they were proof of his continuing relevance in the ever-changing landscape of popular music.

The walkout in Paris was not to define his legacy. Instead, it was a beginning, The world was listening, and Noel Gallagher's High Flying Birds had taken flight.

5

Second Bite of the Apple – Liam, 2012–14

Just as Noel's birds were starting to take flight, Liam was heading into freefall. He'd bundled through the fallout of the Oasis split on cortisol and muscle memory. But the period following the release of Beady Eye's first album had begun to send him into a tailspin and the earth was starting to move very quickly towards him. All the sharp edges in Liam's life had begun to converge and, in 2013, he officially divorced from his wife and mother to his second son, Gene, Nicole Appleton.

It was a pattern he'd drawn before. During his marriage to Patsy Kensit in 1997–2000, when the pair became the face of Cool Britannia, he'd fathered Molly with former Kill City singer Lisa Moorish. Liam steadfastly refused to recognise Molly, born in March 1998, suggesting her mother had an agenda. Liam projected his frustration onto Lisa, and acceptance of Molly was the cost. On the one hand, it was complicated. On the other, it could have been made simple. The Gallagher stubborn streak struck again. Molly was his responsibility, but living in public estrangement a few miles down the road from Liam's Hampstead home. Molly's mother, Lisa, is a kind-hearted person who was part of the indie scene during the 1990s and 2000s.

Perhaps Liam's angst around acknowledging Molly stemmed from the difficult fact that his father, Tommy, had been unfaithful to his mother, Peggy, and fathered another child months after Liam entered the world. Liam and Noel's half-sister, Emma Davies, grew up a few streets away from the Gallagher household. Her mother had met Tommy at a local disco, where he acted as a country and western DJ, unaware he was married with three young sons at the time: baby Liam, Noel and eldest brother Paul. Liam only became aware of this following the huge success of Oasis. He and Noel didn't respond to overtures from Emma to meet and remain entirely estranged.

Branches of the same tree. The Tommy in Liam was poking its head up again.

Liam was antagonised further when Lisa had Peter Doherty's child, Astile, in 2003. He viewed Pete Doherty as the worst type of rock star. A skaghead southerner who made up with pimples what he lacked in style. When Noel invited Pete's new band Babyshambles to open for Oasis on a few dates of their 2005 tour, it was another example of the failures in brotherly empathy the Gallaghers shared. Pete failed to show for the 60,000-capacity concert at the cricket ground in Southampton, opting instead to remain in Paris with his then girlfriend, Kate Moss (one of Noel's closest friends). Liam played the big card marked 'I told you so' and offered the slot to the band of his housekeeper's nephew when they arrived in Newcastle shortly after.

So, a quick recap of high-grade chaos in Liam's life at this time: Beady Eye – not great. Nicole – divorcing him for adultery. An estranged daughter in London and a half-sister for her arriving in New York. Growing speculation about the personal nature of his relationship with a member of his management, Debbie Gwyther. Money in: not a lot. Money out: loads. Big brother: flying high. Not an ideal set of circumstances from which to build on your career.

Liam's divorce from the mother of his second son was reported to have cost him half his estimated £15 million assets. On top of that, he had been named as the father of Gemma by a New York court, with the mother suing for a reported $3 million, plus another commitment to another round of child support to go along with the house, school fees and everything else he owed for Molly. Rock stars of Liam's nature have a high burn rate and the diminishing royalties faced by musicians in the emerging streaming world don't really cut it. Nor do live sales when you refuse to play Oasis's big hits.

It's possible Liam has a degree of social anxiety. That may sound strange for such a charismatic public persona but he often behaves awkwardly in public situations and often retreats totally from the public eye. His attire during these periods is a world away from the flamboyant white furs and Burberry duffel of his peak fashionista phase. For the next decade, when spotted jogging on Hampstead Heath, he'd be shrouded in all-black hooded parkas.

Extended to 2020, when COVID-19 normalised face masks, combined with Stone Island and C. P. Company's integration of hooligan-friendly masks in their attire, then he was able to hide almost completely. Had it not been for that Steven Gerrard-esque cadence, he probably would have gone totally unnoticed on his early morning route of the north London haven. On stage too, his parkas became increasingly baggier. A true northerner, the coat was always the most important piece of the look and regardless of whether he'd be happy to sweat his way through a show in it. But now it was a cloak. Another barrier, on top of the bins and bravado, between him and the world. And a way to avoiding confirming his increasing girth.

In his shell and tired of being bothered by paps and Oasis fans, he'd begun to feel like he was on a 'bad trip'. He also questioned his relevance as a musician, wondering, 'Am I a fucking has-been? Is this it?' With that came financial pressure. He was waiting for his divorce to be finalised and to see what 'pennies they'd throw back' at him. He'd seen his financial worth more than halved. A healthy amount remained by any stretch but not the full Scrooge McDuck. He felt that lawyers were making the situation worse: 'If it wasn't the divorce lawyer, it was the other lawyer. It was fucking grim. They just make it worse. They fucking strung it out, mate. They definitely know how long a piece of string is.' The string in question was apparently £800,000 in length when spread between his and Nicole's teams. Musicians don't love paying those outside of the immediate music sphere, but they really don't like paying solicitors. All this led to him 'drinking too much'. A big claim considering the source. He admitted to 'ruining [his now official girlfriend] Debbie's vibe', by trying to convince her to 'come and be a fucking dosser like me!' rather than go to work. Debbie Gwyther is widely regarded as a highly professional operator in the music industry. She has the ability to really get on it but everything about her work is meticulous. Alongside her sister Katie, they became known as 'the terrible twins' for their impressive abilities in the field of socialising. Besides drinking rock stars under tables, they established FEAR PR, running publicity for music acts and managing or co-managing artists such as Martha Wainwright and, by this point, Beady Eye. Rock 'n' roll was very much the family business, with Gwyther's mother, Elaine, managing Simple Minds. The smallness of the music world throws up another quirky connection: Liam's first wife, Patsy, had been married to Simple Minds frontman, Jim Kerr, before Liam. Together they'd shared a son, James (of 'Little James' notoriety – Liam's first stab at an Oasis song, which occupies a space several leagues below 'Octopus's Garden', Ringo's Beatles effort, in the estimation of Oasis aficionados).

So, while Debbie went to work, Liam was spending time 'sitting at home being Billy No Mates'. Misery may love company but it thrives on isolation.

Beady Eye's debut *Different Gear, Still Speeding* had achieved moderate commercial success and garnered some positive reviews but it failed to really move the critical or commercial needle. Great footballers know when they're in a great team. Great singers know when they're singing a great song. Liam's internal quality control knew this was methadone. Crucially, the difference between Beady Eye and Noel Gallagher's High Flying Birds' font sizes on festival posters and venue marquees was growing.

The answer to Liam's ills is always rock 'n' roll. The medicine can be found in the studio and on the road. Competitive with his brother and driven by a deep-seated need to prove himself, Beady Eye was becoming a source of frustration and, perhaps, drawing out a sense of insecurity to which he would never admit. Publicly, Liam remained defiant, dismissing the comparisons and insisting that Beady Eye was a different beast altogether, a band with a unique sound and vision. They had steadfastly refused to play Oasis songs. Anathema to concert promoters and fans alike. This served to filter their crowd down to the most dedicated. Whereas Noel had created an artistic filter in relation to the past, Liam's was born of stubbornness and the hope he could create something meaningful and lasting without Noel's songwriting and without the Oasis brand name.

The only notable exception to this came during the closing ceremony of the 2012 London Olympics. Beady Eye, motivated by the unique reach of the opportunity, agreed to perform 'Wonderwall' for the event. The band mimed while Liam's vocal was performed live. Noel later claimed to have rejected the opportunity to perform the song himself, implying Beady Eye were second choice. Speaking to XFM, he said he'd asked the organisers why they were insistent on him miming. '"Why do you want me to mime?" and he said, "It's a big gig." Really? I do this for a living. In the end, I was just like, you know what, I'd rather watch it on the telly.' So watch on the telly he did, but not before putting pressure on Liam's involvement purely out of bedevilment. As the song was to be a new master recording performed on a broadcast, it required sync clearance by the songwriter. Noel elaborated in the same chat with XFM, 'They had to re-record it and then send it to me. I did play a bit of cat and mouse with them for a few days – I took it until Friday night at ten o'clock before I said yes and they were shitting it. "Meh, it's all right, I'm not sure with this new string arrangement" and they were like, "Fuck! The gig's on Sunday," so I was like, "OK, all right, you can have it then."'

Noel revelled in the power to throw Liam off where possible. A few days later, while performing at a War Child charity concert, Noel dedicated that very song to 'Stratford's finest Oasis tribute band'. It's a textbook example of what makes Noel's put-downs of his brother so compelling: reducing Liam's career to that of somebody whose skill in aping their former glory is limited to being the best in a single neighbourhood of London. Playing a song he'd had to get approval to perform at an event his brother felt below his calling. If it weren't so mean spirited it would actually be an act of elegant reductionism.

Liam and Beady Eye had embarked on the recording of their second album in a couple of months before the Olympic Stadium singalong. They made a bold decision that signalled a significant shift in direction, enlisting the services of producer Dave Sitek, a member of the experimental indie rock band TV on the Radio. Sitek was renowned for his adventurous, atmospheric production style, his innovative use of electronic textures and unconventional recording techniques. His work with bands such as Yeah Yeah Yeahs and Foals demonstrated a willingness to push sonic boundaries, to defy easy categorisation. It was an interesting move.

This was a marked departure from the straightforward, guitar-driven rock 'n' roll sound of Beady Eye's debut, a clear indication that Liam was willing to take risks to succeed and starting to open up to career advice from Gwyther, his partner and manager. The recording sessions for the new album, which would eventually be titled *BE*, began in the spring of 2012 at London's State of the Ark Studios, known for its vintage equipment and its warm, analogue sound. Sitek's influence was immediately apparent, his presence a catalyst for change. He encouraged the band towards some intriguing moments of weirdness and pushed them to explore uncharted musical territory. In a 2013 interview with *NME*, Liam described the recording process as 'trippy' and 'mind-blowing', praising Sitek for his innovative approach. 'He's without a doubt the best producer I've ever worked with,' Liam enthused, his admiration for Sitek evident.

Sitek's production techniques were unconventional, at least by the standards of a band accustomed to more traditional, straightforward methods. He employed a range of vintage synthesisers, samplers and effects pedals, creating a sonic landscape that was far more layered and textured, more nuanced, than anything Beady Eye had done before.

He encouraged improvisation, often manipulating and distorting the band's performances in real time, creating a sense of spontaneity and unpredictability, capturing unexpected moments of magic. He was a sonic sculptor, moulding and shaping their sound.

Liam was initially hesitant about some of Sitek's more experimental ideas due to his own instinctive preference for a more raw, stripped-down sound, but gradually he embraced the new direction, the sonic possibilities. He later admitted in an interview with the *Guardian* that he'd been wary of Sitek's methods at first, that he had questioned some of his choices, but had come to appreciate the producer's willingness to take risks. Liam acknowledged that they needed to be pushed out of their comfort zones.

The band's studio sessions were, by all accounts, a period of intense creativity and experimentation, a time of exploration and discovery. Anecdotes from the recording sessions, shared in later interviews by band members, paint a picture of a band willing to try new things, to push their musical boundaries and embrace the unknown. Gem Archer, in a 2013 interview with *Guitar World*, described the sessions as 'a real learning experience', praising Sitek's ability to bring the best out in the band and help them find a new voice. Andy Bell, too, took to the experimental approach, incorporating new guitar effects and textures into his playing, expanding his tonal palette.

Liam's role in the studio also evolved, taking on a new dimension. While he remained primarily focused on his vocals, his signature instrument, he became more involved in the overall sound of the band, offering suggestions, contributing ideas to the arrangements, and shaping the sonic direction of the songs. He led the songwriting of some of the tracks, and overall shared equal credit for the compositions along with Gem Archer and Andy Bell. It was a turnaround from their initial working relationship with Liam when a greater sense of job security could be fostered by biting their tongues when asked about songs they didn't love. Now they were the ones creating the tunes and Liam needed them. As for Liam, he was no longer simply the frontman, the singer; he was an active participant in the creative process, a band leader pushing the direction of the music, taking ownership of the band's sound.

Despite the experimental nature of the sessions, the band were determined to create an album that was still accessible and engaging, that would connect with their audience. They were not interested in making a record that was simply weird or avant-garde for the sake of it, an album that would alienate their existing fanbase. They wanted to create something that was both challenging and rewarding, something that would push their boundaries while still retaining their core identity as a rock 'n' roll band, a band that could write memorable tunes. Liam emphasised this in multiple interviews, stating that while they were trying new things, experimenting with different sounds, they still wanted to make 'proper tunes' that people could connect with, songs that would resonate with their audience.

During promotional duties for *BE* Liam continued to poke at his brother. He dismissed Noel's solo work as 'boring' and 'predictable', his words dripping with disdain, while also taking aim at bands such as Kasabian and Arctic Monkeys, who he felt had committed the crimes of being 'corporate' and 'lacking spirit'. These pronouncements, while entertaining for some, often overshadowed the music Beady Eye were making, distracting from the creative process. The media, always eager for a Gallagher feud story and a headline-grabbing quote, focused on Liam's surrealist gems. But the references to Noel only led to the press framing each Beady Eye story in the context of Oasis and Noel's solo success. Simply put, Liam being Liam was doing much better business than Beady Eye ever could.

BE was finally released on 10 June 2013. It was the moment of truth for Beady Eye. The album's cover, featuring a stark black and white photograph of a woman's bare back, was a departure from the more colourful and psychedelic artwork of their debut. It was a visual representation of the band's desire to strip things back, to present a more raw and honest version of themselves, to move away from the familiar imagery of their past.

The album's lead single, 'Second Bite of the Apple', was released in April 2013, a precursor to the album. It was a driving, energetic track with a distinct psychedelic edge, showcasing Sitek's influence on the band's sound, his experimental production techniques. The song received mixed reviews. The experimental feel, while novel, didn't make up for the absence of a strong hook and the single failed to make the UK top 100.

Other notable tracks on the album included the

co-written 'Flick of the Finger', which was a sprawling, experimental track that featured a spoken-word sample from a Tariq Ali speech, a political statement that surprised some listeners, and the Liam-penned 'Soul Love', a more melodic, introspective song that showcased his vocal range, his ability to convey emotion. 'Iz Rite' was a driving rocker with a catchy chorus, while 'Don't Brother Me' seemed to address his relationship with Noel, something he denied in interviews.

Commercially, *BE* performed modestly, a reflection of the sub-Oasis songs and the changing landscape of the music industry. It debuted at number two on the UK albums chart, an improvement on their debut album's number three position, a small victory. But it quickly fell down the charts, failing to maintain its initial momentum. Sales were ultimately disappointing, especially when compared to the success of Noel's double-platinum solo debut.

Following the release of *BE*, Beady Eye embarked on a world tour to promote the album. However, the band faced significant challenges in translating the album's experimental, often layered and textured sound to a live setting. The more atmospheric tracks from *BE* often lacked the immediate impact, the raw energy, of the band's earlier, more straightforward rock songs.

Moreover, Beady Eye struggled to fill larger venues. While Liam's stage presence remained as captivating as ever, the band's lack of 'Wonderwall'-shaped hits made it difficult to maintain momentum and keep the audience engaged. They found themselves playing to smaller crowds than they had anticipated, a stark contrast to the stadium-filling days of Oasis – a humbling experience. The band's touring struggles were documented in various concert reviews, including one from the *Telegraph* that noted the 'lack of atmosphere' at a particular show, a sign that they were not connecting with audiences as they had hoped. The calls for 'Wonderwall' and 'Live Forever' from the crowd became a recurring theme at Beady Eye shows, a constant reminder of a past the band were trying to move beyond, and a source of frustration for Liam.

In August 2013, guitarist Gem Archer suffered a serious head injury after falling down a flight of stairs at home, leaving him with a potentially life-changing injury. This forced the band to cancel a number of shows, including appearances at the V Festival and other high-profile events, disrupting their tour schedule and their promotional plans. While Archer eventually made a full recovery, it was slow progress. Following brain trauma, some skills return more readily than others and Gem wasn't quite himself for a long time afterwards. Beady Eye were forced to cancel their upcoming shows, with the band's official website stating: 'Beady Eye regret to announce that they are cancelling their performance at V Festival and their remaining scheduled shows and promotional commitments in August due to guitarist Gem Archer suffering severe head trauma after an accident on August 1. The band apologise to fans, but under the circumstances feel they cannot perform without Gem and want to focus on supporting him throughout his recovery. Gem was released from hospital yesterday evening and is recovering at home though remains under observation.'

Gem entered the world with the slightly less rock-star-ready name of Colin Archer. The etymology of playground nicknames being what it is, Colin became Gem thanks to the prominence of Scottish footballer Archie Gemmill. Gem joined Oasis as guitarist in November 1999, initially to take lead duties from Noel. Noel had started to agree with the guitar-shop bores who thought he was overrated and delegated solos to Gem. Quite a thing to join Oasis as the man responsible for playing those iconic riffs. It didn't last long. Noel enjoyed the lead role too much and reassumed control shortly after.

Gem was recruited after original Oasis guitarist and barre-chord enthusiast, Bonehead (so named thanks to a less flattering nickname convention), had followed bassist Guigsy out of the band following a row with Noel. Gem was a fan and feared Oasis would split up upon hearing the news. Unbeknown to him, Noel had him in mind to audition. Gem's band, Heavy Stereo, shared a label with Oasis and Noel had sounded out mutual friends about Gem. Gem was happy with Heavy Stereo but getting the call from Oasis in 1998 was akin to a Wigan Athletic striker being the subject of a transfer bid from Real Madrid. The Chief invited Gem to Olympic Studios, where Oasis were mixing their fourth album, the misnomered *Standing on the Shoulder of Giants*. Gem and Noel reportedly went to the pub following Gem's audition. Gem couldn't stand not knowing how it had went and asked what Liam's thoughts were; Noel said it was his band and he'd have who he liked. Noel was right. It was his band now. The departures of Bonehead and Guigsy, four years after drummer Tony McCarroll had been bullied out of the band, left Liam as the only original member of Oasis remaining. Initially Gem was paid a standard session wage, reportedly £85 a gig for the first tour, but did go on to contribute to the writing of some of the band songs going forward. He remained in the band until its demise and became a trusted confidant and collaborator for both Liam and Noel.

In October 2014, after a series of increasingly sparsely attended festival shows, culminating in a performance at the Benicàssim festival in Spain, Liam Gallagher unceremoniously announced the end of Beady Eye, via Twitter. The unexpected tweet was short and sweet, 'Beady Eye are no longer. Thanks for all your support. LGx'

It brought the band's short-lived journey to an abrupt end. Noel later had a pop at him for dropping his bandmates by text while deciding on a solo career. This was the same Noel Gallagher who had lit the internet up by announcing he was leaving Oasis to seek pastures new.

6

You Know We Can't Go Back – Noel, 2012–14

The years following the release of his debut solo album, *Noel Gallagher's High Flying Birds*, were a period of creative exploration, artistic consolidation and personal contentment for Noel Gallagher. Noel had deftly navigated the early stage of his solo career. He'd set the table for something different from Oasis while retaining enough of his trademark anthemic writing sensibility to still connect with his core audience. Crucially, unlike Liam, he had incorporated the Oasis bangers that had made his name into the shows. The initially mooted Amorphous Androgynous album never materialised but the mention of it had helped to tick the experimental box and shift expectations towards that direction just enough. He was gradually building the concept of what the High Flying Birds was. His band evolved both in personnel and in sound. He was gradually refining his audience, sanding off the rougher edges and shaping a crowd who arrived at his gigs wanting to watch Noel Gallagher the solo star rather than a nineties nostalgia trip. It was a strong, thoughtful transition from Noel. Equal parts pragmatic careerism and creative progression.

The success of his debut album and the subsequent tour had instilled in Noel a confidence in his new direction and he wanted to push it further. By his own admission, he was not a natural frontman, but his songwriting prowess and the collective visual of the expanded live band were enough to captivate audiences. Emboldened, he began working on the material that would eventually form his second album.

Unlike his debut, which was partially comprised of songs written during the latter years of Oasis, *Chasing Yesterday*, which was recorded in 2012–14 and released in spring 2015, was almost entirely conceived and written in Noel's post-Oasis life. 'Lock All the Doors' was the notable exception, which he had begun some twenty-three years earlier during his collaboration with the Chemical Brothers, which had yielded the singles 'Setting Sun' (1996) and 'Let Forever Be' (1999). He'd returned to the track after a finding a moment of inspiration among the aisles of Maida Vale's Tesco Express. He returned home from that most unlikely of future blue plaque locations with a new verse melody in the bag next to the semi-skimmed milk. Unexpected item in bagging area indeed.

In interviews during this period, Noel spoke of his desire to push his boundaries, to expand his sonic palette, to experiment with different sounds and styles, to progress as a songwriter. He was no longer interested in simply recreating the anthemic rock of his Oasis days, the formula that had brought him such success. He wanted to create something more nuanced, more textured, more reflective of his evolving musical tastes, his growing maturity as an artist. He expressed this sentiment in a 2014 interview with *Rolling Stone*, saying he'd already done the anthems and stadium rock – now it was time to do whatever he wanted. It was a statement of artistic intent.

The writing process for *Chasing Yesterday* was another solitary pursuit, befitting the self-proclaimed 'bit of a loner', although the realisation of these songs in the studio was a more collaborative affair. He'd returned to past Oasis producers, engineers and session musicians but never actual band members. Chris Sharrock, Gem Archer and Andy Bell had all made their Beady Eye-shaped bed as far as Noel was concerned and a clean break was needed. They'd also been collectively and specifically criticised for failing to offer adequate support to Noel. To be fair, it's hard for junior or non-permanent members of a band as big and established as Oasis to look anywhere other than their shoes when the twin engines are roaring at each other.

Familiar faces like Jeremy and Paul Stacey joined longtime friend and all-round boss Johnny Marr in the studio. The problem with having Marr layer tracks of guitar in the studio is you then have to figure out how to play it live and there's nobody quite like Marr when it comes to doing that. Johnny Marr stands out in the music industry, where everybody who has ever met or dealt with him, with the exception of a notable lone voice in the form of his ex-Smiths bandmate Morrissey, is effusive about their experience of the man. He has added some incredible music to the world and always pushes on with his own creative expression, writing and playing. He's a generous man whose ongoing efforts on behalf of other people enhance their lives in orders of magnitude. Noel too was a recipient of Marr's enthusiastic generosity of spirit and soul. In the early days, Johnny lent/donated (depending on perspective) guitars to Noel and introduced him to his manager, Marcus Russell, who would go on to help Oasis and the High Flying Birds achieve so much. If you ever fancy an exercise in compare and contrast, listen to the audiobooks of Marr and Morrissey back to back. Marr's revisits the past with a philosophical but forward motion, while there is no gripe too slight nor too distant to be omitted from Mozz's recollections.

A significant development in Noel's creative process for *Chasing Yesterday* was his decision to assume full production responsibilities. This was partially due to Dave Sardy's unavailability at the time and partially because, as he said to *NME*, Noel knew 'what I want these songs to sound like. I know what's in my head. I didn't need someone else to tell me what to do.'

He again returned to Paul Stacey for engineering duties and recorded the album at Stacey's Strangeways Studios and the fabled Abbey Road, scene of the wall-shakingly loud *Be Here Now* sessions. Walking into Abbey Road's legendary Studio 2 live room, where the Beatles expanded the very concept of what an album could be, never gets old. There is a reverential hush adopted by people when first stepping on to the parquet floor akin to visiting one of the world's grand old cathedrals. Only way more exciting. You can smell the sixties in the air.

A couple of tracks credited production to Amorphous Androgynous: 'The Right Stuff' and 'The Mexican'. They were stylistically different to anything Noel had made before. 'The Right Stuff' is atmospheric and patient. Its horizon is wide but hazy like Sunday-morning fog over a park football pitch. The mix allows Noel's vocal, which Joy Rose beautifully harmonises with, to be given space and depth in the centre of the track.

Meanwhile, 'The Mexican' was a late inclusion after Noel felt the album's sonic shade needed a little more light. Although generally very dismissive of his efforts on the ill-fated and allegedly deleted Androgynous Amorphous sessions, some of the work did eventually make it into the world. Speaking to *NME* around the time of release, Noel said the basis for the track came while 'playing bass, not liking what I was doing, so [I] started messing about with an effects pedal and played a riff and everybody leapt up and went "what's that?" So they looped it and put a drum beat on it and it's a little different.' This way of writing as part of the recording process was alien to Noel at the time and unintentional. It would become the MO of his later work with David Holmes. Lyrically the song sees Noel offer an alternative resolution to David Cameron's infamous 'hug a hoodie' approach to young offenders. Noel, as an alleged young offender himself, felt they'd be better served by 'a fucking baseball bat right across the fucking skull'. Interesting approach to lightening an album's tone. The song is another example of Noel's often opaque titling style. Although it's not immediately clear who or what 'The Mexican' refers to, it should be noted that he has a long-standing love for holidaying in Mexico. His Oasis album and touring cycle used to finish in Mexico City or on the US west coast, from which Noel would head for a long beach holiday to unwind. He even titled the song he contributed to the 1998 *X-Files* soundtrack 'Teotihuacan'. The trip-hop tune was named such after Noel made a 'spiritual pilgrimage' to the ancient Mesoamerican pyramids.

Despite Noel's 'Chief' persona, which governed the majority of Oasis's musical direction, and his prolific criticism of other musicians, he is actually a keen collaborator under the right conditions. If he gets on with and admires the work of the musician in question, he can be a very productive creative partner.

The arrangements on *Chasing Yesterday* were more complex than on the previous record. They were more layered, with greater use of horns, strings and electronic textures, which created a more diverse sonic landscape. Tracks such as 'Riverman', with its jazzy feel, displayed a newfound sophistication in Noel's songwriting, and pushed his vision of the High Flying Birds further down the musical road. 'Lock All the Doors', though, harkened back to the more raucous style, reminiscent of early Oasis, albeit brighter sounding and with a more polished production.

The album's title, *Chasing Yesterday*, became the latest

in a long line of album names to give Noel a sense of 'buyer's remorse'. Upon release, he said he'd 'literally came up with it [a week earlier and] if [he] could change it [he] would'.

Chasing Yesterday was released on 2 March 2015 to positive reviews and strong commercial success. The album debuted at number one on the UK albums chart, giving him a second consecutive number-one solo album. This achievement is rarer than you'd think for a band member who was not the lead vocalist in a hugely successful band.

The lead single, 'In the Heat of the Moment', released in November 2014, was a driving, energetic track that showcased the album's more experimental sound, its fusion of rock and electronic elements. It received significant radio airplay and reached number twenty-six on the UK singles chart, a respectable showing. The song's success and its popularity on the airwaves further drove anticipation for the album's release, creating a buzz around Noel's new project.

Other singles from the album included the 'Ballad of the Mighty I' featuring Johnny Marr, 'Riverman' and 'The Dying of the Light', each showcasing a different facet of Noel's songwriting, a different aspect of his musical personality. Each single was accompanied by a music video, further expanding the visual world of *Chasing Yesterday*.

Fan reactions to *Chasing Yesterday* were part of the ongoing remoulding of his audience. While many embraced Noel's new direction, appreciating his willingness to experiment and evolve, others longed for the more straightforward, anthemic rock of his Oasis days. This is the dividing line between those who gravitate towards Liam and those who spend their money on High Flying Birds records. There's a paradox at the heart of Oasis's music and their fans. On the one hand, you have a band who were largely defined by their proclamations of love for the Beatles but which never really sounded like them. McCartney-style bass counter melodies, melodic drum patterns and close harmonies are almost completely absent from the Oasis canon. Arguably the defining trait of the Beatles was their desire to evolve, and the rapid rate at which they did so in both musical output and visuals. In 1964, they were clean-cut lads in suits and leather Cuban heeled boots playing pop songs about love. By 1968 they were hairy-faced hippies in plimsoles and knitted moccasins whose experimental push required the invention of new recording equipment to create. Most adamant in his love for the Beatles and yet most resistant to changing the Oasis sound was their singer, Liam Gallagher. For him, it seemed, musical expression never needs to change beyond the second gear. Post-show in Noel's dressing room, you'll hear the La's, Neil Young and all sorts of soul, indie and dance obscurities. This juxtaposition of musical sensibilities had begun to push the Oasis fanbase into tribes and Noel was increasingly happy to shed the more laddish element.

Chasing Yesterday was a commercial success, selling over 89,000 copies in its first week in the UK, an impressive figure in the age of streaming and digital downloads, and it went on to achieve platinum certification. The album also performed well internationally, reaching the top ten in numerous territories.

In March 2015, Noel set out on an extensive world tour with the High Flying Birds, which would stretch over a year and a half. The tour took Noel and his growing band across the UK, Europe, North America, Asia and South America.

The setlists for the tour were a mix of songs from *Chasing Yesterday*, his debut solo album and a selection of Oasis classics, a balance that reflected his desire to perform new material and provide fan service. The economics of moving the High Flying Birds around the world also dictated the same balance. He started to curate a setlist, built on striking a deal with the crowd, which would deliver the fans what they wanted near the end of the set if they came along for the ride in the first half, which was becoming weighted towards the solo compositions. Lessons had been learned from Beady Eye's refusal to perform Oasis numbers.

He told the *Telegraph* in 2015, 'Those songs belong to me as much as they belong to anyone else. I wrote them. I'm proud of them. But I'm also proud of the new stuff, and I want people to hear that too.' It was a tightrope walk between honouring his legacy and forging a new path.

The live performances were a chance to underline Noel's continuing development as a frontman, a role he had not fully embraced in Oasis. While Liam's was static in a mesmerising way, Noel's stillness looked uncomfortable when taking lead vocals. He adopts an almost opposite posture to his younger brother. Whereas Liam's knees are dropped, allowing his neck to reach up to the mic, Noel cranes his neck down, rounding his back and eliminating the possibility of eye contact with the crowd as he sings the lyrics. Neither are great from a technique standpoint but Noel's is significantly less exciting to watch. But he has a great big bag of hit songs and that's really enough.

Despite his awkward singing posture, he was growing ever-more relaxed in the frontman role. He continued to interact with the audience, often insulting them over some shout or placard they were holding, and they received it like an affectionate dedication.

The band, too, had evolved into a tight, cohesive unit, a well-oiled machine. They performed with energy and precision, bringing Noel's songs to life with a dynamic interplay that showcased their individual talents while also serving the overall sound of the music, the nuances of the arrangements.

Standout performances during this period included a triumphant set at the Latitude Festival in the UK. Noel had taken the decision to headline smaller festivals rather than appear lower down the bill at larger events. It was a savvy piece of positioning that retained his perception as a big commercial name while also effectively ensuring a 'home' crowd, receptive to his new material rather than having to win over multitudes who weren't necessarily his audience and who probably wouldn't make time in their fuzzy itinerary for the solo tracks. Better to have a smaller field that adores you than an ambivalent mass.

When Noel launched into an Oasis classic at a solo show, like 'Don't Look Back in Anger' or 'Wonderwall', the crowd would erupt, singing along to every word, their voices coalescing in communal rapture. But the new material was increasingly received with enthusiasm. Noel's solo work was connecting with audiences on its own terms, not just as an extension of his Oasis legacy, but as a distinct and valuable body of work, and a declaration of artistic independence.

In contrast to Liam's more traditional rock sound with Beady Eye, his adherence to a more conventional approach, Noel's solo work was becoming increasingly eclectic and experimental, more adventurous. He was continuing to move well away from the 'lad rock' label that had often been applied to Oasis, a label he now found limiting, embracing a more mature and sophisticated sound that reflected his evolving musical tastes.

He reflected on this difference in a 2015 interview with the *Telegraph*, stating, 'In Oasis, I was always aware of what the fans wanted. Now, I just do what I want.' It was a liberating experience, a chance for the Chief finally to be his own boss, and push himself further now that *Chasing Yesterday* and the subsequent tour had proven that he could stand alone.

While Noel's artistic evolution, his musical journey, was taking centre stage, his personal life during this period also reflected a newfound sense of stability and contentment that had often eluded him in the past. His marriage to Sara MacDonald in 2011, in a beautiful ceremony in the English countryside, provided him with a strong foundation. Noel often spoke of the importance of his family in interviews, describing his wife as his 'rock' and his children as his 'greatest joy'. He was determined to be a present and involved father, in stark contrast to his own dad, who had been abusive before becoming estranged.

Noel had a clear sense of priorities, a recognition that his personal happiness and his family's wellbeing were, in theory at least, just as important as his professional success, his musical ambitions. His ease with Oasis's legacy grew. While he had no desire to reunite the band, he was able to look back on Oasis with pride.

He acknowledged the importance of Oasis in his life and in the lives of his fans, but he was also confident in his ability to move forward and write songs that would stand the test of time. He told *Rolling Stone* in 2016, 'I'm not done yet. I've still got a lot of music left in me. I'm still learning, still exploring.' It was a statement that reflected both his humility and his enduring ambition.

The period between 2012 and 2014, the years following the release of his debut and leading up to *Chasing Yesterday*, marked a crucial stage in Noel Gallagher's evolution as a solo artist. He had successfully established a distinct musical identity but wanted to push it further forward. His second LP, *Chasing Yesterday*, showcased his growth as a songwriter and producer. The album's critical acclaim and commercial success further solidified his position in the music industry, cementing his place as a major solo artist.

7

For What It's Worth – Liam, 2015–17

'I'm a cunt' – Liam Gallagher

Liam now found himself in uncharted depths and just about managing to tread water. After the implosion of Beady Eye, in 2014, he may not have been totally on his arse but his cheeks were uncomfortably close to the floor. His bank account was dwindling and for the first time in over two decades, Liam Gallagher was without a band. The touring and recording that had provided some degree of structure in his life since his early twenties was gone and he was spending more and more time down his local. 'When Beady Eye split up, I could've knocked music on the head. It was like, "Fuck it. I've got a lot of shit goin'. I haven't got a band. I can't be arsed lookin' for a new one,"' he revealed to *Huck* magazine.

The end of Beady Eye left him grasping for something to hold on to, but the past had already let go. This was his last roll of the dice, and he knew it. He had always thrived in a band setting, feeding off the energy of collaboration, the creative tension that fuelled his best performances. Going it alone meant stepping out of the Oasis shadow, out of the comfort zone of Beady Eye, and proving himself as an artist in his own right. It was intimidating but also liberating – an opportunity to be fully in control for the first time in his career.

Besides the career ennui, Liam was also struggling with his divorce from Nicole Appleton. He'd appointed the divorce lawyer of choice for rock stars, Fiona Shackleton. She was known for representing Prince Charles and Paul McCartney in their respective divorces. Shackleton isn't known for her low hourly rates, and when combined with the settlement to Nicole and the settlement to Liza, Liam was really feeling the pinch.

Deflated, he asked if he even wanted to be Liam Gallagher: rock 'n' roll star any more. 'Do I really wanna be Liam Gallagher? Can I be arsed with the bullshit that goes with it? Maybe it's time to walk away and not do anything.' For a time, he considered moving to Spain, contemplating a life away from the chaos. 'I was gonna go and live in Spain and just chill out, get fit, eat nice, bit of sun on me bones and just fucking live.' Debbie wasn't impressed and, despite Liam's rationale that it would only be a couple of hours on a plane, she remained unmoved. 'I got this close to going by myself. Googling properties. It weren't fucking Magaluf, I'm not that broke, but not far off. My kids weren't bothered. They were just asking if it would have a pool or not, the cheeky fucks.'

Noel, watching from afar, commented on Liam's struggles in an *NME* interview, suggesting that such challenges could serve as a chance for reinvention. 'He's making a fucking mess of things at the moment, but we've all been there,' he says. 'I've been there. Something like that can be a great thing because you get to the bottom and you cleanse yourself of a lot of fucking shit baggage and you start again. I'm the kind of person that says, "Fuck it, take it," and I'll start again. And that would be my advice to him.'

Publicly, Liam maintained a low profile. He was occasionally seen out and about in London or spotted at football matches, supporting his beloved Manchester City, on one occasion bumping into Noel for the first time since they'd wished each other a not so fond farewell. Noel described the encounter, which happened the day City won the Premier League at their Etihad Stadium on 11 May 2014: 'I was in the directors box, obviously, and he was outside selling burgers, and one of the directors asked if I wanted to go on the pitch with the team, and I was like, "Fucking yeah" so I went on the pitch and in the tunnel before I said to [club captain] Vincent Kompany "Give us your armband" and he gave me it, so I was wearing it in the bar afterwards, and I was sitting there talking to somebody, and someone came up behind me and tried to take the armband off and I was like, "Fucking get off of it" and it was Liam. And he was like, "Fucking hell man, you knobhead, you shouldn't have that, I should fucking have that." And that's how it started. And I was like, "Oh yeah, alright, and how are you?" Every time I see him he is still being a bit of a fucking cheeky cunt. And he's still putting out the persona of the angry barking dog.'

So they pretty much picked up where they left off. Liam jabbing. Noel ducking and throwing a little kidney shot as he rolled. No sign the pattern of their relationship was about to change any time soon.

Liam needed to be rescued and, luckily for him, he had Debbie Gwyther to show him the way forward. During Liam's period of self-doubt, it was Debbie who ultimately pulled him back from the brink. Liam credits her with not only saving him from himself but also resurrecting his career. 'Debbie saved me. No bullshit,' he told *Q*. 'Debbie swooped me up as I was falling, she just said, "Stop being a dickhead." She got me out of the house, introduced me to all kinds of people outside my world, got me doing new things.'

Debbie made small changes to move Liam out of his rut. His world had become small and he was confined largely to familiar haunts in Hampstead (home to many an ace public house), a place he had called home for years. She pushed him to explore new places and experiences – simple but transformative acts that helped him reconnect with the world around him. 'I've been to Dalston, man,' he joked. Dalston, that most feared borough of London for anti-hipsters, was a step towards the new.

Before this, Liam's days were largely unstructured and often focused on Debbie's plans, or more to the point, trying to disrupt them. 'Just waiting for Debbie to entertain me all day. I'm like her dog. I'm like: "Will you take me for walkies?" Speaking with the *Guardian*, Liam offered a possible explanation. 'I think I've got ADHD, I like to keep moving, man.' Indeed, his brother Paul described the young Liam as 'hyperactive', saying 'everything was a game to Liam' and it often got him into trouble.

Now, if Liam does have ADHD it would explain a lot. Although the neurodiversity is often wrongly described by some as a benign personality trait and subject to a weirdly light-hearted view, it is a progressive condition which becomes increasingly pernicious and can cause major fuckery in the lives of those who have it and everybody in their orbit. There is a disproportionately high level of people with ADHD who find themselves staying at His Majesty's pleasure and on average those with the condition live 6.8 years less than those without. Associated behaviours include self-medication, drug addiction, binge eating, impulsivity, poor financial management and patterns of self-destructive behaviour. Liam may well be calling 'House' on his ADHD bingo card if he's reading that list.

Those close to Liam always had the sense that he was playing at being an adult, but his maturity remained arrested. He wanted control of his career but didn't know what to do once he got it. In Debbie, he had a partner who would take care of everything. Debbie continued to introduce incremental changes. She intuitively knew not to send Liam's system into shock and gradually nudged him towards the light. She helped to provide a degree of structure and a goal to work towards: for him to get back to the business of being Liam Gallagher. Liam was waking at 5 a.m. and heading out to Hampstead Heath for morning runs. Besides this being good for her boyfriend's mental and physical health, it was a crucial step in the comeback. He needed to look like the gorgeous rock star he used to be and she needed to help the industry see he was an investible proposition again. London's nature-loving paparazzi found themselves drawn to the heath and regularly had snaps of Liam jogging published in the national press. It was like *Rocky*, if 'Eye of the Tiger' was replaced by 'Supersonic'.

'I go for a run at six, just to have a bit of discipline. No music, I just run. Chase the squirrels,' Liam said. The ritual was about more than just fitness – it became a way to clear his mind, to reset himself each morning. On his way back he'd bring Debbie her morning coffee, a small token of gratitude. He had a lot to be grateful for.

The continuation of band life with Beady Eye hadn't allowed Liam properly to process the grief of losing Oasis. Now he had the time and support to start to recover and, as the haze cleared, he made his way back to songwriting. 'Without sounding like a hippy, that was when all these songs were coming. The light sorted me out,' he admitted.

By 2016 he'd found himself with a collection of songs which he felt good enough to build an album with. With Debbie's encouragement, they grew it into what would become *As You Were*. The songs had a balance of reflection and confidence, and set the tone for his reinvention.

The level of persuasion and patience required of Debbie to pull Liam back from the brink cannot be overstated. She had recognised that Liam was not being given the focus he required and she had taken him away from Ignition. For the first time, he was the primary focus of those supporting his music career. Fundamentally, Debbie believed in him. Nobody has ever been able to wrangle Liam in the way she has. The holistic approach to their full-life partnership has tied up the frayed edges of Liam's world, and in her he has the partner he never had with Noel or any of his previous relationships. The level of skill and emotional connection required to get Liam to agree to a launch solo career and to write with established pop producers cannot be underestimated. It was a singular act of managerial coercion. Debbie Gwyther: The Liam Whisperer.

Not one for subtlety, when he announced his solo career, he did so in the most Liam way possible – by calling himself a 'cunt' on Twitter, in response to his own declaration that he would never go solo, arguing, 'I'm not a cunt.' Yet, by 2016, he had done exactly that, signing a solo record deal with Warner Brothers. 'Well yeah, the majority of solo stars are cunts,' he told *Vice* that year. 'The ones that split bands up because they need their egos fuckin' stroked are the biggest cunts. If someone said to me, "OK, get Oasis back or go solo?" I'd get Oasis back. There's not enough bands out there. There's far too many fuckin' solo stars. It's shit. This is the last fuckin' roll of the dice for me. For me to go and get another band back together it'd only be compared to Oasis anyway, so what's the fuckin' point? So the solo thing? I'll give it a fuckin' go, man.'

His signing to Warner Bros. was led by veteran executive Mike Smith, the former head at Columbia and a well-respected A & R figure, known for his passion for artists and penchant for sketching line portraits of musicians while watching from the side of the stage. Smith believed in Liam's potential despite his rocky recent history. Liam said he was, 'Very excited to be signing to the mighty Warner Brothers; looking forward to making some super sweet sounds. Keep the faith!' He added that he felt the songs he'd got together had 'flair, attitude, and the melodies are sick. It's chin-out music, not something to scratch your chin over.'

The rebooted Liam Gallagher was booked for the major festivals across Europe, including Reading and Leeds, and a full tour was scheduled. Along the way he'd started to reach a younger fanbase via Twitter. They hadn't grown up with Oasis but were drawn to his unapologetic personality and raw honesty. He was an antidote to cancel culture – someone who spoke his mind, often without a filter, and somehow managed to remain beloved for it.

In 2016, the much-anticipated documentary *Oasis: Supersonic* was released, offering an in-depth look at the meteoric rise of the band. Directed by Mat Whitecross, the doc chronicled the band's journey from their scrappy beginnings in Manchester to their record-breaking Knebworth concerts in 1996. The story of their rise from unemployment to rock titans over a two-year period was told through archival footage and narrated by Noel, Liam and all the key players of the day. It's a great documentary, which captures the essence of Oasis.

Although Noel and Liam actively participated and served as executive producers, Liam confirmed, 'We weren't in communication one bit.' The film prompted inevitable questions about an Oasis reunion. Liam was keen but not optimistic: 'I'd like it to happen, because I miss him and I miss the band and I miss the fans and I miss singing them songs. But it's in the lap of the gods, not Noel Gallagher, as much as he'd like to think he's a bit of a god, but he ain't.'

Noel was emphatic in his stance: 'Not even if all the starving children in the world depended on it'. Liam responded, somewhat contradicting his previous position by saying he wasn't fussed: 'It doesn't hurt me mate, doesn't hurt me. If the guy doesn't want me back in our band then I don't want to either.' His conflicted feelings about Noel were drawn further by his view on their breakup. 'He stitched me up with Oasis. I was the one left to carry the fuckin' blame, and that's it.' In a 2017 interview with *GQ*, Liam elaborated: 'But he set booby traps for me, stuff he knew I hated, all that last year, and me being me I walked straight into them. He knew he wanted to go solo. He knew we weren't selling records. He knew we were on the descent and, yes, we all knew we'd probably peaked at Knebworth in '96. He just didn't have the balls to say he wanted to leave. So he set me up to look like the bad guy.' When asked if he genuinely believed that, Liam responded, 'Without a doubt. I'll tell it to my grave. I heard one record company executive in LA asking Noel to go solo ten years before the scrap. But there you go. The rest is history. But one thing that I will fucking say, I will never, ever be fucking Noel Gallagher's muppet. I started that band with Bonehead and Guigsy, he wrote the songs and I sang them and gave them a bit of spirit and we are both equal as far as I'm concerned. So you want to go fucking solo, go for it, but you take your stupid little fans with you, because I don't want them. They're the ones that ruined fucking Oasis, the cheeky cunts. If it weren't for me there would be no fucking Oasis. He knows he fucking stitched that band up for his own benefits.'

By 2016, the forking paths of Liam and Noel had fully diverged. Noel had leaned further into a more professionalised, industry-friendly world, rubbing shoulders with top celebs. Liam felt Noel's growing position as part of the establishment was a class betrayal worthy of derision. 'Noel lives in a £17 million house. That changes you, I reckon. You have appropriate furniture, appropriate kitchens, appropriate red wine that Bono's recommended. And Damon Albarn becomes your mate. Fair dos, but not for me.' Liam's social circle had always been more insular when it came to industry figures. It revolved around the pub, his partner, his mates and now his children. He had long resented and mocked Noel's 'posh' mates. Why the fuck would he wanna hang out with them when he could hang out with Liam Gallagher?

Time had allowed Liam to become more comfortable with Oasis's legacy. He embraced the songs in his live sets, and acknowledged their importance in making him Liam.

Speaking to the *Guardian* in 2017, he said, 'I am Oasis. That's what I am. And I'm proud of it.' Liam Gallagher remains the world's biggest Oasis fan.

Upon its release in October 2017, *As You Were* debuted at number one on the UK album chart. It outsold the rest of the top ten combined and earned Liam another gold record for his wall, later to be joined by a platinum disc. The album also became the fastest-selling vinyl release in twenty years.

Liam took the album out on the road, starting with a homecoming show at the O2 Ritz Manchester on 30 May 2017. However, the gig carried a deeper significance – it was a benefit gig for the victims of the Manchester AO Arena bombing, which had occurred just a week earlier. The devastating terrorist attack took the lives of twenty-two fans and injured a thousand people at the end of an Ariana Grande concert at the Arena. Besides the life-changing hurt it delivered to its victims, the attack reopened an old wound for the city itself. The Arena on Hunts Bank was originally built after that area of Manchester was destroyed by an IRA car bomb in the nineties. It led to a deep wave of grief throughout the city and an outpouring of support from music fans around the world.

In response, Ariana Grande organised the One Love Manchester benefit concert, held on 4 June 2017 at Emirates Old Trafford, and Liam was involved once again. The concert included pop stars from around the world including Justin Bieber, Coldplay, Katy Perry and

Miley Cyrus, who came together to show solidarity and support for the victims. Liam flew in from Germany to make a surprise appearance. He raised the concert to a spiritual communion when he took to the stage in a bright orange parka and played 'Rock 'n' Roll Star' before performing a duet of 'Live Forever' with Coldplay's Chris Martin. It was an unexpected moment given Liam's long history of slagging off the indie band turned pop stars. 'When I met him [Chris], I said, "Look, I'm sorry about that stuff that I fuckin' said in the past. I was only fuckin' about." And they went, "No, we love it, carry on."' Coldplay went on to perform 'Don't Look Back in Anger' with Ariana Grande. The song had organically become a healing anthem after a lone voice in the crowd spontaneously started singing it at a memorial outside Manchester City Hall following the end of a minute's silence. The thousands in attendance joined in and the Oasis classic took on a new life.

However, this being Liam, the event couldn't be all peace and love ... Notably absent was Noel Gallagher, Liam's estranged brother. The omission infuriated Liam, who publicly called him out for not attending. With an extraordinary absence of irony when it comes to not looking back in anger, he tweeted: 'Noel's out of the fucking country, wasn't there for his people, wasn't there for the gig. Get on a fucking plane and play your tunes for your people, you sad fuck.'

Noel later responded, saying he hadn't been asked and dismissed the criticism from 'ill-informed fuckwits'. Liam responded by posting a screenshot of a text exchange between Noel and his daughter Anaïs, where Noel expressed frustration at the situation he found himself in, texting her, 'Because your astonishing knob of an uncle is doing it and the organisers have now got it in their heads there's going to be an Oasis reunion … What a cunt.' Perhaps not the best example to set when it comes to how to communicate familial feelings to your teenage daughter.

An unlikely, and in Liam's view, most unwelcome defence of Noel came from Lisa Moorish. Lisa claimed that, on the night in question, Noel had been with Liam's estranged daughter, Molly: 'Maybe he's busy looking after his kids and the daughter you've never even met! AS YOU WERE x LM', signing off with a version of Liam's now trademark 'As You Were X LG' signature. Lisa accompanied the tweet with a picture of Molly and Noel together and captioned it, 'Uncle Noel @themightyi with my beautiful girl @mollymoorish #FAMILYFIRST Mol working hard revising for exams so had to miss the fun last week. Belated celebrations soon! @saspg.'

Noel had privately built a relationship around this time with Molly after Lisa reached out. They had become reasonably close, and it was very significant, emotionally, for Molly to be publicly recognised by her uncle.

Meanwhile, Liam's solo career was flourishing and his tour continued to grow in scale. His Glastonbury 2017 appearance became a festival highlight and he closed the set by singing 'Don't Look Back in Anger', a song he had never performed live before in tribute to those affected by the Manchester bomb, albeit allowing the crowd to take over chorus vocals.

Taking a Morrissey-esque approach to his reflection on the song's new meaning he said, 'That song got hijacked. "Don't Look Back in Anger"? You should look back in fucking anger. You should be fucking kicking off.' The yin of Noel's song met the yang of Liam's temperament once more.

By now all aspects of Liam's life were finally moving in the right direction at the right time, and in 2018 he reconciled a major facet of it when he finally met Molly Moorish for the first time.

Molly had grown up a couple of miles away from Liam but never had a relationship with her famous dad due to his grudge against her mother. Speaking in 2018, Liam said 'I've just never got around to meeting her. I've heard she's all right, though. She's doing all right.' But now, after Molly's coming of age, and encouraged by Debbie, Liam reached out and supposedly called the encounter a 'beautiful moment'.

For her part, Molly was ready for that relationship and embraced it completely, later adding Gallagher as a second barrel to her surname. Molly quickly forged a strong relationship with Liam's sons, Lennon and Gene, as well as Noel's daughter Anaïs. She was now firmly in the Gallagher fold and able to enjoy the benefits of Liam's practical advice on life, music and drugs. 'Weed's all right, but even that's fucking stupid,' he told his kids. 'Who are you buying it off? Don't be buying it off idiots. And don't be smoking all different shit, like that spice stuff.'

Liam and been battered by the storm but not bettered by it. He emerged from this period with a renewed sense of purpose and a consolidated family, save his other daughter Gemma and his brother Noel, of course. His relationship with Debbie was both a positive and productive one. The chaos had not disappeared entirely – after all, this was Liam Gallagher – but for the first time in a long time, he was grounded, focused and ready to embrace the future.

8

Keep On Reaching – Noel, 2015–17

Despite being critical of their approach and the resulting masters, the scrapped Amorphous Androgynous sessions seemed to unlock something in Noel. Although *Chasing Yesterday* had been recorded more conventionally, he'd used bits of their work together as B-sides. Maybe he wasn't quite ready to be pushed in that direction so soon after ruling the world with Oasis or maybe their technique was too sharp elbowed. But with his next record, *Who Built the Moon?*, Noel was ready to be pushed far beyond his musical comfort zone.

Looking for a different approach, Noel reached out to Belfast-born DJ and producer, David Holmes, by text. Noel admired Holmes's eclectic work across remixes and film scores and wanted to try working with somebody from a different school of music to his own. He wanted to be challenged as an artist. Holmes was fascinated by the idea of working with one of Britain's most successful songwriters, and the pair met up. When they got together they discussed broad creative themes and philosophies, with Noel describing their first encounter in a 2017 *Q* interview as 'a meeting of minds', saying they 'just clicked immediately'. They had a shared mutual respect from which to build their collaboration.

Holmes challenged Noel to abandon his usual songwriting methods. Whenever Noel would start to play a new song idea, David would tell him, 'We've heard that before in Oasis'. Initially on the backfoot, Noel soon responded to being pushed away from his normal approach. It was an approach that had worked extremely well so it took a moment for him to adjust. Holmes made him play keyboards and instruments other than his usual guitar to help unlock new melodic pathways. He'd have Noel play and would take samples from which they could build entirely new tracks. When Noel wasn't present, David would then build them into new sonic landscapes. Noel would return to the track to find something new and unexpected, and it further pushed him to question what his songs could be.

Searching for something different, Noel had spoken with his long-time friend and occasional collaborator, Paul Weller. Weller, like Noel's other great musician friend, Johnny Marr, was known for pushing forward with each record. Fans of Weller's seminal first band, the Jam, had loathed the Style Council. A natural provocateur, Weller told Noel that the more the Jam fans hated the Style Council, the more he wanted to do it.

Just before the sessions, Noel had been on the road with U2 on their *Joshua Tree* thirtieth anniversary tour. Bassist

Adam Clayton told Noel that U2's fans didn't much care for their stylistic deviations either and although *The Joshua Tree* is regarded as U2's best album now, it was not the case on release in 1987. Noel realised that the 'people who've made these amazing turns in their history are the ones we love and wish were still around.' And he wanted artistic longevity.

Typically Noel had developed and demoed songs before bringing them into the studio, where the question was about how to build them, rather than whether they should be built at all. Although he'd worked with producers before, the sessions with Holmes took on a form more akin to a co-writing partnership. Noel described this process as 'liberating' and 'inspiring' in an *NME* interview. He said it was a totally new way of working for him; he was writing in the studio, which was unprecedented for him.

Despite initially having been 'resistant' to some of Holmes's techniques, he had come to trust the producer's judgement. Reflecting on the sessions, Noel remarked that he was initially sceptical, but that Holmes was usually right.

There were moments of artistic tension, as should be expected in any collaborative endeavour, but Noel and David were able to work through them together. They pushed and challenged each other to bring the best out of the project.

Who Built the Moon? developed into a record far different from anything Noel had done before. It was an ambitious and experimental record woven from a spectrum of influences. Together he and Holmes took a ride through a divergent assortment of styles and influences. They visited psychedelia, electronica soul and even disco on their studio journey. Noel played instruments that were new to him and allowed himself to be guided by Holmes's vision for the sound of the record.

Speaking to *Uncut*, Holmes described his working conditions: 'I suggested making a record from scratch that didn't involve him bringing anything to the studio apart from his guitars and a bunch of pedals.' It forced Noel to be spontaneous. It meant he had to surrender. 'The biggest challenge was allowing myself to let go of control,' he said. 'In Oasis, I dictated everything. Here, I had to trust the process.'

Arriving at Holmes's Belfast studio in the rain, Noel was uncertain about what the process would lead to. David had built ten tracks from loops for Noel to build on top of, and Noel started to craft melodies over them, 'Everything was down to a great vibe and instinct,' Holmes said.

Noel described the studio environment as chaotic, with instruments everywhere and the band just trying things out to see what worked. But the approach was effective and Noel felt able to make music that was completely beyond him previously.

The album's opener, 'Fort Knox' was a bold signpost to a new sonic direction. The Kanye West-inspired track immediately signalled a departure from Noel's previous work. Noel viewed it as a necessary palate cleanser.

'Holy Mountain', the album's first single, released in October 2017, followed in a similar vein. It's the most outright joyous song Noel has ever written. An up-tempo glam rocker, reminiscent of Dexy's Midnight Runners, T. Rex and early Bowie, capped off by a real earworm of a flute hook. The track's boisterous energy and playful lyrics make it look a right laugh for Noel to play and sing.

'It's a Beautiful World' was the album's most progressive track. An atmospheric production that featured a French spoken-word passage, recited by Charlotte Marionneau of the London-based band Le Volume Courbe, against a haunting, widescreen soundscape.

The recording process and the resulting album were big creative and commercial leaps for Noel to take. It was by far his most adventurous and, to date, most polarising album.

When *Who Built the Moon?* was released on 24 November 2017, it was met with bewilderment and, in some cases, outright hostility by swathes of Noel's fanbase. It was a polarising album. It was designed to be so.

The album debuted at number one on the UK albums chart, becoming Noel's third consecutive number-one solo album and his tenth consecutive including Oasis. He has the record for most consecutive UK number-one albums by any artist in history. It's an extraordinary achievement. But despite topping the pops the record performed poorly in comparison to the previous High Flying Birds LPs, with lower sales overall.

Noel turned his cheek to criticisms from parts of his audience. He told the *Independent* in 2017, 'I'm not trying to please everyone. I'm trying to please myself.'

It was a statement of artistic integrity, a declaration of independence.

When Ignition told Noel they felt *Who Built the Moon?* had 'split his fans in two', he took satisfaction. 'That was the intention.'

His strongest feelings were revealed during an interview with *Q*, where he called the variety of Oasis fan who hated the new record 'parka monkeys. little 15-year-old snotty cunts with polka-dot scarves'. He wanted to shed that element of his audience. He was happy to leave them to Liam. Liam predictably embraced them, taking possession of the phrase and turning Noel's pejorative into an unofficial name for his fandom. After all, he is King Parka Monkey.

Warming to his theme, Noel claimed, 'The parka monkeys are going to be like, "A fucking French bird on a track? No mate, not having it. It's not rock n' roll." Well no, it isn't. Who's saying it is?' 'That's not where I am now,' he said. 'I know that's what people want, but fuck what they want.'

Noel Gallagher's dismissive attitude towards certain sections of his audience was not just reactionary – it was strategic. By deliberately alienating fans who clung to his Oasis-era sound, he could approach those who remained as being genuinely invested in his artistry.

The idea that Gallagher was on a mission to wrongfoot his followers was further upheld in October 2017 when the High Flying Birds appeared on BBC's *Later . . . With Jools Holland* with new member Charlotte Marionneau, who seemed to serve as a muse-like figure for him. Gallagher recalled his first conversation with Marionneau about her role in the band: 'She's French and she's eccentric to say the least. I said to her, can you play the tambourine? She said, [adopts French accent] "I cannot play the tambourine." I said, "Oh right. Shaker?" "Non. I can play the scissors."'

And play the scissors she did ... a surrealist conceit that even made the BBC news. Gallagher had made his request whether she could maybe play percussion during rehearsals for 'She Taught Me How to Fly', so she'd have something to do. When she insisted she would only play the scissors, Gallagher was so amused and impressed by the originality that he embraced it wholeheartedly: 'She brought them in and I was looking at my bass player going, if that's not the greatest thing you've ever seen then tell me what is. A French bird in a cape playing the scissors? It doesn't get any better than that, does it?' Bonehead she was not.

Noel loves Marionneau's sense of individualism and artistry, and the reflected sense of those traits it brings to his band. 'I adore that girl, she's amazing. She means it, this is not a joke.'

The *Later ... With Jools Holland* appearance also revealed that Noel had introduced former Oasis members Chris Sharrock and Gem Archer into his band, bridging his past musical identity with his present.

During this period, Liam's solo career was taking off with the release of *As You Were*, a record that, in contrast to Noel's, played heavily on classic Oasis-style anthems. When asked about Liam's music, Noel dismissed it outright: 'I'm not a fan. I'm not going to learn anything. He doesn't write his own songs, so it means nothing to me.' Artists who use other songwriters rank about two levels below karaoke singers in Noel's estimation. The Beatles are to blame for that. Before the mop-tops came along all bands basically just recorded other people's tunes.

When the topic of reuniting Oasis was inevitably, tediously raised, Noel predictably stuck to his guns, which at that time were far from silent. He told Q magazine: 'I've been very consistent about it. I don't need the money, I don't need the glory, I don't need to relive the memories. If I was to get Oasis back together tomorrow and then do a tour, I'd have a hundred million dollars in the bank but I'd have learnt fuck all.' It didn't fit his MO as an evolving artist. He couldn't exactly launch an album drenched in musical discovery by harking back to the past. It wouldn't be good business.

Plus he felt he'd completed rock 'n' roll with Oasis. 'We did it. We fucking did it, and then some. It's done.'

The expanding sonic universe of Noel's new 'cosmic pop' album was reflected in the band's growing lineup. Alongside longtime members like guitarist bassist Russell Pritchard and keyboardist Mike Rowe, now joined by old mates Gem Archer and drummer Chris Sharrock, the band incorporated additional musicians: Charlotte Marionneau (percussion, tin whistle, aforementioned contentious scissors), YSEE (vocals), and a full brass section featuring Ben Edwards (trumpet), Steve Hamilton (saxophone) and Alistair White (trombone). The increased flock gave the High Flying Birds a distinctive live presence.

To support *Who Built the Moon?*, Gallagher embarked on the 'Stranded on the Earth World Tour', starting on 2 April 2018 at L'Olympia in Paris and spanning multiple continents before concluding in late 2019. The tour was one of his most extensive solo outings to date, covering North America, Europe, South America and Asia, and included a run of co-headlining dates with Billy Corgan's Smashing Pumpkins in 2019.

The tour setlist prioritised Noel's new solo material, with Oasis classics sparingly woven in. Songs like 'She Taught Me How to Fly' and 'It's a Beautiful World' showcased the band's bigger sound. Despite this, Oasis mainstays 'Wonderwall' and 'Don't Look Back in Anger' remained staples. They formed part of a pact between performer and audience: you listen to my new stuff and I'll give you my old stuff as a reward.

The tour played to packed crowds worldwide, with notable performances at London's SSE Arena Wembley, New York's Radio City Music Hall and Manchester Arena. Gallagher also took on prominent festival slots, including the Isle of Wight Festival, Mad Cool Festival in Madrid and Rock Werchter in Belgium. His North American leg saw sold-out dates in major cities. The setlist remained fluid, sometimes including deep cuts such as 'Dead in the Water', an acoustic track recorded spontaneously during an Irish radio appearance. Noel later recalled that the song was captured while he was idly playing his guitar, waiting for a sound engineer to fix an issue in the studio.

The raw, unfiltered nature of the performance gave the track an emotional immediacy that resonated with fans, making it one of the standout moments of his solo career, an acoustic ballad that became a fan favourite.

As his artistic journey evolved, so too did his relationship with his daughter, Anaïs Gallagher. Born in 2000 to Noel and his first wife, Meg Mathews, Anaïs was raised in the big O-shaped shadow cast by Noel's band and their gigantic fame.

She went on to develop a career as a model and social media personality, but remained in awe of her father's musical legacy. Speaking to the *Evening Standard* in 2017, Anaïs admitted that watching her father perform live moved her to tears: 'It's only now, as I've got older and understand the scale of things, that I almost tear up seeing my dad play on stage. Now, I go and see my dad and pop over to his studio and say, "I'm so proud of you."'

Growing up Gallagher hadn't always been easy for Anaïs. 'It's very hard trying to find your own way, dealing with people saying you're only doing it because of your parents. I've had stuff written about me since the moment I was born.' Despite this, she shared her father's taste in music and love of artists such as David Bowie, the Beatles and the Smiths. 'My knowledge of music has always been good because I think my dad would disown me if it wasn't.'

Unfortunately for Anaïs, she wasn't immune to attacks from close family members. Inevitably, Noel and Liam's verbals filtered down to their children. In 2017, Liam's second lad, Gene, made headlines. Following Anaïs's appearance in a Tommy Hilfiger fashion show, Gene tweeted his unsolicited opinions on her look: 'U look like ur dad with a blonde wig on.' It underscored the point that family toxicity and conflict can trickle down the generations. Gene went back in, criticising the decision to cast her in the collection in the first place, saying the person responsible was 'a complete doughnut who should have gone to Specsavers'. Hello Mr Pot. I'm Mr Kettle. Gene's modelling career, much like Anaïs's and his own siblings Lennon and Molly's, benefitted enormously from the distinctive eyebrows and surname inherited from their respective fathers. Despite their youth, they showed the maturity that remained beyond the Gallagher patriarchs and quickly reconciled.

Anaïs had always loved her dad but he had been emotionally distant and they only became really close in the recent past. She was fully aware of his blunt nature and how spiky he could be, but saw him as, at heart, a dedicated and loving parent. 'I wouldn't want people thinking he's a really bad parent, because he's not – he's a really good parent. But that's [not] how the media would portray it.' Unlike her dad and uncle, Anaïs retained a sense of family reputational responsibility: 'I can't do anything too crazy or say anything too crazy because it's going to reflect back on to my dad.'

As Anaïs began to carve her own path as an influencer she embraced Noel's music. 'I bang out Oasis and Noel Gallagher's High Flying Birds in my room super-loud all the time.' Anaïs Gallagher's relationship with her father remained complex yet deeply affectionate. While navigating the pressures of fame and family conflict, she was emerging as a well-balanced young woman.

9

Why Me? – Liam, 2018–19

The phenomenal success of *As You Were* had not just resurrected Liam Gallagher's career. It had catapulted him back into the spotlight, reaffirming his status as one of the most iconic frontmen in rock 'n' roll history.

Riding the wave of *As You Were*'s success, Liam was making up for lost time, determined to capitalise on the second wind his solo career had been given. Almost immediately after his successful tour, he began working on new material. Energised by the positive reception to the album, he was eager to prove that he wasn't a one-hit wonder.

For his second solo album, Liam returned to enlist the talents of producers Greg Kurstin and Andrew Wyatt. The chemistry between Liam and this production duo had been a key ingredient in the success of *As You Were*, and Liam was keen to continue the collaboration. Kurstin, with his pop sensibilities and meticulous production style, brought a polished sheen to Liam's raw rock 'n' roll energy. Wyatt, with his knack for crafting infectious melodies and memorable hooks, helped Liam refine his songwriting and create songs that were both personal and universally appealing.

The recording sessions for *Why Me? Why Not.*, which took place in London and Los Angeles, largely with a different set of musicians to the previous album (although guitarist Mike Moore and multi-instrumentalist Dan McDougall featured heavily on both), were reportedly even more focused and productive than those for *As You Were*. Liam was more confident in his role as a solo artist, more assertive in expressing his ideas, and more involved in the overall creative process. He was not just the singer; he was the driving force behind the album, the one who set the tone and direction of the music.

In interviews during this period, Liam spoke of his desire to create an album that built on the foundation laid by *As You Were*. He told *Rolling Stone* in 2019, 'I wanted to make a record that was even better than the first one. I wanted to push myself, to see what I could do.'

Liam's vision for *Why Me? Why Not.* was to create an album that was both anthemic and introspective, an album that reflected his personal growth and his evolving perspective on life, love and the world around him.

Why Me? Why Not., released on 20 September 2019, was a more diverse and emotionally resonant album than its predecessor. While it retained the classic rock influences that had always been a hallmark of Liam's music, it also incorporated elements of psychedelia, pop and even a touch of gospel. The album was marked Liam's growth as a songwriter.

The lead single, 'Shockwave', released in June 2019, a formulaic stomp elevated by his world-class rock vocals, touched on themes of defiance and resilience. The lyrics seemed to reflect Liam's own journey back from the wilderness. Suggestions that he had been held back and treated like a stepping stone alluded to the ever-present tension with Noel.

'Once', another key track on the album, was a more introspective, ballad-like song that showcased Liam's vulnerable side. The song's stripped-down instrumentation, featuring delicate piano chords and subtle strings, allowed his raw vocals to take centre stage, enhancing the emotional weight of the lyrics. The melody's melancholic yet nostalgic quality further reinforced the song's introspective nature, making it one of the album's standout moments. Once more taking to Twitter, Liam described the song as 'one of the best songs I've ever had the pleasure to be part of'.

'Now That I've Found You' was a tender, heartfelt ode to his daughter Molly Moorish, following their reconnection the previous year. The song's lyrics expressed Liam's joy at finding his daughter and his determination to make up for lost time. It was 'a really special song' to Liam, which he hoped resonated with others who had been in similar situations.

Why Me? Why Not. debuted at number one on the

UK albums chart, becoming Liam's second consecutive solo album to reach the top spot. It also performed well internationally, reaching the top ten in several countries and further solidifying Liam's status as a global rock star.

The success was a further vindication for Liam. It proved that his solo resurgence was not a fluke and that he still had the chops to connect with audiences on a global scale. To prove as much, he set off on a major world tour in the summer of 2019 and continued into 2020. He performed to sold-out crowds in arenas and stadiums across the UK, Europe, North America and Australia.

As had now become familiar in both of the Gallaghers' concerts, the setlists were a mix of songs from the albums of solo material and a selection of Oasis classics. Liam had found a balance between honouring his past and embracing his future, a balance that resonated with both long-time fans and those who had discovered him through his solo work. This time, the Oasis songs included 'Rock 'n' Roll Star', 'Morning Glory', 'Champagne Supernova' and 'Live Forever', which inevitably created moments of pure euphoria in the crowds. And as with the first solo album, the new material, particularly 'Shockwave', 'Wall of Glass', 'Once' and 'The River', managed to stand on its own two feet, underscoring the fact that he was creating new anthems for a new generation.

As the tour reached England he played a series of sold-out shows at the O2 Arena in London, which cemented his status as one of Britain's biggest live acts. The scale of his tours was getting closer to those with Oasis, a feat that largely eluded his brother.

It wasn't all perfect for the re-energised Liam Gallagher during the period. Pretty Green entered administration in 2019, marking the end of the fashion label Liam had launched a decade earlier. Despite its early success, the brand had struggled to adapt and eventually collapsed under the weight of the challenging retail market. JD Sports acquired Pretty Green, marking Liam's exit from the brand. He was genuinely passionate about the label, stating, 'It was about more than clothes; it was about an attitude, a way of life.'

Pretty Green's origins lay in Gallagher's deep-rooted connection to fashion and British youth culture. Long before he launched the brand in 2009, he had been celebrated not just as a rock star but as a bona fide style icon. His effortless cool – a fusion of mod heritage, rock 'n' roll rebellion and Mancunian grit – made him a natural figurehead for a brand that embodied those very elements. The name, borrowed from a Jam song (despite Liam's beef with Noel's bestie, Paul Weller), perfectly encapsulated Gallagher's aesthetic: British, nostalgic and effortlessly cool.

From the start, Liam was involved in shaping Pretty Green. It gave him an outlet and relevancy during breaks from the studio. 'While I wasn't doing any music, it was important. Because it's still creating. And they're mint clothes, man,' he said in a 2018 interview. His creative vision and personal brand were at the heart of the label.

His status as a fashion icon had long been established, but the brand allowed him to channel his aesthetic into something tangible. It was also, in a way, a reflection of his journey post-Oasis. Interestingly, as we touched upon earlier, Pretty Green itself played a role in Oasis's demise, with Noel Gallagher claiming that a dispute over a Pretty Green advertisement in the V Festival programme was one of the sparks that ignited the band's final meltdown. He later recounted on Radio X, 'I had enough when Liam and Bonehead – and this is true – started arguing over a leather jacket. I am not even kidding. I can dress it up more than this, but this is what happened.' Further cranking tensions, Noel alleged that Liam's insistence on advertising Pretty Green in Oasis's tour programme led to a final explosive argument in Paris, with Noel demanding commercial rates. Noel was seemingly unable to allow a little gratis space for his brother's newly spread wings. It was a classic Noel poison pill: he'd agree but Liam would have to pay the same rate as any other business.

Liam was now a man staring down the barrel of the big five-oh and the inevitable questions life raises when somebody eyes the half century. High on the list of things he wished he'd done better was his relationship with Molly. Their relationship continued to blossom, and he maintained close relationships with his sons, Lennon and Gene.

The release of *Why Me? Why Not.* and the subsequent

'Shockwave' tour marked the culmination of a remarkable comeback for Liam Gallagher. He had emerged from the wilderness years following the demise of Beady Eye a changed man, both personally and professionally.

10

This is the Place – Noel, 2018–19

Noel Gallagher's High Flying Birds experienced some commercial head winds as they came home to roost following 2018's year-long tour. Liam's debut album, *As You Were*, had sold 103,000 units in its first week, and he sold out Finsbury Park in London, with over 30,000 fans in attendance. He was steadily ticking off the old Oasis venues. Meanwhile, *Who Built the Moon?* ended its first week with 78,000 sales, a success by most measures but a far cry from Noel's previous tallies. And Noel was playing to a 12,500-seat Wembley Arena, where face-value tickets were available on the day. Again, he wasn't exactly struggling but our heroes' trajectories were heading in demonstrably different directions.

Another event designed to increase the peace was Noel and Sara's move to Hampshire, not far from the site of their New Forest wedding, in 2019. The move was also partially motivated by the desire to get their children into desirable local schools.

Noel had seemed noticeably quiet in the media in 2018. It seems like he'd conceded to Liam's chart superiority. When *Who Built the Moon?* was released in November 2017, he did two mainstream print interviews and then he cracked on with the business of being an artist. Sometimes the publicity department of a label see which way the wind is blowing and decide to keep their powder dry for the next release, but Noel was now releasing music via his own label so the silence would have been a conscious choice on his part.

'I'm genuinely not competitive,' Noel insisted, hard. 'OK, I was in the '90s. Then we won – we won the '90s! Then it was, "I'm not arsed any more." [Sighs] Liam's record comes out, and if the journalist isn't asking a question about me, [Liam's] inventing one for them to ask about me. He's setting the agenda. When I do interviews it's always, "I was on your brother's Twitter account this morning; he doesn't like your wife very much." I'm like, "I haven't come all the way to Peru to talk about that penis." That would be a daily occurrence. Then when my album came out and I'd gone on the road, I said to my office, "Look, I can't be arsed." If I don't take a back seat here, this will go on for ever, and it's belittling. It's beneath me. All that fucking squabbling brothers, you read about it, and it's so juvenile. I'll let the music do the talking and whatever will be, will be.'

It was a belatedly mature stance and one which lasted right up until the next sentence he uttered. Responding to Liam's Finsbury Park triumph, Noel added, 'Good luck to him. [Pause] Listen, I know the true story of Beady Eye and how it fell apart. He left the band by text! The Prince of Darkness, The Man, he didn't even have the balls to phone his bandmates. Because he got a solo deal, it was, "See you later, lads." Then when he got his deal with Live Nation, no one was telling him, "Don't do any Oasis songs, do your new stuff, that's what you're good at." He's got his thing now – which is effectively my thing – and when he's headlining Finsbury Park I'm sitting there watching *Match of the Day* getting a PRS cheque for him playing my songs. But instead of making him happy, it's made him worse. It's made him even angrier [laughs].'

Noel followed his artistic nose when it came to following up *Who Built the Moon?*. Having escaped the orthodox album recording process he now also wanted to escape the normal album campaign cycle. He made his next releases a series of EPs rather than a conventional album. The EP was a largely antiquated format but beloved by indie bands in the nineties and was slowly making a coming back in the streaming world.

Noel loved the format because he wasn't constrained by a fixed concept or sound. The trilogy of EPs each had an identity distinct from the next. First off the rank was *Black Star Dancing* in June 2019. The title track, a pulsating, disco-infused anthem, drew inspiration from artists such as INXS, U2, Queen and David Bowie. It felt a natural follow on from the electronic elements of *Who Built the Moon?*.

The EP also featured 'Rattling Rose', which lures you in with some traditional acoustic guitar and a driving Americana rhythm before blooming into a sci-fi carnival breakdown. Noel's voice sounds as silky as he ever has as he croons. That marriage of soulful indie and a sweet groove harks back to Doves' early work. After the sound of rainfall subsides, 'Sail On' swoons with the immediately relatable simplicity of Noel's most powerful acoustic moments – but this time with a (no kidding) folk sea-shanty vibe. 'I might have been watching too much *Top of the Pops* recently ... anyway, it's "dope" ... not my words, but the words of Nile Rodgers who literally danced in the studio when he heard it!' The mix of styles demonstrated his refusal to be confined to any single genre.

The reception to the EP further nudged those fans who'd found the preceding album not quite their cup of tea. Speaking to *Rolling Stone* in 2019, Noel reiterated: 'I'm not trying to please everyone. I'm trying to make music that I find interesting.'

Just three months later, in September 2019, Noel dropped *This Is the Place*. It was a diverse mix blend of atmospheric psychedelia and traditional songwriting. The lead track, named after the poem read by Tony Walsh in remembrance of the Manchester Arena bombing, is a fast-tempo number marked by soaring and swooping female backing vocals. It could have been recorded by Primal Scream.

Tucked away in the track listing is another absolute peach of a Gallagher rarity, 'A Dream Is All I Need to Get By', which Noel imagined as a Smiths B-side. It more closely resembles how the La's may have sounded had Lee Mavers preferred weed to skag. It's probably Noel's most wistful song. His voice floats across the twinkling percussion and castanets. It's the sound of Noel Gallagher daydreaming. All Noel's writing influences are present in this song. Bacharach, Lennon, Mavers, Head, Marr. And they're all getting along just fine among the clouds of Noel's hinterland.

The trilogy concluded in March 2020 with *Blue Moon Rising*. Noel kept some of the electronic and experimental elements of the previous releases but the writing was much closer to his more traditional heritage songcraft. In fact, the title track felt like it could be an Oasis-era number. The music video for the lead track was released on 30 January 2020 and was filmed at the Scala in London by Dan Cadan and Noel's old mate, Scully (Jonathan Mowatt). It features the actress Gala Gordon and *Skins* actor Jack O'Connell alongside Noel Gallagher.

Noel's moral-highroad press strategy when it came to Liam was about to be permanently kiboshed. Over on Twitter, things were escalating from verbal argy-bargy to deeply personal attacks on family. Noel's wife, Sara MacDonald, had been exploring Worthy Farm at Glastonbury on Friday night, 28 June 2019, and posted photos of Stormzy's magnificent headline set, captioning the post 'fucking dude'.

According to *NME*, when one fan asked if she'd be 'Staying for Liam's set?' she replied, 'Think I'm going to swerve that. The fat twat doing his tribute act, balancing a tambourine on his head, is going to look pretty dated after Stormzy.'

Noel then accused Liam of sending a threatening

message to his nineteen-year-old daughter, Anaïs. The text featured a screenshot of Sara's Twitter post with the warning: 'Tell your step mam to be very careful.'

For Noel, this wasn't just about defending his daughter – it was an assault on his core values of family loyalty and protection. 'That crossed a line,' Noel said. 'It's not just banter when you involve my daughter. Some things you can't just brush off.' This particular beef put more distance between the brothers than ever, with Noel firmly (at least seemingly) closing the door on ever reuniting with Liam.

Noel publicly shamed his kid brother. 'So you're sending threatening messages via my teenage daughter, are you now? You were always good at intimidating women though, eh?' Noel was alluding to an incident in 2018, at Chiltern Firehouse in Marylebone. The Chiltern is Noel's London bar of choice. Liam, hearing Noel was there, headed down, looking to confront Noel. When he arrived Noel was gone and the little devil on Liam's shoulder was plying the angel on the other with shots. It was alleged in the next day's tabloids that Liam had grabbed his girlfriend Debbie by the throat, and the papers published leaked CCTV footage from the highly private establishment. According to the reports, Debbie was in tears and 'shaking' after Liam appeared to grab her by the throat and shout, 'She is a witch. It was her fault. She is a witch. She is a fucking witch.'

Liam staunchly denied the claims, saying he 'had never and would never' put a hand on a woman, and Debbie insisted they were just 'messing around'.

Peggy and her three sons, Noel, Paul and Liam.

The Gallagher brothers' childhood home in Burnage, Manchester.

The original Oasis lineup in 1993.

The Gallagher brothers in Manchester City shirts, 1994.

Oasis at Knebworth.

Liam and Nicole in 2001.

Noel and Meg Mathews.

Liam and Patsy Kensit.

Lisa Moorish.

Backstage with Noel and co.

PJ. The indie years. Don't Believe
The Truth tour 2005.

LG and PJ. City of Manchester stadium.
Side of stage as we watched The Bees.
Don't Believe The Truth tour July 2005.

PJ and Andrew Loog Oldham.

Various Oasis passes and tickets.

Author provided

Liam at Glastonbury in 2004.

Noel's 'broken' guitar, restored in 2011.

Beady Eye during the closing ceremony of the London Olympic Games.

Liam opening the Pretty Green clothing store in Glasgow in 2011.

Liam wearing Burberry during London Fashion Week, 2018.

Noel with the Captain's armband at the end of a Manchester City match.

Liam performing the opening gig of his Underplay tour, raising money for the 'We Love Manchester Emergency Fund'.

Liam and Chris Martin performing in the 'One Love Manchester' benefit concert in 2017.

Noel performing at the Teenage Cancer Trust charity gig in 2003.

High Flying Birds performing at Warwick Castle in 2024.

Noel and daughter Anaïs at the 2019 BMI London Awards.

Siblings Lennon, Molly and Gene.

Noel and Sara Macdonald attending the Adidas Originals dinner.

Liam and Debbie Gwyther attending the *Q* Awards.

Liam followed the denial with a tweet: 'Firstly I have never put my hands on any woman in a vicious manner. Secondly there is only 1 witch and we all know who that is as you were LG x'. Implying your sister-in-law is a witch while defending yourself against claims of serious misogyny isn't a textbook PR move, but there you go.

Liam later issued a public apology to both Anaïs and the brothers' mother, Peggy Gallagher, tweeting, 'My sincere apologies to my beautiful mum Peggy and my lovely niece Anaïs for getting caught up in all of this childish behaviour. I love you both dearly. LG x.'

This chapter of the Gallagher spat, which could be a book long enough to rival *The Lord of the Rings* in volume, confirmed to Noel that revisiting the past was futile, as personal animosities had spread to family members. When asked if it had now got past the point of making up with Liam, Noel nodded, telling the *Guardian*: 'Because I've got one fatal flaw in my otherwise perfect makeup as a human being, which is I don't forgive people. Once you start texting my children – and his two sons have been going for her, too – and legitimise my wife being bullied on the internet, where she has to shut down Instagram accounts because of the vile shit being written about her and my daughter, then it ain't happening.'

Noel has always placed a high value on order, routine and professionalism, with trust and respect being central to his relationships. He maintains a close-knit circle of friends and family, where loyalty is paramount. Trust must be earned, often over a long period, and once broken, there is little chance of reinstatement. Those within his circle are his trusted confidants, the ones he feels comfortable around. His strong value system means that once a boundary is crossed – especially one involving his loved ones – there is no turning back. This was particularly evident in his unwillingness to forgive Liam. That said, his logic does remain internal at times. He has publicly criticised both of Liam's wives in the past, even calling Patsy Kensit 'a fuckwit of the highest order' in one interview.

Liam, on the other hand, thrives in chaos. He craves mayhem and disorder, and when it doesn't exist, he will create it. This is partly driven by a need for attention, as he is easily bored and feeds off negativity. His public outbursts and social media antics ensure he is always being noticed, especially by big brother. It was a performance he'd developed in childhood: acting out was his way of being seen, a child who misbehaved simply to gain parental attention. As an adult this MO had been rewarded handsomely with all the attention and money he could dream of. But his failure to develop a healthier coping mechanism in adulthood made him volatile, easily riled and prone to dramatic reactions.

In Liam's world, boundaries exist solely to be broken – and this latest example of boundary blurring was too much for Noel, who is far more measured and deliberate. Noel found Liam's unpredictability frustrating and a disruption to the ordered and peaceful life he values.

'People keep asking about an Oasis reunion, but I've moved on. It's never happening. We're not those people any more,' he stated bluntly. 'Yes. Now, it's fucking no way, mate. Not a cat in hell's chance [that Oasis will re-form]. At the beginning, I would have said to my management, "There's a magic number. If it reaches that magic number, I'll do it. Give me a shout." A couple of monster gigs. Even a tour of the big cities, a world tour, stadiums, burn a load of money, buy a yacht, and a plane, and another new house, then go back to what I'm doing. Easy. I wouldn't even have to travel with the cunt. I'd get me own helicopter, dial it in, see you later ... That thing about my kids and my wife. No way. If I had 50 quid left in my pocket, I'd rather go busking. No way, I can't do it.'

Despite the ever-deepening animosity with his former bandmate, Noel did briefly reflect on Oasis and the legendary Knebworth shows in 2019 interviews about the documentary film covering the pair of legendary concerts at rock's favourite stately home. Speaking nostalgically, he admitted, 'I can't believe we did that. I can't believe it was that big. We were young and had no real understanding of what we were doing at the time.'

Unable to believe the scale of the event and how tightly they performed, Noel somewhat emotionally pinpointed the event as the moment he truly began to emerge as an artist, even joking it was time for him to buy a scarf and hat.

11

One of Us
2019

White ash falls, returning whatever was incinerated to the earth, and drawing our eye to three empty chairs in the middle of this post-heartbreak landscape. Three chairs for three brothers. The 2019 video for 'One of Us', a track from Liam Gallagher's second solo album, *Why Me? Why Not.*, is more than just a promotional tool; it is a poignant, visually arresting meditation on a fractured brotherhood, a public airing of a very private grief.

It's black and white but the depiction of the emotional weight and abrasive Greater Mancunian landscape is in glorious technicolour. The North York Moors are the lungs that help Manchester breathe. From the right spot, you can survey the entire city. The weathered red bricks and faded grandeur of the Industrial Revolution are punctuated by a rapidly increasing number of early twenty-first-century generic skyscrapers as they reach to meet the heavy northwest skies. It's a world away from the Burnage council estate Liam grew up in. But it is the perfect vantage point for reflection and perspective.

Ten years ago. The end of Oasis, the end of a fraternal bond and the end of an identity. The video for Liam's 'One of Us' arrives a decade to the day he and his brother finally put one straw too many on the camel's back. The song and the video don't bother themselves with subtext and metaphor. This is an open letter to his lost sibling. The strongest yet in a series of attempts by Liam to reconnect with Noel and perhaps provoke a response. The younger brother alternating between negative and positive attention strategies as the older brother consciously keeps him on the naughty step. Noel's silence ensures the moral high ground, but both siblings know it's all part of the same game. This is the pattern of their shared existence, ever since Liam's arrival.

Liam emerges from the long grass as rain joins the ash on its journey to the barren terrain. This vision of northern nature is almost apocalyptic. Partially an aesthetic watermark from the director. Partially a reflection of the scorched fraternal bond. Even the biggest of northern figures appear small in the wilderness of the moors. He makes his way up the hill and strides into shot protected by a waxed Barbour cagoule and holding a very un-Liam brolly. The coat is an extension of the singer. A second skin. A heritage British brand with a contemporary cut. He meets the camera's gaze with an expression that rolls between menace and sincerity like a roulette ball settling on black or red. He wears the umbrella well. It was a last-minute accessory choice to defend the most precious of all the singer's gifts — apart from his voice — from the rain: his hair. 'It's fucking raining. I don't mind the cold. It's when it's raining you just look like a twat, don't you? I mean, doing videos in the Moors, you're asking for it, aren't you? You know what I mean?' he told *GQ*'s Olive Pometsey in September 2019.

At the summit is a graveyard of memories. Photographs from his childhood, sparsely arranged, stretch out to the horizon as smoke simmers and the ash of burned memories fall. We've always seen this man as a raucous adult but here, in the 'One of Us' video, titled *The Ballad of the Blue Eyed Boy*, we see the child. The younger brother born into a tough household in a tough part of a tough old city. The part of him that still reaches for his big brother. As the camera returns to Liam we see him as a young boy with angelic blond hair and seventies hand-me-down chic. It should be said that a jacket is the single most important item of clothing a northerner can ever possess and we will wear it inside or out no matter the weather. Often the only investment item in our wardrobe. We see here that Liam Gallagher has always had a cool coat.

His eyes linger over the images of 'happy memories' that fill the placards: Liam and his brothers as babies, little boys and young men. All smiles. Family holidays to their parents' homeland of Ireland. The simple surrounds and furnishing of a typical working-class home where the only things that matter are money, food and love.

In the next cut we see his two older brothers, Paul and Noel, walking with the famously fixed Gallagher scowl, trailed by the much younger and smaller Liam. Liam still innocent and playfully swinging a stick, not yet embittered by the indelible trauma of domestic violence and borderline poverty. He has always followed his brother.

Now we return to the adult Liam walking the same path alone. He never wanted to be a solo act. He never wanted his relationship with Noel to break, no matter how far he tried to bend it. As he takes his seat on one of the three wooden dining-chair thrones from their family kitchen he looks across to Noel and is met by a look of tangible resentment. It's a look and a feeling he has had to live with to varying degrees since he came into this world. Noel's unfair but inescapable resentment of Liam for having the audacity to have been born later and thus escape the beatings from their father, Tommy. Liam's bravado may appear bulletproof but any older brother knows they always have a shadow to manage when it comes to their kid brother. Noel's looms especially long. The camera returns to Liam, now back as the child, receiving that same look with confused heartbreak weighing the corners of his mouth into a black rainbow of a frown.

The protection of being one of three is not to be underestimated. The schoolyard is full of 'my brother will twat you' threats. The walk home can be fraught. An older brother can relax the fight-or-flight. Extended to the amplified predators of the nineties British tabloid media who fed on cruelty, it helped Liam to have his big brother there to shoulder the burden. Another reason he didn't love the idea of being a solo act. Oasis or 'The Gallaghers' is a broader shield than 'Liam Gallagher' alone. This is Liam Gallagher the lost boy. Vulnerable and making a home movie for an audience of one rings heartbreakingly clear. The meaning of the song and accompanying imagery are clear to anyone who's paid attention to their long, tangled story. The bond they once had, the camaraderie eroded by years of feuds, taunts and stony silences.

Written and directed by the brilliant tandem of Steven Knight and Anthony Byrne, who brought the Shelbys to life in such singularly vivid fashion, this could well be the story of a character from the *Peaky Blinders* universe. A man who has risen from nowhere to the top but is still wrestling with the past and present.

The music of 'One of Us' swells, sparse and wistful at first, then growing into something more insistent. It's a curious mix of melancholy and defiance, mirroring the complex emotions at play. The drums are steady, anchoring the song with a simple, almost primal beat, reminiscent of Ringo Starr's understated work with the Beatles. The bass is melodic, weaving its way through the chords, providing a solid foundation. A piano adds a touch of classicism, while strings strengthen and recede, tugging at the heartstrings. But it's Liam's voice that takes centre stage, that signature Mancunian drawl, imbued with a vulnerability that's rarely been so exposed.

These days, Liam stands at a crossroads. It's 2019, and he's nearly a decade on from the implosion at Rock en Seine in Paris, where Noel walked out and ended Oasis on the spot. Liam thinks back to that moment often. In 2009, it felt like the end of everything stable. For all their fighting, Oasis gave the brothers a structure – songs to sing, stages to share, a purpose that transcended their individual egos. In Oasis, they created something bigger than themselves. Without it these two brothers, who are so different, may have drifted from each other's lives completely.

Now, as Liam walks through the video's field of metaphors, he knows he's trying to break through something dense and layered: Noel's emotional walls, the fans' endless speculation, his own pride. He's well aware of his reputation as the loudmouth. His tendency to be the one who would get drunk and get in scraps. But hasn't he changed since then? He's more settled now, engaged to Debbie Gwyther, reunited with his daughter Molly. He wants to stop perpetuating cycles of absence and anger.

In interviews, Liam emphasises that he's open to making amends. He mentions that 'One of Us' is about 'someone you love who isn't around', answering questions with a mix of honesty and deflection, acknowledging the song's personal significance while also maintaining a degree of ambiguity. 'It's about family, innit?' he says in one radio interview, his voice tinged with a hint of melancholy. 'About people you love, people you miss. It's about wanting to put things right, but not knowing how.' The video for 'One of Us' stands out as a crack in Liam's armour, a glimpse of his vulnerability.

Liam is proud of 'One of Us', an aural and visual representation of the brothers' shared history, the memories that bind them together, and the pain that keeps them apart. It's a reminder of the human cost of their feud and the emotional toll life has taken on both of them, and on their family.

The song takes him back to Burnage, to the council house where he grew up with Noel and their eldest brother Paul, to their mother Peggy's unshakable warmth, and yes, even to the darkness cast by their father Tommy and the conflicting moments of joy and love felt with an abusive parent.

How had the two brothers, who had such an intense, shared background, developed such different outlooks, such different standpoints, to the point that it seemed they could never be reconciled?

12

Bring it on Down – Noel and Liam, 1972–93

To understand the fractured brotherhood of Liam and Noel Gallagher, the seemingly irreparable rift that destroyed Oasis and continues to fascinate and frustrate fans in equal measure, one must journey back to the crucible of their shared past... starting in 1970s Burnage, a sprawling network of council estates and red-brick semis. Burnage was more than just a place – it was the backdrop of the Gallagher brothers' earliest identity struggles. Their childhood home was both a sanctuary and a battleground. The emotional impact of their childhood echoed long after their rise to fame, defining their artistic and personal conflicts, and never fully fading from their music – or their relationship – even after they had conquered the world.

Very little about the seventies was romantic for those in south Manchester, save a couple of FA Cups for those of a sky-blue persuasion. The council estate surrounding Cranwell Drive in Burnage cast a long shadow over their youth. It was a place where the cliché 'football is religion/

music is an escape' was true, albeit as a 99:1 ratio. It was significantly easier to enjoy a hassle-free walk down the street carrying a football than a guitar. The threat of violence around each street corner and behind many sets of curtains was met with the mix of pride and scorn adopted by many from a similar background.

The Gallaghers' childhood homes, modest council houses, were a microcosm of the larger social and economic forces that shaped their personalities, their music and their complex, often volatile relationship. It was there, amidst the backdrop of a turbulent family life, that the seeds of both their extraordinary success and their enduring conflict were sown. The trauma of their father's abuse cast a shadow far longer than either brother could acknowledge. Noel's relationship with their mother, Peggy, was built on shared survival. Together, mother and son had weathered Tommy's rages, forging a bond from which Liam often felt excluded, perceiving that they had a shared experience without him. Noel, on the other hand, saw Liam's chaos as an echo of their father's unpredictability.

Peggy Gallagher, mother of Liam and Noel Gallagher, was the steadfast force behind the brothers' turbulent upbringing. Born Margaret Sweeney on 30 January 1943, in Charlestown, County Mayo, she was one of eleven children in a large Irish family. 'My father was a labourer who worked for the local council. He came from Sligo. As a family, we were very poor,' she recalled. Hardship defined her early years – her mother's poor health and father's absence forced Peggy to leave school and work as a cook and cleaner at a seminary, handing over most of her earnings to support her family. This early struggle instilled in her a deep sense of resilience and responsibility.

In 1961, at eighteen, Peggy emigrated to Manchester, England, working as a housekeeper and childminder. At the time, there were a lot of Irish immigrants in Manchester and Peggy met Tommy Gallagher in 1964 whilst dancing at the Astoria Club. He was a fellow Irish immigrant, a builder and small concrete business owner from County Meath. The couple married in 1965 and settled in a small council house in Longsight, where they raised their three sons – Paul (born 1966), Noel (1967) and Liam (1972) – moving to nearby Burnage after Liam was born.

Despite the challenges of family life, Peggy remained a quiet yet unwavering supporter of her sons. In a rare 1996 interview, she credited their musical roots to her family's Irish heritage, recalling uncles who played traditional instruments. Though she avoided the spotlight, her sons never hid their admiration for her. Noel has called her the 'real hero' of their family, while Liam famously described her as 'the coolest woman that's ever walked this fucking planet'. Through hardship and sacrifice, Peggy Gallagher shaped her sons into the men they became. Her strength was a defining influence on both Noel and Liam. Peggy's quiet presence was a reminder that, despite their differences, both brothers were shaped by the same foundational experiences of trauma and resilience. She worked tirelessly as a school dinner lady to provide for her children, to protect them from their father's abuse, and to instil in them a sense of hope, a belief that they could escape the confines of their difficult circumstances. She was, as Liam described her in a 2017 interview, 'a saint', a woman who held the family together through the most difficult of times, a woman who never gave up on her children. 'She's the most important person in my life,' Liam stated in an interview with the *Sunday Times* in June 2020.

The Gallagher brothers' childhood was steeped in volatility. Tommy Gallagher wielded alcoholism and violence like weapons, a domineering man who created an atmosphere of chaos and fear. Paul Gallagher later described their father bluntly: 'Ah, Dad wasn't a great bastion of morality. He gambled, drank, smoked, was violent, bossy, adulterous – and he was a top scally.'

Peggy Gallagher reflected on her relationship with Tommy. With hindsight, she couldn't find any redeeming qualities in him – he was tight with money and had a quick temper – but at the time, she had fallen for his charm. By the time she started to see his negative qualities, she felt it was too late – the wedding had been organised.

She recalled the physical and emotional abuse she endured, saying, 'One time there was a big row; he kicked and smashed and dragged and beat me. It was terrible. He'd come back home, taking it out on me and the kids, and yet still be the perfect gentleman to everyone outside.'

Domestic violence became a grim reality for Peggy and her children. Despite her hardships, she remained steadfast, enduring the abuse while going out to work and trying to provide a loving home for her sons.

According to Peggy, the brunt of Tommy's violence was

often directed at Noel, the second eldest of the three musical brothers. As a child, Noel was, by his own admission, a sensitive and introverted boy, a dreamer who found solace in books and music. He was an easy target for his father's rage, a convenient outlet for his frustrations. The physical and emotional abuse that Noel endured during his formative years left deep scars, shaping his personality and his worldview in profound ways. He became withdrawn, guarded and fiercely independent, developing a thick skin and a sharp tongue as defence mechanisms.

Peggy was all too aware of the damage being inflicted upon her son. She saw how he struggled with self-confidence, how he recoiled from confrontation, and how he internalised his pain. He struggled with a pronounced stammer as a child, a condition that he and Paul shared. In those days, a speech impediment was an invitation for bullying from classmates and tutors alike. Both boys attended speech therapy sessions every week for four years, as Peggy was determined to help them overcome their impediments. Paul later recalled how their stammers were so severe that they sought solace in sweets, which became a comfort mechanism during those years. The difficult and chaotic home environment likely played a significant role in the development of their speech impediments. Thankfully, with consistent therapy and Peggy's unwavering support, they were eventually able to overcome the challenge, though the scars of their childhood struggles remained.

When Peggy eventually left Tommy in 1984, she whisked the boys away in the middle of the night to relocate to a council house on Cranwell Drive, nearby in Burnage, where she resides to this day.

Noel later reflected on this period in the 2016 documentary *Supersonic*, stating, 'It made me who I am. I wouldn't change it, but it was tough.' He once told Peggy, 'I'll be famous one day, Mam, and you'll be proud of me. I wasn't put on this Earth to dig holes. I was put on this Earth for something special.'

It was the last time Noel ever saw his dad until the *News of the World* had the spectacularly awful idea of gatecrashing an Oasis aftershow in Ireland at the height of their success. Talk about traumatic. When the world's least welcome gatecrasher, Tommy Gallagher, arrived with News International as his plus-one, it was Liam, the one who was never beaten, who wanted to fight him. This unfinished business from childhood manifested in his constant aggression, the fight he longed to have as a child but never could. Noel, however, disengaged entirely, going to bed rather than reacting. He reportedly told Liam that he had made his peace with it – that his songs, not his father, were what's important. This moment underscores the fundamental difference between them – Noel compartmentalises pain, while Liam externalises it.

Liam, the youngest, was originally less affected by his father's behaviour in some ways, as he was too young to fully comprehend the violence at the time. However, he grew up watching it all unfold, and the impact of their father on the Gallagher brothers was profound and long lasting. The trauma of his abuse created a rift between the brothers that ran deeper than music. With Noel and

Peggy enduring the worst of Tommy's violence according to Peggy, Liam not only felt excluded from their shared narrative of survival, but guilt over his inability to protect the mother he idolised, compounding his feelings of inadequacy. In *Supersonic*, Liam said, 'I'd rather have taken a slap than witnessed it.' When asked about his father years later, Noel remarked that he had made his peace with it and his dad didn't matter anymore. Liam's response was tellingly different. For him, the wounds were still raw. The fury he harboured towards Tommy remained unresolved, surfacing in confrontations with Noel and others as an echo of the battles he longed to fight as a child but couldn't.

The experience of growing up in a violent household instilled in Liam a fierce loyalty to his mother and a deep-seated distrust of authority. It also hardwired a lifelong rebellious streak, his tendency to lash out, to challenge those who tried to control him, to assert his dominance. He was, as he often described himself, 'a fighter', someone who had learned to stand up for himself from a very young age, someone who was not afraid to confront his adversaries, whether it be his father, his brother or the music industry establishment. Speaking about his unhappy childhood home in 2019, Liam pondered on the impact his abusive upbringing may have had on him: 'God, I don't know, man. I guess there's the old one where you go: "Look, I'm never going to be like him," but I have been like him. Not in a violent way, just … relationships, doing things I shouldn't have done. So that carried through, but I'm not blaming him for it, it's my doing. But abusive? No, not abusive, man. I'm straight up with the kids, I'm like: "Look, you've got to get up for school, mate, come on." But I'm pretty chilled. I'm cool. I don't even know what it was like to have a dad, really, so I wouldn't know if he was a good one or a bad one. But I never lacked a crack round the head or a bollocking. Because my mam would do that. There are some mams out there that are just drips, but she's Irish. I think she did both roles.' In the context of the era 'cracks around the head' were considered part of good parenting and many remain almost sentimental about that part of growing up. Smacked arses and clipped earlugs, when deployed fairly, fell outside the purview of domestic abuse.

Noel took refuge in the sounds of the Beatles, the Rolling Stones, the Kinks, T. Rex and the Smiths, bands that offered him a glimpse into a different world, one beyond the confines of Burnage. He taught himself to play the guitar, picking up an old acoustic that his father, when he was still around, had one day mysteriously brought back from the boozer, and painstakingly learned the chords and riffs of his favourite songs. Encouraging his hobby, Peggy bought him a guitar of his own from Kays catalogue. Catalogue purchases at this time tended to be layaway or weekly payments, so Kays provided a way for working-class families to acquire what would otherwise be an investment piece. Music became Noel's obsession, his driving force. He spent hours in his room, writing songs, driving his mother to distraction. 'Will you stop playing that bloody guitar?!' Peggy would shout. But Noel honed his craft and dreamed of a life beyond the council estate. He saw music as a way out, a path to a better life, a life filled with purpose and meaning: 'Everything I needed was coming out of those speakers.' He was to make something of himself, telling *Esquire* in 2018, 'I had to get out. Music was the only way.' To those not from those parts or that time, statements such as these may seem a little extreme. But it was a truism and remains so. Boxing, football and music were the lottery-ticket escape routes for poor lads who were not academically gifted. Genuine meritocracies that didn't discriminate against class or ilk. Girls didn't even have those options, their aspirations further limited.

Liam, meanwhile, was not at all arsed about music until he was 'hit over the head with a hammer' and his sonic epiphany arrived. Noel, steering well clear of the more traditional reaction of brotherly concern and empathy, commented in *Supersonic*, 'Somebody knocked the music into him. That person's got a lot to answer for.' Speaking to Howard Stern, Liam elaborated on his origin story. 'I was 14, 15, having a cigarette with my mates, and a few lads came down from another school, hoods up, and one of them whacked me on the head with a hammer. I thought music was for weirdos, man!' Howard pushed back, 'Right, you never sat there in your room and listened to Beatles and Stones, and sort of became one of those record nerds or anything like that? Noel was off learning the guitar, trying to get his shit together. You're off doing your thing, this kid hits you in the head with a hammer, and you say you wake up and suddenly, what, you heard music?' 'No, it wasn't instantly,' Liam explained. 'I had just always gone ... I think it was Madonna's "Like a Virgin". I was going, "That's a fucking tune, actually, man." So, a week before, I'd be going like that [disdainful look]. It wouldn't have even got close, you know what I mean?' It is a tune, to be fair.

Describing the weapon to the *Guardian*, Liam said: 'Not a big, massive mallet – one of those little small ones. I ended up in hospital and, after that, I just started hearing music differently.' The hammer in question was probably a lump hammer, a weapon of choice for hooligans at the time as it was easily concealed in a jacket pocket. It seems crazy now, but it wasn't uncommon for kids from rival schools to arrive tooled up, mob-handed and wade into unprepared boys.

It's interesting, given the Gallaghers' abusive home life, that they both attribute their musical ability to violence. In *Supersonic*, Noel claimed his father 'beat the talent into me'. Maybe it's their way of rationalising some degree of justice or sense in this trauma of body and mind. Post-head injury, Liam developed a love for bands such as the Stone Roses, the Jam and the Sex Pistols, drawn to their rebellious spirit, their swagger, their working-class authenticity. These bands, particularly the Roses, became symbols of Mancunian pride and working-class identity.

While Liam didn't initially share Noel's all-consuming passion for playing and writing music, he possessed a natural charisma, a powerful voice, an innate ability to connect with an audience and the spirit of rock 'n' roll. He was a born frontman from childhood. He loved to sing, to perform, to be the centre of attention. His mother said he was very different to both Paul and Noel; he was always attention-seeking and wanting to be the 'cock' of his class. He loved being noticed. That side of Liam's personality feasted on the adulation and public gaze that came with being front and centre during Oasis's rise. Each act of rock 'n' roll misbehaviour brought more attention. More love. Liam is 'love hungry'. He needs the ego stroke he gets from being on stage. The 'love and adoration' he perceives he is getting from the audience fills a void left by lack of love from his father. Liam cultivated a rebellious rock-star image, characterised by his swagger, confrontational attitude and volatile behaviour. This persona, however, masked deep insecurities. As Oasis entered the public discourse, the general view on the brothers was 'Noel's the talented one' and 'Liam is the wild rock star'. Liam's talent never really entered the conversation. It left him feeling he needed his star to burn more brightly than Noel's, feeling overshadowed by his brother's songwriting skills and seeking validation through other means.

For Noel, songwriting was a form of therapy. He struggles to show vulnerability and express emotions directly. He expresses his emotions through his songwriting. 'The music speaks for me,' he has often said, and fans saw this vulnerability in tracks such as 'Talk Tonight'. Mark Coyle, a close collaborator, described Noel as 'almost childlike' when writing – pouring his fears and frustrations into melodies that served as emotional release. That's because writing and playing guitar is where Noel's inner child lives. Liam, by contrast, used performance as his outlet. On stage, he was larger than life, projecting an image of defiance and invulnerability. Yet behind the bravado lay the same yearning for connection that defined Noel's music.

Both brothers found solace in music, but their approaches reflected their contrasting personas – one introspective, the other explosive.

The Gallagher brothers' schooldays were, unsurprisingly, far from conventional. Neither Liam nor Noel were particularly academically inclined. They were, as Liam put it, 'more interested in bunking off and having a laugh'. School was seen as a constraint, an obstacle to be overcome, rather than a place of learning and growth. Noel's academic struggles were, in part, a consequence of his difficult home life. He found it hard to concentrate on his studies when his home life was so turbulent, so unpredictable. He often skipped school, preferring to spend his time reading, listening to music or simply wandering the streets of Manchester. He was eventually expelled for throwing a bag of flour over a teacher, an act of rebellion that seemed to seal his fate as an academic underachiever. Noel, however, would later see this as a turning point, freeing him to focus on his true passion: music.

Liam's school experience was similarly chequered. He was, by his own admission, a bit of a rebel, always getting into trouble, always pushing the boundaries. He was more interested in football, fashion and socialising than he was in his studies. He was a popular figure, known for his charisma, his wit and his ability to make people laugh, and he was often the ringleader, the one who instigated pranks and mischief. He was expelled for fighting, something which would become a recurring theme in his life. The mutual disagreement with academia didn't prevent the Gallagher boys from going on to huge things.

Noel's musical journey took an unexpected turn in 1988, in his very early twenties. He landed a job as a roadie for the Inspiral Carpets, a local band that was beginning to make waves on the national music scene. It proved to be a pivotal moment in Noel's life, a turning point that would ultimately set him on the path to superstardom. Touring with the Carpets gave Noel a first-hand look at the inner workings of the music industry. He learned about life on the road, the technical aspects of live performance, the importance of professionalism, and the realities of being in a touring band. He absorbed the experience like a sponge, storing away valuable lessons that he would later apply to his own career. As he stated in *Supersonic*, 'It was the best apprenticeship I could have ever had.' The job also provided him with a sense of purpose, a direction that had been lacking in his life. He saw in the Inspiral Carpets, who had top-ten albums in both 1990 and 1991, a tangible blueprint that he could follow. He'd been 'bitten by the bug' and infected with a burning ambition.

Meanwhile, back in Manchester, Liam's life also took a turn towards a career in music. In 1991, he had, somewhat unexpectedly, joined a band called the Rain, featuring his school friend Paul 'Guigsy' McGuigan and Paul 'Bonehead' Arthurs, who was seven years older. The Rain were a far cry from the polished, ambitious band that Noel was working with. They were raw, inexperienced and, by most accounts, not particularly good. They played the occasional gig in local pubs to small, often indifferent audiences. Liam, however, brought something unique to the Rain. He had charisma, attitude and a voice that, while untrained, possessed a raw power, a distinctive quality that cut through the noise. He was a natural frontman, a born performer, even if he didn't yet have the songs to match his stage presence. As Bonehead later recalled in an interview with the *Guardian* in March 2006, 'Liam was just a natural. He had that swagger, that voice. We knew he was special.' The Rain, despite their limitations, provided Liam with an outlet for his energy, his ambition and his burgeoning musical talent. It was a chance to perform, to be in the spotlight, to experience the thrill of being on stage. It was also a chance to learn, to develop his stagecraft, to hone his vocal abilities.

The stage was now set for the fateful meeting that would change the course of British music history. Noel, having returned from touring with the Inspiral Carpets, went to see his brother's band perform at the Boardwalk, a legendary Manchester music venue that had hosted countless up-and-coming bands. The exact details of that night in August 1991 have become shrouded in myth and legend, embellished and distorted over the years by countless retellings. However, the basic facts remain undisputed. Noel, by his own admission, was not impressed by the Rain's musical abilities. He found their songs to be derivative, their performance sloppy, their overall sound lacking in originality. As he recounted in *Supersonic*, 'I thought,

"He's all right, the singer. The songs are a bit shit."' He saw something in Liam, a spark, a raw talent, an undeniable charisma that transcended the band's limitations. He recognised in his younger brother a star quality, a natural ability to command a stage, to connect with an audience. He also saw an opportunity, a chance finally to realise his own musical ambitions, to put his songs in the hands of a singer who could truly bring them to life.

Neither brother can agree on who asked who to join the band, but it was agreed that Noel would join, but only on his terms. He would be the band's sole songwriter and the one who called the shots. He recounted the moment in Paolo Hewitt's 1997 book *Getting High: The Adventures of Oasis*: 'I'll join your band, but I'm taking over.' The other members of the Rain, recognising the quality of Noel's songs, acquiesced. If your mouth is writing those sorts of cheques and cashing them in with a song like 'Live Forever', it's a pretty straightforward negotiation.

With Noel firmly in control, the band underwent a transformation. 'The Rain' was deemed too dreary and uninspired a name, and was replaced with 'Oasis', a name suggested by Liam, inspired by an Inspiral Carpets tour poster that hung in the brothers' shared bedroom, a poster that listed the Oasis Leisure Centre in Swindon as a venue. The Rain was dead. Long live Oasis.

The lineup was set: Liam on vocals, Noel on lead guitar and backing vocals, Bonehead on rhythm guitar, Guigsy on bass and Tony McCarroll on drums. The dynamic would both propel them at warp speed to unimaginable heights and ultimately contribute to their demise: Noel, the introverted and meticulous songwriter, the architect of their sound, the brains of the operation, and Liam, the extroverted, charismatic frontman, the voice, the attitude, the heart and soul of the band.

Oasis began rehearsing relentlessly, rigorously, in the cramped confines of the Boardwalk's rehearsal rooms. Noel's songs, infused with the influences of the Beatles, the Sex Pistols and T. Rex, were instantly anthemic. They were social commentaries about escape, about ambition, about the dreams and frustrations of working-class youth, themes that resonated deeply with their audience. These songs would go on to define a generation.

During these early days, everybody was pulling in the same direction. When opposite behavioural types work together harmoniously, it's a great combination and can lead to extraordinary creativity and results. Each has a strength that the other may lack and they each contribute to create a whole which is far greater than the sum of its parts. However, if there is discord or disharmony and they start to aim for different things and pull apart, rather than together, the results are explosive and destructive. For the time being, the Gallagher brothers' dynamic was still in the upward swing.

Oasis began playing gigs in and around Manchester, starting in the small, sweaty clubs and pubs that formed the backbone of the city's vibrant music scene. Their early performances were raw, energetic and often chaotic, powered by a potent mix of youthful exuberance, raw ambition and the sheer thrill of playing their music to a live audience. Liam's charisma, his undeniable stage presence, quickly became a focal point, captivating audiences with his natural swagger, his every move, every snarl, every perfectly timed vocal phrase. Noel, in contrast, was the stoic, focused guitarist, the anchor of the band, his guitar work providing the sonic foundation upon which Liam's performance could soar.

The band's reputation for explosive live shows grew rapidly. Word of mouth spread through the Manchester music scene, whispers of a new band, a band with great songs, a killer frontman and an undeniable energy. Their following grew with each gig, as more and more people were drawn to their raw power, their anthemic songs and their authentic working-class attitude. They were, as many who saw them in those early days described them, 'a force of nature', a band that demanded to be noticed.

Stories from this period abound, tales of chaotic gigs, drunken brawls and the band's unwavering self-belief. They played every show as if it were their last, pouring their hearts and souls into every performance. They were hungry, ambitious and determined to make it, to escape the confines of their background and conquer the world. One often-recounted story involves a gig at the small Hop and Grape in Manchester, where Liam, in a fit of pique, threw a tambourine at a heckler in the audience. The incident, while minor in itself, became a symbol of the band's raw energy, their unpredictability and their refusal to be ignored. These stories, often embellished and exaggerated over time, contributed to the growing mythology surrounding the band, a mythology that they themselves were not afraid to cultivate.

A pivotal moment in the Oasis story, which would

forever alter their trajectory, came in May 1993. The band, still relatively unknown outside Manchester, travelled to Glasgow to play a gig at the legendary King Tut's Wah Wah Hut, a small but influential venue. The story of how they secured the gig has become part of the band's legend. They had heard that various record label scouts would be in attendance to watch a mixed bill of bands, and they were determined to play, to seize the opportunity to showcase their talent to a wider audience. They travelled to Scotland with barely enough money for petrol, their instruments crammed into a battered van, and their persistence, their sheer audacity, paid off.

Alan McGee, the founder of Creation Records and one of modern British music's true catalysts, attended the gig out of sheer bedevilment. Going through a breakup, he'd decided to try to unnerve his ex-girlfriend, Debbie Turner (one-third of the all-female trio Sister Lovers). Debbie, now Debbie Ellis, a great music and fashion photographer based in Stockport, may not have proved to be McGee's soulmate, but she did lead to him meeting another that evening at the Wah Wah Hut, in the unlikely form of five Mancunians who had threatened their way on to that evening's lineup. McGee, a man known for his keen ear for talent and his impulsive nature, was instantly captivated by Oasis's raw energy and undeniable swagger.

'They were so volatile, but I loved it. Everything I had always dreamt of releasing with Creation,' McGee recalled in his autobiography, *Creation Stories*. 'They were rock 'n' roll, they had a psychedelic edge, but it was tougher and more working class, and they had those anthems.

They also had Noel and Liam, who were about to be the two most famous people of the decade. They had the charisma and the whiff of danger, especially when they were together, which was pure excitement.'

He approached the band after their set and was effusive in his praise, telling them that they were the best band he had seen in years. He offered them a record deal on the spot, a contract that would change their lives for ever. 'I knew I had to sign them. They were the real deal. They had the songs, the attitude, the swagger. They had it all.'

The band, initially stunned by McGee's offer, quickly accepted. It was a dream come true, a moment they had been working towards since they first picked up their instruments. The signing with Creation Records was a turning point for Oasis. It was a validation of their talent, a recognition of their potential and a gateway to a wider audience, a chance finally to escape the confines of their everyday lives and launch their assault on the music world. Creation, at the time, was one of the most influential independent labels in the UK, home to bands such as Primal Scream, My Bloody Valentine and the Jesus and Mary Chain. Creation were to give Oasis the launchpad they needed to go supersonic.

13

Supersonic – Noel and Liam, 1994–6

With the backing of Creation Records, a label that understood their vision, Oasis entered the studio in 1993 to record their debut album, *Definitely Maybe*. The recording sessions, which took place in various studios in Wales and England, including the iconic Monnow Valley Studio in Monmouthshire, were fraught with tension and given a nervous energy by the brothers' volatile relationship, Noel's inherent perfectionism and the band's inexperience in the studio.

Creation staff and close friends believe no outsider can ever understand the dynamic of the brothers during that part of their lives. Two siblings growing up in such difficult conditions and then going from the dole to millionaire rock gods in just over a year was too unique for non-Gallaghers to grasp. The council estates of Manchester may only be 200 miles from London's celebrity circuit but they may as well have grown up on Mars judging how alien life was becoming.

Being around Noel and Liam at this time was electrifying and the energy was incredible, but their relationship was enigmatic and dangerous. Eldest brother Paul observed how the band's rapidly growing success amplified their differences and how the pressures of fame exacerbated their existing tensions. He described Noel as becoming increasingly withdrawn and controlling, while Liam became more erratic and unpredictable. The turbo injection of cash, fame and adulation were starting to drive the twin engines' torque inwards. The counterpoints of their personas that drove Oasis's magic were creating more and more friction and they'd never really recovered their sibling synergy.

Definitely Maybe quickly became the defining sound of a generation. The making of the album, however, was fraught with difficulties. Before the version that the world came to know and love hit the shelves, it was scrapped, re-recorded and mixed multiple times. The escalating recording costs soared past £50,000, threatening to shelve the project altogether.

There were arguments, fights, disagreements over arrangements, production choices and even the choice of studios. There was a particularly heated debate over the drum sound on 'Supersonic', with Noel demanding a more polished sound and Tony McCarroll struggling to deliver. There was even a brief departure by Noel after a particularly heated disagreement with Liam, a fight that reportedly involved a cricket bat. The incident, recounted in numerous interviews and books, became another chapter in the growing legend of the Gallagher feud.

Originally working with producer Dave Batchelor at Monnow Valley Studio, the process was frustrating. 'We were a live band, we shouldn't have been thinking about that production shit. We should've just gone in and fucking banged it out,' Liam Gallagher lamented. The sessions were fraught with challenges, from excessive guitar layering to further struggles with McCarroll's performance. Eventually, a second recording attempt at Sawmills Studio, led by Mark Coyle, proved more productive.

As the album neared completion, Owen Morris stepped in to refine its sound, transforming it into the anthemic record it became. 'Liam was a live wire who talked non-stop shite, but when he sang, he was extraordinary,' Morris said. His work helped cement the album's raw, unfiltered power.

Upon release on 4 September 1994, *Definitely Maybe* shot to number one in the UK charts, selling over 86,000 copies in its first week and becoming the fastest-selling debut album in British history at the time, a record that stood for over a decade, eventually beaten by the last great British band, Arctic Monkeys. It eventually surpassed 10 million sales worldwide. Reflecting on its impact, Noel boldly stated, 'Probably the greatest debut by any band, ever.'

Oasis had arrived. The album was not just a soundtrack but an ethos – one that resonated with disillusioned youth searching for escapism. It became one of the few positive legacies of the preceding decade of Thatcherism, as Britain emerged from a period of economic recession and social unrest. *Definitely Maybe* was so drenched in attitude that putting it on a turntable risked spattering swagger over everybody in the room.

The album's anthemic songs were at odds with the prevailing grunge scene that had dominated the American rock charts. Noel can be melancholic at heart but his songs are always optimistic. He wasn't going to gaze at his shoes or write mopey music like his US contemporaries. One thing he did share with the grunge crowd was a tendency to wear pretty awful baggy jumpers. Liam hopped on the big-jumper bus too but they just hung better from him. The album's success propelled Oasis to the forefront of the burgeoning British guitar scene, which would later label disparate bands as 'Britpop', a cultural phenomenon that celebrated the expression of Britishness in music, fashion and art.

Tracks such as 'Supersonic', with its driving rhythm and instantly memorable guitar riff, 'Shakermaker', with its Beatles-esque melody and Liam's sneering vocals, 'Live Forever', a soaring anthem of hope and defiance, and 'Cigarettes & Alcohol', a raw, raucous ode to working-class escapism, became instant classics. Liam's distinctive Mancunian drawl, Noel's soaring guitar riffs, his knack for crafting unforgettable melodies, and the band's raw energy captured the spirit of the times, a spirit of optimism, rebellion and a renewed sense of British identity.

The album's success was not limited to the UK. It also achieved significant commercial success in Europe, Australia and even made inroads into the US market. Oasis were suddenly a global phenomenon, their music spreading across the airwaves, their faces adorning magazine covers, their every move scrutinised by the media.

If *Definitely Maybe* had sent the band supersonic, their second album *(What's the Story) Morning Glory?* sent them supernova. The recording sessions, which took place in 1995 in Monmouthshire's Rockfield Studios, were even more strained, particularly between Liam and Noel. The pressure to follow up their successful debut, coupled with the constant media attention and the excesses of the rock 'n' roll lifestyle, exacerbated the already strained relationship between the brothers. Liam was increasingly rebelling, culminating in the evening when Noel recorded his vocals on 'Don't Look Back in Anger'. Liam nearly brought the band to an end after inviting a gaggle of randoms from the local pub back to the residential studio. The scene descended into carnage, the studio's quaint farmhouse hosting a Tommy and Jerry-style royal rumble. Oasis photographer Michael Spencer Jones summarised the chaos, 'It was a serious falling out. There were cricket bats, air rifles – and I remember [Liam] getting into a car and going with me running up the drive shouting.' Noel's view was 'I'm here to make a record' but Liam wanted to live the life of a rock 'n' roll superstar.

'Most of the band left the recording sessions while I was still at the studio – and people felt they might not finish the album for sure,' Liam remembers, conceding: 'Now, I realise I'm not the easiest person to work with, but when you join a rock 'n' roll band, for me, there are no limits – you drink, you take drugs, you party, you mess up, you stop. And then you think about it and move on. That all seemed to go out of the window with Noel. He was the sensible one, I get it, but you can be too sensible. As far as I'm concerned, a big rule book came out and he started ticking people off one by one.'

Despite the internal strife, *(What's the Story) Morning Glory?*, released in October 1995, was an even bigger success than Oasis's first album. It debuted at number one in the UK, selling over 340,000 copies in its first week alone, solidifying Oasis's position as the biggest band in the country. It went on to become one of the best-selling albums of all time in the UK. It also achieved significant international success, topping the charts in several countries and reaching number four on the US *Billboard* 200.

The album was a more polished and ambitious work than *Definitely Maybe*, showcasing Noel's growing confidence as a songwriter and the band's increasing musical maturity. It featured some of Oasis's most iconic tracks, including 'Wonderwall', 'Don't Look Back in Anger', 'Champagne Supernova' and 'Morning Glory'.

When the band released the song that would go on to define them, 'Wonderwall', it became a global anthem. Despite only reaching number two in the UK charts, it made the Gallaghers household names and broke them into the American mainstream.

Noel had written the song while living in Camden's Albert Street. He took the demo tape into Creation and played it for his girlfriend Meg Mathews, who was working on the band's artist liaison and publicity, telling her he'd written it in her honour. As the final chord decayed into the air, Meg remained unwowed. She eased out a diplomatic 'Oh, really? Great. Thanks,' as envious co-workers watched on. Meg was an industry professional and her own entity. She wasn't easily impressed by Noel's work, or if she was she understood the benefits of concealing it.

In the more recent past, Noel has obfuscated the song's origin story, claiming he'd told Meg it was about her to cheer her up following the dissolution of her own music management company, Flavour, but actually it's about a number of people. It's his way of asserting emotional ownership over this best-known composition. But it was 100 per cent about Meg Mathews.

Oasis followed 'Wonderwall' with 'Don't Look Back in Anger', which became the band's first single to feature Noel on lead vocals. It built on the 'Wonderwall' juggernaut and became another anthem for the masses. Its lyrics are difficult to interpret but everybody in Britain seems to know them all and believe in their sentiment. Noel's singing brought an unspoken Gallagher fissure to the fore. He's technically a better singer than Liam and this particular song benefitted from his range. When they were recording, he'd told Liam he could only sing one of 'Look Back' or 'Wonderwall'. Obviously this was a confusing and unsettling ultimatum for the lead singer. Following a predictable tantrum, Liam plumped for 'Wonderwall', leaving the 'Let It Be'-style anthem to Noel.

It created an unavoidable moment in every Oasis set that followed. As soon as the *Imagine*-inspired piano hit the opening C chord, Liam would wander off stage and leave Noel essentially fronting the band. Unlike his Fab Four heroes, Liam didn't have an instrument to play while his bandmate belted out the top line, and he felt embarrassed to be rendered redundant in such a public manner.

The *Morning Glory* sessions had been a battlefield for the escalating Gallagher power struggle. In Liam's view, Noel had taken over his band and seized control, but his older brother was backed in this by his management, Ignition, and his label, Creation. In Noel, they saw a hugely talented writer and an investible star they could depend on. Liam was hard work and his behavioural protests were becoming increasingly damaging and erratic, not helped by his almost constant drug use. At the heart of this was creative control, money and ego. Noel absolutely governed the band's direction and decisions. Everything ran through him. He had complete control of Oasis and, like a dog chasing a car, Liam wanted it even if he wasn't sure what to do with it once he got it.

Another example of Liam's disruption came when he failed to show for *Morning Glory*'s cover-art shoot. Sean Rowley had to fill in, taking Liam's place on the now iconic album cover. Noel was coming to the conclusion that he just couldn't rely on Liam to do anything that he was supposed to do any more. It became a huge problem, a barrier in the brothers' trust.

The clear favouritism towards Noel from the label and management was really starting to piss Liam off. He'd imagined them as being equals when Noel joined the Rain. He hadn't seen the role of frontman as becoming secondary to that of writer. A rapidly expanding financial gulf had opened up between the brothers too. At the start, the whole band had been on wages. The money began to come in very quickly and in huge quantities. Noel made more than everybody else from the mechanical royalties (royalties from album sales) due to playing multiple instruments, and received the entirety of the publishing royalties, being the sole songwriter. He reportedly received a cheque for £19 million from Sony ATV for his publishing rights and celebrated alone at an Angus Steakhouse. He was not one for sharing the wealth. Noel seemingly inherited his father's tight fist to go with his sharp tongue, and gained a reputation for being notoriously stingy. The recently nouveau riche Noel now had a financial platform from which to further assert his control.

The favouritism and financial disparity were further highlighted when Alan McGee gifted Noel a brown Rolls-Royce in front of his bandmates at a Creation Records party. He rewarded Liam with a Rolex. Ordinarily, a Rolex would be a brilliant gift but, in this instance, it was a horological slap in the chops.

Noel's rewards were justifiable. He was the one putting the shift in at the studio. He was the one writing those amazing songs. He started to see the rest of the band as dispensable and riding on his coattails. Noel had complained to Ignition that he wasn't happy with the way anyone was playing or singing while at Rockfield. He'd stayed up all night, every night for a week, while the other lads went to the pub, leaving Noel to redo every instrument to get it right. He felt entitled to the lion's share, and he enjoyed the dominion over Oasis afforded him by his songwriting and growing piles of dosh.

The increasingly obvious financial hierarchy had begun to cause a huge amount of tension, and there was also a growing resentment over creative control. Liam wanted to be a greater part of the creative process and wasn't allowed to be. In the lead-up to the *Morning Glory* sessions, Liam had tried to make his case, telling Noel and his label he had five songs and they were just as good. He wanted to know why he wasn't being given a chance. Every voice that came back was saying no.

The band had an amazing singer in Liam and an amazing songwriter in Noel, and together it was mega. But if you allow the gaps to widen in such a pronounced way, you're looking for trouble. The divide between the brothers was deepening. Liam was growing resentful, feeling like he was being boxed out of the creative process, while Noel saw himself as the only one capable of steering Oasis towards continued success. It wasn't just about songwriting any more – it was about control, power and legacy.

Noel's desire for control had started to push towards ruminations on a solo career, and Liam could feel it. It was the stick Noel left in the corner of the room when the carrot failed to get Liam in line. When Liam skipped out on vocal duties at an *MTV Unplugged* session, Noel took over and delivered a set that became a classic to Oasis fans. Noel wasn't prepared to let Liam's disruptive protests derail his career. That night, he showed he could carry the band if Liam ever went too far, and the Gallagher power dynamic solidified for ever.

Despite denials, Noel had always wanted to be a frontman. Looking back during an interview with *Q* in 2016 he maintained, 'no, I never stood in front of the mirror with a tennis racket, it never occurred to me', yet he had originally auditioned to be the lead singer of the Inspiral Carpets, who – like Dick Rowe's infamous 'no ta' to Brian Epstein and the Beatles – decided he'd be a better fit as a roadie. Noel was growing increasingly frustrated. According to a source, he told Meg he wanted to be the singer and that he should have split the band up after *Definitely Maybe* and made *Morning Glory* his debut solo record. He said that they were his songs, that everyone loved them and wondered why he wasn't the one out there singing them. The ego was growing.

Meanwhile, Liam was clashing more and more with Noel's value system. 'Liam is chaos,' Noel would later quip. 'He's the guy who smashes the door down, and I'm the one who fixes it.' Liam thrived on volatility. He believed that rock 'n' roll was as much about bad behaviour as it was about good tunes. 'It's not just the music,' he declared in an interview. 'You need the mayhem.' To Noel, this mindset felt like a threat to everything he had worked to create. Liam's refusal to respect boundaries wasn't rebellion – it was an attack on the very foundations of what kept Noel grounded, his meticulous songwriting and studio work demonstrating his desire for precision and autonomy. It was a clash of incompatible values and views on how to navigate the world.

Liam can suck the energy out of any situation or environment – he feeds off it. He needs it like oxygen.

Confrontation with the press, with the fans on stage – he loves it. Noel, on the other hand, withdraws. He doesn't need that energy and feels uncomfortable around it. It's not a power struggle in the usual sense; it's a need for chaos versus a need for order. The brothers' rivalry is rarefied oxygen and it's zero-sum. What feeds one starves the other.

(What's the Story) Morning Glory? had solidified Oasis's position as the biggest band in the world, the undisputed kings of Britpop, and the summer of 1996 saw them embark on a massive, sold-out tour in support of the album. They played to packed stadiums and arenas across the UK, Europe and the US, culminating in two historic concerts at Knebworth House in Hertfordshire, England, on 10 and 11 August 1996. These concerts, attended by a staggering 250,000 people over two nights, were the largest outdoor concerts in British history at the time.

The Knebworth concerts were more than just gigs; they were cultural events, a moment that captured the zeitgeist. They were a celebration of Oasis at the peak of their powers, a testament to their connection with their fans and a defining moment for a generation. Over 2.5 million people applied for tickets, roughly 4 per cent of the British population, highlighting the band's immense popularity.

The atmosphere was electric, a sea of faces stretching as far as the eye could see. The crowd sang along to every word, their voices echoing across the vast expanse of the park. It was a moment of pure euphoria, a collective experience that transcended the music itself. It was, as many who were there described it, 'a once-in-a-lifetime event'. Fans interviewed in the *Oasis: Knebworth 1996* documentary called the experience 'life affirming' and 'the best weekend of my life'. The film provides a vivid record of those historic nights, capturing the energy of the performances, the passion of the crowd and the sheer scale of the event. Noel Gallagher himself, looking back at the footage, expressed a mixture of pride and disbelief at what the band had achieved.

For Oasis, Knebworth was the culmination of everything they had worked for. They had started as a small band from Manchester. Now, they were headlining the biggest concerts in British history. Even more than that, they had conquered the world. But while the period between 1991 and 1996 was undoubtedly Oasis's golden age, it was also a time when the seeds of their eventual destruction were sown. The intense pressure of their rapid ascent to fame, the constant media scrutiny and the excesses of the rock 'n' roll lifestyle took a toll on the band, particularly on the already strained relationship between Liam and Noel.

The brothers' contrasting personalities, which had initially been a source of strength, were now a source of conflict. Their increasingly frequent physical fights failed to even raise an eyebrow among Creation's staff and were indicative of a deeper tension, a fundamental difference in their approach to music, to fame and to life.

Paul Gallagher, in his book *Brothers, From Childhood to Oasis* and subsequent interviews, offered a unique perspective on the brothers' dynamic during this period. He observed how success amplified their differences, how the pressures of fame exacerbated their existing tensions. He described Noel as becoming increasingly withdrawn and controlling, while Liam became more erratic and unpredictable. Paul also spoke of the difficulty of being caught in the middle, of trying to mediate between his two warring brothers. He was often the one who had to pick up the pieces after their fights, to keep the peace and keep the band together. He was, as he described it, 'the referee in a never-ending boxing match'.

Despite the growing tensions, Oasis continued to produce great music. Their creative partnership, while fraught with conflict, was still incredibly productive. They were a band that thrived on tension, a band that seemed to need the friction between Liam and Noel to spark their creativity. However, the cracks were beginning to show, and the very dynamic that had propelled them to stardom was now threatening to tear them apart.

Knebworth, in hindsight, was not just the peak of their success; it was also the beginning of the end. The crowd's roar, the euphoria of that shared moment, would soon be replaced by the sounds of a band breaking apart, a brotherhood fractured, and a legacy that would for ever be marked by both triumph and tragedy, by both brilliance and bitterness.

14

Some Might Say – Noel and Liam, 1997

The afterglow of Knebworth, while brilliant, a moment that seemed to encapsulate the zenith of British music in the nineties, was tragically brief. The concerts were a fleeting glimpse of a band at its peak before the inevitable descent. Oasis, having reached the summit of their ambitions, having conquered the world, found themselves on a precarious precipice, teetering on the edge of an abyss. The monumental success of *Definitely Maybe* and *(What's the Story) Morning Glory?* had cemented their place in music history, had made them icons, but it had also created a pressure-cooker environment, exacerbating the already volatile dynamic between Liam and Noel Gallagher, pushing their relationship to its breaking point. They both found some solace in the developing relationships with their future wives Meg Mathews (Noel) and Patsy Kensit (Liam).

Noel first met his future 'Wonderwall' in 1994 at Meg's Maida Vale flat, where she lived with MTV presenter

Rebecca de Ruvo. At the time, Noel had just been signed to Creation Records and was dating Meg's flatmate Rebecca, but she wasn't all that keen on the boy from Burnage. As Rebecca's interest faded, a new, more profound connection began to form between Noel and Meg.

They started as friends but it didn't take long for something deeper to emerge. Meg was already an established industry figure in the music PR and management world. Her company, Flavour, had helped build the careers of dance acts such as Betty Boo, and she moved within a tight-knit circle from London's clubbing scene – Danny Rampling, Pete Tong, Paul Oakenfold and Fat Tony (Anthony Marnoch). Acid house and ecstasy-fuelled all-nighters at Notting Hill's Subterranean defined her social world before cocaine emerged as the drug of choice. It accelerated a scene that already moved fast and burned bright.

Noel was a serial monogamist who sought stability during his dizzying ascent. In Meg, he found a partner who could match his energy and who understood the industry. She was savvy, sharp and as much a part of the rock 'n' roll circus as he was.

Their bond deepened quickly and they became inseparable. When Flavour disbanded, Meg threw herself into supporting Noel, eventually securing a role at Creation Records as part of the company's Oasis-specific office. It wasn't just a job – it was a statement of how entwined their lives had become. Meg applied for the role via an ad in the *Guardian* and gained a strong referral from Noel, who told Alan McGee to 'Give my missus a job.' She handled publicity, artist liaison and – most importantly – helped hold things together as the Oasis machine surged forward at breakneck speed.

As Oasis cemented their status as the biggest band in the world, their relationship had taken on the same kind of momentum. Meg moved into Noel's Camden flat on Albert Street but, before long, they were upgrading. A townhouse in St John's Wood served as a temporary base while their real dream home – an opulent Primrose Hill mansion destined to become Supernova Heights – was undergoing renovations. The house would become an infamous Britpop palace, hosting an endless, delirious party where the famous, the infamous and the utterly reckless passed through its doors day and night. The house's regulars included Goldie, Nellee Hooper, Massive Attack, journalist Paolo Hewitt, actors Jonny Lee Miller and Jude Law, and the ever-present Sadie Frost. The home to the sound of the nineties also provided accommodation for the face of the nineties, Kate Moss. She was Meg's best friend and took up residence there for a while, extending the invitations to her then-boyfriend Johnny Depp who would later provide guest guitar work on Oasis's *Be Here Now* album.

For all Kate's charms, she doesn't follow the norms of houseguest etiquette. In addition to nicking Noel's crisps, she also had a weakness for famous indie boys and was very flirtatious with Noel. Noel was feeling awkward about Kate's flirting. Meg took it in her stride and had a word with the star of the 'heroin chic' look – this was their world, a chaotic blend of fame, love, loyalty and the occasional complication.

By 1997 marriage was inevitable: Noel and Meg were inseparable, their relationship having blossomed despite the madness of fame and the demands of a global rock band, and they eloped to Las Vegas.

Let's take a moment to celebrate the most famous rock 'n' roll house since Elvis took a shine to a colonial-style mansion in Memphis: Supernova Heights ...

The house was tucked on a quiet, treelined street between Primrose Hill and Belsize Park in northwest London. While the front door was impressive, it wasn't often used. Most people preferred the side entrance, which led directly into the kitchen. However, for those who entered through the front, they were met with an extraordinary sight.

Inside, the hallway was striking. The dark-brown wooden corridor set a rich, elegant tone, complemented by a sweeping staircase on the right side. The staircase featured a dark mahogany banister, which wound gracefully upwards. The walls were adorned with a creamy rag-rolled finish – an incredibly popular effect at the time – while the marble flooring added a sleek, polished touch.

One of the most eye-catching features was on the left-hand side: an eight-foot tank, filled with vibrant fish swimming in a mesmerising display, made up the wall. On the other side of the fish tank was the living room, a statement of excess. There were four enormous leopard-print sofas and a massive brown square coffee table sitting centrally, anchoring the space. Against one wall, a huge fireplace added warmth and grandeur. Adorning the walls were several iconic Sex Pistols artworks – striking, rebellious and entirely fitting for the house's rock 'n' roll aesthetic.

The grand staircase was carpeted with a bubble pattern, contrasting the otherwise regal setting with a psychedelic sixties vibe, leading to Meg and Noel's first-floor bedroom. The entire floor was dedicated to that one bedroom, dominated by a gigantic, navy-blue, leather-studded bed. Two bay windows overlooked the back of the house, framed by huge sweeping velvet curtains that draped luxuriously. Directly in front of the bed, a large TV was mounted on the wall. As well as a walk-in dressing area, there was a bathroom that housed a mosaic target bath – one of the house's most iconic features – along with golden sinks and shower. The top floor featured additional bedrooms, which were more modest compared to the rest of the house.

Heading back down, past the fish tank, you would reach the kitchen and dining area. This entire space was open plan, designed for both dining and socialising. A grand dark oak dining table sat near the large back windows, which led out to the garden. The floor also featured a more casual living area with two leather sofas. This was where everyone would naturally gravitate – whether after a night out or just for an evening in. Tucked underneath the grand staircase was a running machine, as Meg was a keen runner.

Everything about Supernova Heights was big – big furniture, big tables, big chairs, big sofas. It was designed to feel extravagant, opulent and unlike anything most people had ever seen. Massive chandeliers adorned each room, while dip candles contributed to the ambience. Every inch of the home radiated luxury, excess and an unmistakable rock-star aesthetic.

Supernova Heights wasn't just a house – it was an Austin Powers fever dream come true.

While Noel was falling for Meg, Liam had landed a teenage crush in the form of Patsy Kensit. The Pretenders' Chrissie Hynde had unwittingly enabled the love connection between the actress and rock star, having decided she liked Liam and calling Patsy to come along as her wingman. Chrissie was unaware that both Liam and Noel had posters of Patsy on their walls as teenagers. It was a strategic error and, unsurprisingly, Liam only had eyes for Chrissie's pretty, blonde IT-girl friend. Liam wasted no time in declaring his intentions. The next day, reputedly, he excitedly bragged to his mates, 'Patsy fucking Kensit! I've got her number. She's mad for it!'

Patsy Kensit had entered the fame game much earlier than Liam. She was a child star who graduated to roles in films such as *Lethal Weapon 2* and *Absolute Beginners* in the mid to late 1980s. In addition to acting, Kensit had a brief career as the lead singer of the pop group Eighth Wonder, achieving moderate success in the same period.

The pair quickly became inseparable. Kensit, who was fresh from her divorce from Jim Kerr of Simple Minds in 1996, was accustomed to the demands of being with a rock star. Liam, meanwhile, was used to being the centre of attention, and their relationship played out like a whirlwind, intense and dramatic from the very beginning. Following her divorce from Kerr, Patsy had a large house in St John's Wood, which she sold so she and Liam could buy a mansion in Elsworthy Road on the edge of Primrose Hill. The couple moved into the imposing townhouse and became part of the infamous Primrose Hill set. Their new pad was every bit as mental as Supernova Heights, but the brothers' social circles remained separate. There was a clear divide emerging between House Liam and House Noel, despite being only a five-minute walk from each other. It wasn't helped by the fact Meg didn't like Liam and Noel didn't like Patsy. Meg had to mitigate the risk of fraternal fisticuffs and would tell friends in reference to Liam, 'Don't bring him around here,' when they'd call enquiring about a boozy Gallagher get-together.

Liam's parties were legendary – wild, chaotic and laced with excess. However, Patsy was often resented by the women on the Liam Gallagher scene, and she found the Primrose Hill set exhausting. She had spent her early fame in more exclusive, high-end circles in the 1980s and wasn't accustomed to the chaotic house parties and constant media attention that followed Oasis and their crowd. Liam's unpredictability and volatile personality were at odds with the domestic life Kensit had envisioned. Their London mansion had become a hub of debauchery, with a different cast playing out the same scenes found at Noel's Supernova Heights.

One of the most infamous moments of their relationship came in 1996 when Liam pulled out of Oasis's US tour at the last minute – just fifteen minutes before his flight was due to leave – claiming he had laryngitis and had to go house hunting with Patsy. It was an act of top-tier self-sabotage that enraged Noel and baffled Oasis fans. That tour was supposed to be the moment Oasis conquered America and Liam torpedoed it.

Liam's absence was catastrophic. The band's momentum was severely impacted, and their reputation in the US took a significant hit. His decision to bail fuelled rumours of an impending breakup, and a furious Noel Gallagher was forced to take centre stage when Liam didn't turn up in Chicago, and sing in his brother's place. The press was quick to speculate about tensions within the band. It was a crazy decision from Liam that messed everything up for everyone related to the band.

The brothers' in-fighting had escalated dramatically in the time leading up to Liam's decision to familiarise himself with the local Foxtons estate agency. There were a lot of arguments, with the resentment, the bad feeling – 'you're making more money than me' – making Liam increasingly unhappy. In the end, it seems, he derailed the tour in protest. Liam did later rejoin the band, but by then the damage had been done – both to Oasis's American ambitions and to Liam's reputation as an insurable frontman. Liam's last-minute decisions and unpredictable nature were already a source of endless frustration for Noel, who was more focused on Oasis's global domination, and the situation was now even more heightened. The band's future teetered on the edge like a bus full of bullion.

If there was one event that encapsulated the tension between Patsy, Liam and Noel, it was a 1997 *Vanity Fair* cover shoot. Featuring Liam and Patsy lying semi-naked under a Union Jack bedspread, the image was meant to represent the peak of Cool Britannia. But to Noel, it was an absolute betrayal of the Oasis brand.

Noel had always been unhappy with any photo shoot that went on outside of Oasis, and he didn't like any public display with the wives and girlfriends (although he obviously softened his stance when agreeing to a photo spread with Meg in *Hello*, which pictured the pair looking like hostages forced to advertise Pot Noodle). He particularly disliked this shoot because he felt '[Oasis] were bigger than all that'. Noel apparently felt the Cool Britannia tag was beneath his band and said 'they're not using us to sell their fucking magazine'. And ultimately, as he didn't like Patsy in the first place, he probably wouldn't have liked her influence on his brother in any case.

The *Vanity Fair* cover became one of the defining images of the decade, but it also drew criticism, including from Noel. In an interview for *Don't Look Back in Anger*, Noel mocked the cover, saying, 'Liam looked like an absolute fucking idiot with a nipple on his head, looking like a fucking baby bottle with his fucking missus in a Union Jack bed, topless [which she wasn't]. Ooh. Rubbish.' He later claimed that Kensit had coerced Liam into the shoot, asserting, 'Liam's missus fucking got him in a headlock! She was like, "I'm going to be on the cover, but they'll only put me on the cover if you're on it." Liam's a weak man, so he went along with it.'

Liam and Patsy's relationship progressed quickly. On 7 April 1997, they married in a low-key ceremony at Marylebone Town Hall – following in the footsteps of two of Liam's idols, Paul McCartney and Ringo Starr. Marriage, however, did little to stabilise their relationship.

15

Fade In-Out – Noel and Liam, 1997–2009

The honeymoon period lasted approximately a week before Liam invited trouble to paradise. Within the first fortnight of holy matrimony Liam disappeared off without trace for a week, leaving Patsy disoriented and shaken. And only a month or so later, he rekindled a previous dalliance with Lisa Moorish, the singer of Kill City, which effectively killed their nascent marital bliss.

On 18 June 1997, Meg Mathews was contacted by Lisa Moorish, who she knew from Kill City's days on Creation Records. Lisa, who had had a fling with Liam before he met Patsy, was in San Francisco and hassling Meg to be put on the guest list and given an aftershow pass for the Oasis show at the Oakland Coliseum that night, where they were opening for U2. Molly was born nine months and eight days later on 26 March 1998.

Patsy later reflected on the betrayal, saying, 'After he married me, he went to Los Angeles and slept with that girl, Lisa Moorish, and got her pregnant. What a son of a bitch.' Liam was angry and unfortunately Molly paid the price, as he didn't see his daughter until she became an adult. Liam's off-stage drama was the latest in a growing list of incidents for Oasis's US adventures. Even getting into the US in the first place was hard to arrange due to Noel having a drugs-related offence on his record, meaning a laborious visa application process, which continues to this day, and multiple secondary interviews with the charming officers who work for America's Customs and Border Protection.

Liam and Patsy's relationship had started with what she described as 'fireworks' – a deep connection filled with excitement and passion. However, as time went on, the moments of joyful intensity were increasingly punctuated by periods of distance and tension. Despite the shared love and deep conversations that spanned nights, the reality of being part of the rock 'n' roll circus meant facing temptations and the relentless pace of celebrity life, which inevitably hurt their marriage. Liam would continue to disappear for days at a time, leaving Patsy distraught, and eventually turn up in a right mess. Patsy lost it at one point and kicked a BMW. Her relationship caused her to suffer anxiety attacks, and she even had to check into a hospital to help her recover.

Kensit later admitted, 'I cried every day of my marriage' in response to Liam's volatile behaviour, fuelled by excessive drinking, drug use and frequent fits of anger. Infidelity was a recurring theme in their relationship, with Liam regularly engaging in extramarital affairs and going AWOL. The couple's friends Pearl Lowe and Danny Goffey, of Supergrass, would spend weekends propping Patsy up during Liam's dalliances.

Liam's recklessness was changing the lives of everybody around him, and it upended his marriage to Patsy before it had even begun. The couple had been happy in their very early days, especially Patsy. 'We just clicked on every level,' she recalled. 'He was protective and loving. When we were together there were fireworks, and a chemistry that lasted to the end.' Their bond was immediate, and after weeks of being inseparable, their connection felt unbreakable. 'In many ways, it was the perfect relationship I'd dreamed about when I was 16,' she reminisced. 'On our first dates, we just stayed up all night talking and sharing secrets. We even dressed the same – in Gucci duffle coats and desert boots – a bit like teenagers.' But as Liam's star was rocketing, his behaviour was spiralling. He was lost in the drugs and booze that came as part of life as Britain's biggest rock star.

Liam was a loose cannon who couldn't be relied on. Liam told friends, 'You know, the dark – I can't drink the dark stuff. Whisky. No. Go fucking mental.' And it's true. On whisky, he'd lose it and become very aggressive. His relationship with drink underscored the destructive impact of his choices, not only on his personal relationships but on his public image and professional commitments.

Bravado and showing off – Liam seemed to think that was 'Alpha male' behaviour as he'd never had a good male role model growing up. All he saw from his father was drunkenness and violence. Toxic masculinity was his childhood experience and that had become his blueprint. He needed to be the cock of the walk, the big drinker, the hard man. His walk, his demeanour, was all about projecting an image of toughness. He would run headlong into trouble where Noel was non-confrontational. You could see the difference on stage: in moments when Liam was acting up, Noel would stay at his spot and continue to play the guitar, almost refusing to acknowledge what was happening. But Liam's hard-man image would prove to be a brittle shell that masked deep insecurities.

Patsy separated from Liam following news of Liam fathering Molly, but they reconciled and Patsy became pregnant. The birth of Lennon Gallagher in September 1999 was a beacon of hope for them amid their tumultuous marriage. Liam's words to *Q* shortly after his son's arrival highlighted a yearning for stability: 'I'm a father now. I've had a gap in my life and the baby is here to fill it. I've got to look after him and I want to be there to feel it. I want to be straight-headed about it.' Yet, the shadow of past indiscretions loomed large. The birth of their son coincided with escalating professional demands and personal temptations. The pressures of life on tour, the constant media attention, and Liam's sporadic presence at home soon tested the bonds of their relationship again. Patsy herself noted the dichotomy of their union: intensely connected when together, yet often separated by Liam's commitments to Oasis and his lifestyle. But Patsy was desperate to make it work. In fact, she later revealed she was so desperate to make their tempestuous five-year relationship work that she turned down the biggest opportunity of her life – to play Ross's girlfriend Emily in hit US comedy *Friends* – on Liam's advice. He told her it would be a mistake to play the love interest who replaces Rachel in Ross's affections as she'd be hated. Reflecting on this time, Patsy told a friend she'd had breast implants at the time, which she subsequently removed. She said that everything she did in the last 18 months of their marriage was about trying to get Liam's attention.

Their marriage hit the rocks again in 2000, and this time the breakup would be for good. Less than a year after Lennon's birth, Patsy left Liam and the couple divorced. Looking back on the relationship, Patsy surprisingly admits regret at not having stood by Liam longer. She feels she was too concerned about what other people thought of their relationship. She regretted walking out almost immediately. She said she thought he had moved on whilst she still had feelings for him; her heart was broken into a million pieces.

To Patsy's credit, she was able to overcome her emotional toll and build a friendship with Liam's new girlfriend, Nicole Appleton of All Saints, and later described Nicole as 'a terrific stepmother' to Lennon. Patsy also built bridges with Molly, who she thinks of as a 'lovely girl'. To this day, Patsy describes Liam to friends as the great love of her life. She's said she doesn't think she's ever loved anyone like she loved him.

After their separation, Liam offered less warmth. When asked if co-parenting was difficult for him, Liam bluntly responded, 'I don't have to deal with her [Patsy]. I see my son every week, I'll bell her what's going on. And I have to make sure she gets her money which pisses me off but that's life.'

Liam would continue to collapse his world in similar fashion when he brought about the demise of his marriage to Nicole in 2013. His self-destructive wheel of misfortune landed in the same place it had with Patsy. The similarities are spooky. He had again been happy with a pretty, blonde star who adored him. He had again cheated on her and conceived a child with somebody else while working away in the US. Nicole, blissfully unaware of the grenade Liam had lobbed in to her life, was playing a game of 'guess who' with her sister Natalie and their friends from the scene when she found out. The girls had heard about a big scandal that was going to break in a US tabloid and were trying to figure out which mystery rock star impregnated a US journalist behind his poster wife's back. If this were a game of Cluedo most people would be feeling confident in their next accusation but Nicole's faith in her husband came with blinkers attached.

After the breakup of Liam Gallagher and Patsy Kensit's marriage, Noel, who had never been a fan of Patsy's, said, 'Liam's better off without Patsy Kensit, because she was a fuckwit of the highest order.' In 2001, Noel even attributed Liam's bad behaviour to Patsy, saying, 'Liam used to really annoy me, but now I think he's a comic genius, the funniest guy I have known in my entire life. I believe that in the old days, he was difficult and drinking so heavily because of his ex-wife. She made him unhappy, and he used to take it out on the rest of the band.' He'd cast Patsy in the Yoko Ono role.

By 1998, Patsy wasn't the only Oasis wife Noel had lost enthusiasm for. He and Meg were heading for the rocks...

When Noel married Meg, he was smitten and wanted to be by her side for ever. At the height of Oasis, the legendary Knebworth concerts in August 1996 symbolised their invincibility, and the band's peak was mirrored by the couple's happiness. Meg explained in the *Guardian* in 2008, 'The Oasis Knebworth concerts were very happy days for me. It was the biggest gig of their lives and that morning Noel went missing. Everyone was worried. He'd gone to a jeweller and bought me a Cartier watch with the inscription "Forever and a day". I've kept it for Anaïs.'

Yet, behind the scenes, the relentless party lifestyle was taking its toll. Excess, fuelled by drugs and rock-star indulgence, set a dangerous precedent. As the band became more and more successful, the atmosphere at Supernova Heights became heavier and heavier under the weight of drugs. Meg would get really fucked up and caused concern at the label. She was becoming increasingly loose-tongued, and the Creation PR offices had to work hard to limit the damage.

By the late nineties, cracks in the marriage had begun to widen. As Noel got more settled, his view on the wife's role became more traditional. They were still partying together with their friends and, initially, had loved the craziness of it all, but he wanted it to stop. He needed more balance. Meg began to choose her friends over Noel, and the party rolled on. Noel, exhausted by Oasis's chaotic existence, pulled away from the hedonistic lifestyle that had defined his years with Meg.

In 1998, he made the snap decision to give up cocaine following a respectable tenure as Primrose Hill's go-to party host. Noel's brilliantly excessive Supernova Heights, the tallest house on one of the biggest hills in London, had filled a gap in the neighbourhood's members club market. In a pre-internet moment of inspired self-doxing, Noel crowned the front door with a stained-glass sign, removing any doubt that this particular height was supernova. A moment that he repeated when replacing the sign after a brick was lobbed through the ornate glass by what he suspected to be a disgruntled Romanian football fan, following some uncomplimentary thoughts on their side's France 1998 World Cup appearance. This time he opted for a sleek font set against frosted glass. This design made the house name even more visible. It was a move which raised expectations about the night each reveller was going to have upon crossing the threshold. Additionally, it guaranteed the callbox on his front gate would be the busiest buzzer this side of *Catchphrase*, with fans congregating like the Beatles' Apple scruffs to interrupt Noel's hangover recovery sleep – not sustainable for a person trying to work at the pinnacle of their craft. And not at all helpful for the famously paranoia-fertile grounds of cocaine use/abuse (delete at reader's discretion). So Noel, the rock star and purveyor of the phrase 'let's have it ... back at mine', a statement three syllables beyond optimal, was heading for a come down. It was too much. Life had simply become too crazy. In 1998, Noel suffered a massive panic attack; he was unable to breathe, collapsed and required an ambulance. He then decided, 'No, I'm not doing this any more.'

Oasis's *Standing on the Shoulder of Giants* album track, 'Gas Panic', documented his experience with the side effects on his health. It was a divergence both sonically and lyrically. Spooky and devoid of positivity, it represented the moment Noel decided to knock the class-As on the head. At least at scale. He told himself and friends that he was giving it up as it wasn't fun anymore, in fact it was becoming too dark. And after that particular domino fell it wasn't long before Noel decided he didn't really know his wife outside of intoxication. In fact, Meg estimated they spent nearly £4,000 per night on drugs. Speaking to the *Guardian* at the time, Noel explained, 'We met through drugs. Our relationship was surrounded by drugs. We got married when we were pissed, though we weren't drunk when we decided to get married. When I decided I was going to come off it and change the way I lived, in the beginning it was like – how's that gonna be with our relationship? Am I still gonna like her?'

He decided he and Meg had to leave London permanently and move to their countryside home, 'The Sheiling', an eight-bedroom house in Chalfont St Giles, Buckinghamshire, in an effort to embrace a more stable lifestyle.

As Noel retreated into a more reserved existence, focusing on songwriting and an attempt at stability, Meg started to feel increasingly isolated by country life, and the differences between them became more pronounced. While she thrived in social settings, he sought solitude. Amid this turbulence, in January 2000, Meg gave birth to their daughter, Anaïs. The arrival of their child was a brief moment of unity. The relationship had been struggling, and the excessive role of drugs and alcohol had damaged them both. When Meg became pregnant, it brought them back together for a while and made it easier for them to keep off drugs together. Noel was thrilled to be an expectant father and, for a short time, their shared excitement over Anaïs's birth provided a reprieve from their mounting tensions. The baby bubble burst prematurely when Noel packed his guitars and left for a tour. Meg recalled, 'I had the baby in January. Noel went on a six-week tour just 10 days afterwards.'

Newly drug-free, Noel was also increasingly interested in getting healthier. The Gallagher genes seemed vulnerable to weight gain, and Noel had gone through what he described as a 'fat Elvis' phase while promoting *Be Here Now*. Meg claimed it all started when Noel began seeing himself in newspapers and noticing how he looked. Since then, he had maintained a stricter diet.

Meanwhile, following Anaïs's birth, Meg had returned to partying. She grew sick of living in the country and escalated her alcohol and cocaine use. The final nail in the marital coffin came when Noel questioned the compatibility of Meg's heavy drinking at home. That was it. Noel's line had been drawn and crossed.

Their split was officially announced in September 2000,

with Noel publicly stating that the relationship had run its course. In the months that followed, he reflected on their time together with a mixture of regret and relief that it had ended, admitting that their marriage had been built on unstable ground. The finalisation of their divorce in January 2001 was a quiet affair, a stark contrast to the high-profile whirlwind that had brought them together. Their split settlement was reported to be significant, with Meg receiving a payout of £4 million plus a house. The *Daily Mirror* claimed Noel offered Meg £500,000 not to file a custody suit, but Meg refused. Their former home, Supernova Heights, was sold as part of the settlement. The only thing Noel truly fought to keep was their country home.

Meg's finances were further aided by an unlikely source – Liam Gallagher. Even when Liam wasn't the cause of Noel's frustrations, he still managed to compound them. Nothing was safe from his younger sibling's reverse Midas touch. Following a paternity test that confirmed Liam was indeed Molly's father, Ignition set up monthly maintenance payments to be sent to Lisa. Shortly after that, a journalist friend of Meg's found out and informed her. When she discovered Lisa was also getting a monthly stipend, she dug out her solicitor's business card and instructed them to go back for more. Noel was livid.

Noel doesn't like to pay for anything. When the big money first flooded into Creation, Noel's friends implored him to take care of his brother, Paul. In the end, Noel purchased an estimated £200,000 flat, but he never transferred ownership to Paul's name.

Meg later expressed frustration over Noel's distance from their daughter to friends. She was annoyed at the lack of contact.

Meg also told friends of her anger that Noel would not pay for an expensive party for Anaïs. Meg further accused Noel of being tight-fisted towards her, adding another layer of bitterness to an already fractured relationship. Though the legal process was discreet, it was a painful conclusion to a relationship that had once seemed inseparable. After their split, Noel fiercely criticised Meg, saying, 'That woman has taken me to court and I abhor it. It is all so unnecessary. But if somebody wants their pound of flesh that badly, there is nothing you can do to stop it. If it means that much to her that she is going to drag me through the courts and have our lives splashed all over the newspapers again because she can't keep her mouth shut, then fine.'

Speaking to the *Guardian* in 2008, Meg reflected on that phase of her life, saying, 'I never got over my divorce. That's what I discovered in rehab. I was trying so hard to be strong and say "I'm fine" and it caught up with me. It's still the longest relationship I've had.' She later revealed that being in the spotlight, with her constant presence in the media, had left her with PTSD.

Since the breakup, Meg has been open about her struggles with drinking and depression. Talking to the *Sun* in 2019, she said she reached a point where she realised she had to 'grow up and stop partying' as she had Anaïs to look after. She attended rehab, where she acknowledged 'I was heartbroken about me and Noel but I couldn't let anyone see how badly it hurt me so for five years I pretended that it didn't matter. I had to learn to let all that go, all the anger and bitterness and emotion.'

Noel has an ability to draw the line with anybody; once drawn, he just completely shuts them out. As had happened with a girlfriend before Meg, Louise, and former bandmate, Tony McCarroll, it was now happening to Meg. He refused to speak with her directly for the next twenty years, instead handling communications through lawyers and their daughter, Anaïs. Noel can be very difficult to be around at times or to maintain a friendship with. He has the ability to make people feel very on edge, even people close to him. He can be efficient with words and leave silences hanging. In fact, when Meg first started getting to know Noel she admitted he had the same effect on her, saying, 'Oh my god. You know, he's just got this way about him that makes you feel a little bit like … scared.' Besides being a generational writing talent, Noel is a world class scowler and the weather of his face can change in a flash.

After the divorce, Noel was quick to recharacterise Meg. She was no longer his 'Wonderwall' – he refused to play the song on the next Oasis tours and started claiming it wasn't written for her. He also presented her as a shopaholic party girl, sneering about the party-planning company she launched with her friend Fran Cutler. 'The party girls and all that shite. Grow up and get a proper job,' he sneered. Years later, live on XFM, when asked by close mates Matt Morgan and Gordon Smart what his most expensive mistake was, Noel replied, 'My first marriage.'

Some may have viewed Meg's event-planning business as a continuation of her former 'proper job' working for Oasis at Creation Records, where, among other duties, she arranged the band's album launches and extensive hospitality plans for Knebworth. Added to the fact that she was now independently wealthy and didn't actually need to work, it's hard to understand Noel's gripe. Continuing to describe the mother of his child, Noel added, 'After I had split up with Meg, some people said: "How did you end up with that lot?" Well, I don't particularly like them.'

Looking back on their divorce in 2008, Meg told the *Guardian*, 'Me and Noel are fine now. I couldn't see myself growing old with him ... not the happiest of people.'

Shortly after the pair's divorce, Liam followed in the grand Gallagher tradition of adding insult to injury when he allegedly falsely questioned the paternity of Noel's daughter Anaïs. Noel responded by adding actual injury to insult and bust his brother's lip.

By the time the divorce was finalised, with Noel admitting to adultery, he was in a relationship with his next wife, Sara MacDonald.

During the brothers' mutual marital merry-go-round, Oasis released their third album, *Be Here Now*, in August 1997. It was a watershed moment for Oasis. Anticipation was incredibly high, driven by the band's previous successes, their global domination and a well-orchestrated publicity campaign that hyped the album as their magnum opus. The album, partly recorded at the legendary Abbey

Road Studios, was a sprawling, ambitious and, in many ways, excessive work, a product of its time, a reflection of the band's status as the biggest rock band in the world, a status that allowed them to indulge their every creative whim.

Be Here Now was initially met with a wave of positive reviews, with many critics hailing it as a masterpiece. The album's lead single, 'D'You Know What I Mean?', an eight-minute epic with swirling guitars and a defiant message, topped the UK charts. The album itself debuted at number one, selling over 420,000 copies in its first day alone, breaking the record they had set with *Morning Glory*. It was a commercial juggernaut, further solidifying the band's global dominance.

However, the initial euphoria surrounding *Be Here Now* soon gave way to a more critical reassessment. Many critics and fans began to find the album overblown, bloated and lacking the raw energy, the emotional honesty and the melodic simplicity of its predecessors. The songs were often criticised for their excessive length, their heavy use of production effects, the layers of guitars that seemed to obscure the melodies, and their lack of subtlety. The album, once hailed as a masterpiece, became derided as a symbol of the band's hubris, a victim of its own ambition.

Noel himself later expressed his own reservations about *Be Here Now*. He admitted that the band had been caught up in the hype surrounding them and that the album had suffered as a result. He attributed the album's excesses to a combination of factors, including drug use, exhaustion from relentless touring and a lack of objective perspective.

Later, he described *Be Here Now* as 'the sound of a bunch of guys on coke, in the studio, not giving a fuck', a blunt assessment that revealed his own dissatisfaction. He later disowned the record, calling it ridiculous and stating that he couldn't even listen to it any more.

The backlash against *Be Here Now* was a significant blow to Oasis, a chink in their armour. It marked the first time the band had faced widespread criticism, the first time their creative choices had been questioned. It exposed the fragility of their position at the top of the music world. The criticism also seemed to affect Noel deeply, his usual confidence shaken.

The *Be Here Now* era also saw a shift in the band's internal dynamics. Noel, who had always been the band's primary creative force, began to exert even greater control over the songwriting and recording process, further marginalising the other members. This increased control, while perhaps understandable given the need for clear direction, further alienated Liam, who felt increasingly frustrated by his lack of creative input. Liam's behaviour during this period became even more erratic, fuelled by a toxic mix of frustration, resentment and substance abuse. He was often late for rehearsals and recording sessions, his performances marred by his volatile temper. The tension between the brothers escalated to new heights, threatening to derail the band.

The tour in support of *Be Here Now*, while commercially successful, was fraught with difficulties, plagued by cancellations and controversy. Liam's voice was often strained, his on-stage behaviour unpredictable. There were several incidents where he walked off stage mid-performance or failed to show up at all, leaving Noel to take over lead vocal duties. The band's management had to cancel several shows due to Liam's 'illness'.

It was the beginning of a slow but steady decline, a period marked by creative stagnation, internal conflict and a growing sense of disillusionment. The backlash against the new album, the shifting dynamics within the band, and the increasing pressures of fame all contributed to a sense of unease, a feeling that the band was losing its way.

While Oasis continued to release the commercially successful albums *Standing on the Shoulder of Giants* (2000), *Heathen Chemistry* (2002), *Don't Believe the Truth* (2005) and *Dig Out Your Soul* (2008), all of which topped the UK charts, they failed to reach the same critical or cultural heights as their earlier work. They were met with mixed reviews, a growing sense that the band was treading water, creatively, and a feeling among critics and fans alike that the spark that had ignited their early work had dimmed.

The band's lineup also underwent several changes during this period, reflecting the growing instability within the group. Original members Paul 'Bonehead' Arthurs and Paul 'Guigsy' McGuigan left Oasis in 1999; their departures finally removed Oasis from the romantic gang mentality of the early days. They were replaced by Gem Archer and Andy Bell, respectively. Drummer Alan White, who had joined in 1995, was replaced by Zak Starkey, son of Ringo Starr, in 2004, and later by Chris Sharrock.

Despite the internal turmoil, Oasis remained a major live act, capable of selling out stadiums around the world. However, their performances were often marred by Liam's behaviour and his ongoing feud with Noel. The brothers would often refuse to speak to each other off stage, communicating only through intermediaries. The recording of *Dig Out Your Soul* in 2007–8 was, by all accounts, a particularly difficult process. The sessions were marked by arguments, walkouts and a general sense of creative stagnation. Noel, in later interviews, described the recording process as a nightmare, saying that everyone was burnt out and running on fumes.

Despite the difficulties, *Dig Out Your Soul* was a creative high point in the band's later years, a brief resurgence of inspiration. It was a more experimental and psychedelic album than their previous work. Tracks like 'The Shock of the Lightning' and 'Falling Down' were praised by critics for their energy and adventurous spirit. The album debuted at number one in the UK, peaked at number five in the US *Billboard* 200, and was generally well received by fans.

The success of *Dig Out Your Soul* was not enough to save the band. The tensions between Liam and Noel had reached a breaking point. The constant fighting, the personal attacks, the fundamental differences in their personalities and their vision for the band had finally taken their toll, all leading to that infamous final act of the Oasis drama, played out backstage at the Rock en Seine festival in August 2009, when Noel walked away.

In later interviews, it became clear that for Noel it

wasn't just that one incident that prompted him to leave. It was a build of many years of tension beginning in their childhood. He just couldn't do it anymore.

It was not just a professional fracture but a personal one, symbolising the culmination of decades of emotional strain between the brothers.

Bandmates, family members and close associates later reflected on the inevitability of the breakup. Many expressed a sense of sadness, a sense of loss, but also a sense of relief that the constant fighting was finally over. Andy Bell, in a 2013 interview with *NME*, described the breakup as 'a long time coming', stating that the band had been 'on the verge of collapse for years'.

Paul Gallagher, in his interviews, suggested that the breakup was, in some ways, a necessary step for both Liam and Noel, a necessary separation. He believed that they needed to escape the confines of Oasis, to forge their own identities, to find their own paths. He also expressed a hope that, one day, the brothers might be able to reconcile. He saw the breakup as a chance for both brothers finally to grow up, to find some peace. The breakup of Oasis was not just the end of a band; it was the fracturing of a family.

The demise of Oasis in 2009 on that fateful night in Paris marked the end of an era in British music. It was the final chapter in the story of a band that had defined a generation, a band that had captured the spirit of the times, a band that had risen from humble beginnings to conquer the world.

The legacy of Oasis is complex and multifaceted. They were a band that inspired millions with their anthemic songs, their raw energy, their unapologetic attitude. They were also a band that were plagued by internal conflict, by a rivalry that was both their greatest strength and their fatal flaw. The story of Oasis is a reminder that even the most successful bands are ultimately made up of individuals, with their own flaws, ambitions and personal struggles. It is a story about the power of music to unite and divide, to create and destroy, to lift people up and to tear them apart. It is a story about brotherhood, rivalry and the enduring power of family, even in the face of seemingly insurmountable odds.

The echoes of their music, the memories of their explosive performances and the ongoing saga of the Gallagher brothers' feud continue to resonate, ensuring that the Oasis story, in all its chaotic glory, will never be forgotten. The final years were a slow burn towards an inevitable end, a stark contrast to the explosive energy of their rise. Yet, even in their decline, Oasis remained compelling, a band whose internal combustion mirrored the turbulent social and political landscape of the late 1990s and early 2000s. Their breakup was the end of a cultural moment, a turning point in the history of British rock 'n' roll, the closing of a chapter. The end of Oasis was the final note of an era defined by Britpop, by a resurgence of national pride, and by the rise of a band that dared to dream of conquering the world – and for a brief, glorious moment, actually did.

The music the Gallaghers created together, the memories

they forged and the legacy they left behind continue to resonate, underlining the enduring power of rock 'n' roll, and the complex, often contradictory, nature of brotherhood.

After such a tumultuous breakup followed by a long war of attrition, could the seemingly impossible ever happen? Could the Gallaghers ever stand on the same stage again?

16

Too Good for Giving Up – Liam, 2020–1

OK ... back to the future ... 2020. The release of Liam's second solo album, *Why Me? Why Not.*, in September 2019, became his second consecutive UK number-one album. It represented another confident step forward. Gone was the intentionally jarring artwork of Beady Eye's debut album, which challenged the buyer. This continued the trend set by his debut, which framed him as an icon. It was Che Guevara by way of Warhol's Factory, the posterised gaze of Liam peering at the viewer in classic hero shot. This and the artwork from *As You Were* positioned him as a contemporary rebel with a distressed, noir punk texture. Contemporary but with heritage. The preceding cover had been shot by former Celine and Yves Saint Laurent creative director, Hedi Slimane. It had visually established Liam as the icon his label and his fans wanted him to be. He'd truly embraced the role and let go of the baggage he'd carried out of Oasis and into his solo career.

The record's critical and commercial success bolstered his position as a solo star and a commercial force to be reckoned with. It proved his resurgence was not a fleeting moment of nostalgia, but a sustained third act in a brilliantly managed solo-career arc. As 2019 drew to a close, Liam's star was continuing to ascend, his live shows were selling out and his new songs were getting strong radio support. He'd pulled off the hardest trick of all in that respect – he had maintained cultural relevance while transitioning from band to solo act, even though he was now in his forties. Liam had transcended his original core fanbase and attracted younger fans simply by being himself. His unique brand of charisma, immune to cancel culture, was as captivating and controversial as ever but now he had Twitter and Instagram through which to express it. And express it he did. His tweets are frequent, witty and surreal.

Over the last few years, he had worked hard to bring his family together, rebuild his career and reconnect with his own power. He developed his writing ability, with the help of intelligently chosen collaborators, and could still command a stage with the same charisma and energy that had made him a star. Noel Gallagher could give the fans the songs, but only Liam Gallagher could give fans the Oasis experience, especially now that he had embraced his past.

The accompanying tour was a victory lap for Liam, a celebration of his resurgence. He performed to sold-out crowds at big venues and festivals around the world, delivering electrifying performances that confirmed his status as one of the greatest frontmen in music history.

Fan reactions to the tour were a wave of positivity. They embraced the new songs from *Why Me? Why Not.*, singing along to every word, and they sat well next to the Oasis anthems. There was a sense of shared experience, of community, among those who attended the shows, with stories of fans travelling from all over the world to see Liam perform, of grown men and women moved to tears by the fresh air his voice had breathed into those classics. A master of his craft who knows how to create moments of intimacy and euphoria, on his day Liam can make a stadium feel too small for it all.

As 2020 dawned, Liam was preparing for another busy year of touring and festival appearances. Then the COVID-19 pandemic swept across the globe, bringing with it lockdowns, travel restrictions and unprecedented disruption to the live music industry.

It was a challenging time for an artist with such momentum to take an enforced timeout. For some people, time in enforced lockdown loomed large and brought their problems to the surface. The devil makes work for idle hands after all. Especially acts who thrive on the pace and connection of live performance. However, Liam was not one to be defeated by adversity. He adapted to the new reality, finding innovative ways to connect with his fans and continue performing, even in the absence of traditional live shows. He embraced social media to an even greater extent. His stream-of-consciousness public service announcement videos on Instagram were a particular highlight. In his kitchen he'd sing a newly adapted version of 'Supersonic' for the twenty-second process we'd all been made familiar with on social media during the pandemic's first movement.

On a significantly larger scale, he staged a unique livestream performance, 'Down by the River Thames', in December 2020. The event, which was broadcast globally via pay-per-view, saw Liam and his band performing on a barge as it travelled down the River Thames in London. The show looked and sounded fantastic and was accompanied later by a vinyl pressing, the cover of which invoked the Sex Pistols. It was an innovative and ambitious project, a testament to Liam's determination to continue making music and to provide his fans with a unique experience, despite the restrictions imposed by COVID. In an interview with Radio X in November 2020, he described the event as 'a bit of rock 'n' roll madness' and a way to 'give people something to look forward to' during a time of uncertainty.

The logistical challenges of staging a live performance on a moving barge were considerable. Especially when you account for London's weather, which isn't renowned for helping outdoor performances during winter. The production team had to contend with the unpredictable nature of the river, the technical complexities of broadcasting live from a moving vessel, tracked by a helicopter for aerial footage, the choreography of where exactly each song would happen during the cruise, the need to create a visually compelling show and making a great audio mix in what is essentially a sound engineer's anxiety dream. The event was meticulously planned and a lovely moment of shared experience for Liam's fans who logged in en masse (albeit alone) to catch his performance.

The setlist for 'Down by the River Thames' was a mix of songs from *As You Were* and *Why Me? Why Not.* alongside iconic Oasis tracks such as 'Hello', 'Supersonic' and 'Champagne Supernova'. There were also a few surprises, including the live debut of a new song, 'All You're Dreaming Of', a wistful, Lennon-esque ballad. This previously unreleased track was lauded in reviews, with *NME* describing it as a 'touching festive ballad' that showcased Liam's songwriting evolution. The *Guardian* called the event 'a triumphant return to live performance' and *Rolling Stone* described it as 'a powerful statement of resilience'. The 'Down by the River Thames' livestream proved to be a warming cultural moment. A musical oasis (ahem) in the cultural desert of lockdown. It was a reminder of the power of music to bring people together, even in the most challenging of times.

The pandemic, while disrupting his touring plans, also provided Liam with an opportunity for reflection. He spent more time at home with his family, sometimes dressed as a wizard in the garden tipi. He reconnected with his children and enjoyed a sense of relative normality that had often eluded him during his years on the road. He was able to be more present in their lives. In interviews during this period, Liam spoke of the importance of family and the grounding influence they had on his life. Particularly Debbie. She had helped create a stable professional and personal environment for Liam, which brought the best out of him. She can reach him in ways others never seem to have been able. Besides curating his solo career, she had helped reconcile his relationships with his children.

When COVID took hold, Liam had only recently established a relationship with his daughter, Molly, and expressed a tearful, long overdue apology to her when they eventually met at Highgate's Red Lion & Sun pub the preceding summer. He regretted not having made it happen sooner, especially in the knowledge he'd probably have to repeat the experience one day with his now five-year-old daughter, Gemma. He told the *Sunday Times* in June 2020, 'I've made a lot of mistakes, but I'm trying to learn from them. I want to be a good dad.' He seemed to have found a new sense of purpose outside of the spotlight.

The pandemic also impacted other aspects of his perspective, forcing him to slow down and appreciate life's simpler aspects. He talked about the importance of mental health, the need to stay positive, and the power of music to provide solace during difficult times. It was a more introspective Liam that emerged during these interviews, far removed from the intoxicated, guarded and often unintelligible frontman of the early days.

Twitter became an even greater preoccupation and his feed was a constant source of entertainment and controversy. He would often engage in playful banter with fans, respond to critics with his trademark wit, and offer his profoundly unfiltered opinions on everything from music to politics to football. Of course, he also continued to use the platform to keep the Gallagher feud alive, regularly taking jabs at his brother Noel. A reductionist classic of his microblogging oeuvre contained a photo of Noel accompanied by the word 'potato'. One of his more enduring Noel put-downs, fans would regularly be seen holding 'potato' placards at gigs. The chink in Noel's steadfast avoidance of Liam was to meet negative attention with his own negative attention. For his part, Noel occasionally would grace Twitter with gritty pearls such as, 'Silence is golden ... and just in case you weren't already aware, someone still has a new single out called "Once" which is the exact amount of times it should be played.' For Liam, the fact Noel had acknowledged and heard his single probably more than outweighed his critique. And on the cycle of psychodramatic slapsies goes ... One of the compelling things about it is just how funny the Gallaghers are when slagging each other off. The American comedian Bill Burr expressed his admiration for their comedic ability, saying the material they spouted when bored in an interview was funnier than most stand-up sets.

Liam's 2020 *MTV Unplugged* album, recorded live at Hull City Hall, added to his extraordinary run of solo album success as it became the first *MTV Unplugged* record ever to top the charts. It was also a chance to remedy a decades-old wrong when, back in 1996, Liam had sat out the Oasis *MTV Unplugged* set. At the time, *Unplugged* was a significant step in a band's career and Noel refused to allow it to become another example of Liam ankle tapping the band's march towards American supremacy. So Noel took lead vocals and did an excellent job in less than ideal circumstances. It became one of the defining Oasis performances and was arguably the moment when the seed was planted in Noel's head that he didn't actually need his brother to play this game. It may have been the second such seed planted in Liam's, following Noel's star lead-vocal turn on 'Don't Look Back in Anger'.

Wearing the latest in a long line of ill-fitting jumpers from his wardrobe of the day, Noel tenderly reworked the Oasis classics while his younger brother, the same younger brother who was supposed to be singing them had it not been for his laryngitis, heckled Noel between swigs of bottled lager from one of the Royal Festival Hall's boxes. Surreal for the audience, but imagine how it was for Noel. The story of Liam having a sore throat and there being an implication of the problem actually relating more to alcohol may already seem familiar in these pages, but this was the night when it first became part of Oasis lore.

Anyway, Liam had now, some twenty-four years later, made up for one of his misdemeanours by finally putting his voice to an *MTV Unplugged*.

Among all the solo success, there were already increasing signs, on top of the 'One of Us' video, that as part of his renaissance as a family man and righting the wrongs of his past, making up with Noel was firmly on Liam's mind, despite the sometimes deeply vitriolic jousting with Noel and his family. He felt a certain heaviness when he thought of Peggy. He remains very close to his now elderly mother, and he has always known how it breaks her heart to see her sons at odds. Liam publicly stated he'd like to make peace with his brother before their mum passes away – he framed it as almost a moral obligation. But whenever he raised the possibility of a reunion, Noel's response was silence or sarcasm. In one interview, he was more direct, stating that he'd love to see Oasis reform, but that the ball was in Noel's court. 'He should call me,' he said, a familiar spark of defiance in his eyes. But he doubted that Noel wanted the reunion, as 'he [had] got his own thing going on.' The hints that he wanted a reconciliation were so clear that they might as well have been neon lit.

Noel's interviews revealed no sign of budging, and Liam, though he continued to dish out insults on Twitter and in the press, perhaps couldn't shake the ache that things weren't how they should be – that two brothers who once shared a room, a life and dreams, could barely share civil words.

17

Back the Way We Came – Noel, 2020–1

Noel enjoyed the relative calm of the government-enforced downtime, but like everybody else he wasn't immune to the fluidity of emotions created by this unique period in our history. Everybody's lockdown experience was bespoke. He now had the luxury of his country gaff in Hampshire, not far from the New Forest where he and Sara MacDonald had married in 2011, nine years earlier. He spent time cycling around the rural lanes, and said that initially he'd found the downtime a welcome break to spend time at home. Those fortunate enough to have scenery, outdoor space and financial stability during COVID-19 were better set up and there was an initial novelty to the experience among many. Others had to contend with far less ideal living conditions to which they were confined for eighteen months on and off. Nobody could begrudge Noel the liberating sense of space offered by his very big house in the country, though, especially when contrasted to the boxed-in nature of the family homes he grew up in, where physical threats loomed and escape was only possible via six strings. But regardless of the lifestyle circumstances each person faced in lockdown, they also had to contend with the challenge of having lots of idle time to themselves and lots of time in close quarters with the people they shared their life with, and whatever demons or gripes each was in possession of. Many performers and many people with a difficult relationship with substances – the Venn diagram for which would probably resemble a Mastercard logo – found it extremely hard.

By June 2020, Noel had started to become frustrated, telling Radio X, 'I miss playing live. It's what I do. It's what I love.' Despite the restrictions, Noel remained prolific. He continued to write and demo. He was not working towards a specific album or release date, and allowed himself simply to follow his creative instincts. Noel has a strong work ethic and discipline when going about his craft. He plays and writes every day, often strumming whichever guitar is serving as his muse that day as he lets daytime TV wash over him. And when that guitar doesn't have any more songs to give, he requests another from his vast collection, which is held in the unglamorous surrounds of a large shipping container stack. He has always understood the balance between inspiration and application that greatness requires.

One piece that emerged around this time was the demo 'We're Gonna Get There in the End', released on New Year's Eve, 2020. The song, a hopeful and uplifting anthem, could be taken as a direct response to the pandemic, and in typical Noel Gallagher fashion combined resilience with optimism. Noel makes it his business to be a man whose glass remains half full. The release was met with an overwhelmingly positive response from fans.

Noel also used his time during lockdown to revisit older, unfinished material. He delved into his archives, rediscovering forgotten demos and half-finished songs. This process of rediscovery led to the completion and release of several tracks that might otherwise have remained unheard.

As 2021 approached, Noel marked a significant milestone in his solo career: ten years since the formation of Noel Gallagher's High Flying Birds. To commemorate this anniversary, he announced the release of *Back the Way We Came: Vol. 1 (2011–2021)*, a compilation album that served as both a retrospective of his solo work and a pointer towards his future.

The compilation, released in June, was not a simple 'greatest hits' collection. It was a carefully curated selection of tracks that showcased the evolution of Noel's sound, his willingness to experiment and his growth as a solo artist. It featured well-known singles such as 'The Death of You and Me', 'AKA ... What a Life!' and 'Holy Mountain' alongside deeper cuts like 'Riverman' and 'It's a Beautiful World'. Noel is very hands-on when it comes to putting together compilations or playlists. They matter to him and he lingers on the correct track listing.

The inclusion of tracks such as 'Black Star Dancing' and 'This Is the Place' from his more experimental EPs demonstrated Noel's commitment to his artistic evolution. He was showcasing the breadth of his artistry, beyond the confines of his Oasis legacy. The album was widely praised by critics and seen as a celebration of his solo work.

The compilation also featured two new songs: 'We're on Our Way Now' and 'Flying on the Ground'. These tracks offered a tantalising glimpse into the future direction of Noel's music. 'We're on Our Way Now', released as a single in April 2021, was a reflective, mid-tempo ballad with a soaring chorus and introspective lyrics. It was a song that seemed to acknowledge the challenges of the past year while also expressing a sense of hope for the future. It was a mature, thoughtful piece of songwriting that resonated and found its place in his live sets. The song was well received and described as a classic. 'Flying on the Ground', released alongside the compilation album, was a more upbeat, soulful track that featured horns and backing vocals, reminiscent of some of the material on *Who Built the Moon?*. It highlighted Noel's continued willingness to experiment with different genres.

The release of *Back the Way We Came* provided Noel with an opportunity to reflect on his solo journey. In interviews promoting the compilation, he acknowledged the challenges of stepping out of Oasis's shadow and establishing himself as a solo artist, but once again he also emphasised the creative freedom and artistic fulfilment he had found in his new role. In interviews and in his own book, *Any Road Will Get Us There (If We Don't Know We're Going)*, there was a clear sense of pride in everything he had done with the High Flying Birds. He also addressed the inevitable questions about Oasis, reiterating that the band was over and that he had no plans to revisit that chapter of his life. The distance had given him space to speak with a mixture of fondness and finality about his time with the band, acknowledging its importance in his life and in the lives of his fans, but also re-emphasising his desire to move on.

Despite his lyrical positivity, Noel's spoken-word output is often a tad harsh. During the pandemic, he started to become a vocal critic of government policy, especially around rules on mask wearing. At the time, this was anathema to those of a liberal bent. For many, the mask mandate had become the most visible of both virtue signalling and government control. Noel's view that the government should allow each individual to make their own decision, expressed in typically candid terms, was met with groans of disappointment among swathes of his fanbase. He felt the whole process had been a continuation of what he viewed as an erosion of civil liberties. At the time, he seemed a little out of touch with the prevailing mood. Explaining his issues with the inconsistent logic of mask-wearing rules to close friend Matt Morgan, Noel said, 'The whole thing's bollocks. You're supposed to wear them in Selfridges, yet you can fucking go down the pub and be surrounded by every fucking cunt. Do you know what I mean? It's like, "Oh actually, we don't have the virus in pubs but we have it in Selfridges?" I was going up to Manchester the other week [on a train, where masks were mandatory] and some guy's going, "Can you put your mask on, because the transport police will get on and fine you a thousand pounds? But you don't have to put it on if you're eating." So I was saying, "Oh right, this killer virus that's sweeping through the train is gonna come and attack me but see me having a sandwich and go, leave him, he's having his lunch?"'

He also expressed his frustration with the government's wider handling of the crisis, particularly its perceived lack of support for the arts.

Although these views were divisive in the contemporaneous environment, they have become more aligned with the mainstream retrospective view on the government's reaction to the pandemic. The Overton window in relation to masks, vaccinations and lockdowns has shifted significantly over the past few years.

Like many during this period of mandated quality time for married couples, the small cracks in love's crazy paving became more noticeable. Absence may make the heart grow fonder but familiarity often breeds contempt, as the saying goes, and for couples, housemates and lockdown bubbles around the world the newly plentiful proximity had become an undiagnosed symptom of coronavirus. For Noel, Sara and his daughter Anaïs, tensions were growing.

Noel had experienced a somewhat comparable period of spousal 'rediscovery' during his first marriage to another publicist, Meg Mathews, when he went cold turkey. Twenty years later, COVID had exposed Noel's relationship with Sara to a similar period of examination.

18

Just Another Rainbow – Liam, 2022–4

Thanks to Debbie, Liam had really started to get his shit together, and with the release of *C'Mon You Know*, his third solo album, he reached heights nearing his Oasis peak. This was capped by a triumphant return to Knebworth, and he was also making further moves towards the reconciliation of his family. In 2020, Liam made another insult cum overture to Noel for an Oasis reunion, saying it will happen 'very fucking soon' because he believes Noel is 'greedy and he loves money and he knows that it's got to happen soon or it won't happen.'

C'mon You Know, released on 27 May 2022, underlined the renaissance of a career that had already spanned decades on the cultural frontline. The album debuted at number one on the UK albums chart, marking Liam's third consecutive solo album to achieve this feat. The record's success was not limited to the UK. It reached the top ten in several other countries in Europe and Australasia.

Critically, *C'mon You Know* was hailed as Liam's most

accomplished and diverse solo work to date. Reviewers praised the album's energy, its ambitious scope and Liam's willingness to experiment with different sounds and styles. *NME*, in a glowing review, called the album 'a triumph'. 'Everything's Electric', 'Diamond in the Dark' and 'More Power' became instant fan favourites and staples of his live set. 'Everything's Electric', co-written with Dave Grohl of Foo Fighters, was a particularly powerful statement of intent. It was a driving glam rocker with a snaking chorus hook, showcasing Liam's vocals at their rawest. 'Diamond in the Dark', with its psychedelic-tinged sound and its introspective lyrics, demonstrated his willingness to push his musical boundaries.

The album's title track, 'C'mon You Know', was a call to arms for a world emerging from the pandemic and yearning for connection and collective experience. The title was classic Liam – an invitation and a challenge all in one.

On the home front, Liam was more settled than he'd ever been and his relationship with Molly was going from strength to strength. The newly united father and daughter followed their initial tearful meeting at a pub with a trip to Ibiza, where Molly accompanied Liam, Debbie, half-brothers Gene and Lennon, Uncle Paul and Grandmother Peggy on a private jet.

Molly, who has built a career as a model, is a sociology and politics graduate and ambassador for Centrepoint, a homeless charity. She adopted an impressively philosophical attitude towards her father, saying that she holds no resentment towards Liam and telling *The Times*, 'It's all happened the way it was meant to happen. We just got on and I'm happy to have him now.' The father and daughter's newfound closeness highlights how Liam has matured over the years, striving to mend past rifts and be present for his children. He was also supporting his sons' creative paths – Lennon in music and modelling, and Gene in forming his own band.

Back in May 2019, Gene Gallagher made a headline collaboration of his own. Gene (then twenty), along with Sonny Starkey (twenty-one), grandson of Ringo Starr, and their friend Noah Ponte, briefly popped Hampstead's veil of tranquility when they caused a bit of bother at the Tesco Express. When the matter went to court it was explained that Ponte had attempted to purchase alcohol after hours and began a confrontation with the staff. It developed into a physical thing, with Gene and Sonny being accused of affray. Ponte was found not guilty and in April 2022, the charges against Gallagher and Starkey were dropped as evidence emerged they were acting in self defence, but they received a telling off from the judge for their 'entitled' and 'out of order' behaviour. Not only had Gene followed in the Gallagher tradition of starting a band, he'd made his first alcohol-related headline.

On a happier note, speaking to Jonathan Ross about Molly, Liam said, 'I met her just last year ... it was terrible that we left it that long. But we've met up now and it's the best it's been now. Me and her are always hanging out. It's cool man, like we have to draw a line under the past. Terrible that I didn't see her.' Liam also explained how he hadn't met his other daughter, Gemma, now aged six, saying it was a case of 'Waiting, just let it happen, you know what I mean? I've no plans [but] I'll definitely leave the door open. We'll see. It's complicated.'

Molly was present at Knebworth to see Liam take to the stage for ever tied to Oasis's historic 1996 concerts. It carried immense significance. Liam had sat out the promotional campaign for the recent Oasis Knebworth concert film, leaving it to Noel to propel the sense of nostalgia. Shortly after the film's release, Liam announced he'd be returning to the site the following summer. It was a masterclass in marketing and one-upmanship. Returning as a solo artist twenty-six years later was a defining statement in his post-Oasis journey, a full-circle moment. The two sold-out Knebworth shows in June 2022, attended by over 170,000 people, were an undeniable success. Liam delivered electrifying performances, with an atmosphere rich in nostalgia and celebration as fans sang along to every lyric from Oasis classics to earlier solo hits like 'Wall of Glass' and 'Shockwave' and tracks from *C'mon You Know*, including 'Everything's Electric'.

The Knebworth shows were documented in the film *Knebworth 22*, capturing the emotional weight of Liam's return, as well as a live album of the same name. The documentary provided a behind-the-scenes look at a rock 'n' roll icon revisiting the pinnacle of his Oasis career and redefining his legacy as a solo star. There were some notable gaps in its soundtrack. Performances of music compositions on screen require the songwriter's permission, and as things weren't exactly tickety-boo between the brothers Gallagher, Noel revelled in giving the request a big thumbs down. He explained the delicacy of his thought process to *Variety*: 'Oh, I turned it down, yeah. If some fucking moron is going to make a film slagging me off, calling my wife a cunt, after trolling my kids on the internet, after being a filthy little misogynist sexist prick who cannot keep his fucking mouth off Twitter, and then call me to ask me a favour, I'm like, "Wow. You are as dumb as you fucking look. I don't give a fuck what music you have in your film; you're not putting any of mine in." It's like, "Can I ask you a favour?" No, you can't. Go fuck yourself.' Although Noel had expressed his respect for Liam's newfound solo success, he can't have enjoyed the idea of Liam's commercial appeal growing to such towering heights while his own pulling power dwindled with each LP.

Liam's 2023 Glastonbury performance was another landmark moment. Though he had played the festival before with both Oasis and Beady Eye, this was his first solo set on the Pyramid Stage – a booking that affirmed his standing as one of the most important artists of his generation. The set was powerful and emotional. His voice was in fine form and his connection with the audience as strong as ever.

Debbie Gwyther was now Liam's fiancée following a romantic proposal in 2019 during a getaway to Italy's Amalfi Coast. The couple had planned to marry in Lake Como in 2022, but their wedding was postponed due to Liam requiring hip surgery. She remained a constant pillar of support. Describing her as his 'rock' and 'best friend', speaking to *GQ* in 2022, he also later said 'I've met my soulmate.' In the 2019 documentary *Liam Gallagher: As It Was*, she stated, 'The Liam I know and the Liam that's in the public eye are totally different. He sometimes drinks too much, he's impulsive and foul-mouthed, but that doesn't mean he can't be tender at the same time. He's very responsible with the family. The way he behaves with me, with my family members, with his children and with his mother, is the reason I love him.'

Debbie's influence in Liam's life goes beyond personal support – she has played a key role in reshaping his public persona. Known for her no-nonsense attitude, fierce loyalty and sharp business sense, she helped steer his solo career to success, earning him both a new wave of fans and critical acclaim. She also played a pivotal role in healing his relationship with Molly, encouraging him to reconnect after years of estrangement.

Liam needed double-hip replacement surgery as a result of arthritis, which had been causing him chronic pain. He initially delayed the operation because he didn't want the stigma associated with it. Eventually, in 2023, he had the surgery and shared updates about his recovery with fans. 'Morning Rastas so I had my Hip operation last wk all went well and RESPEK to all the doctors n nurses who looked after me,' Liam wrote in a post. 'Big shout out to the A team for getting us home safe n sound you know who you are and Florence guru I love and adore you Riverdance here I come LG.'

As Liam's personal life evolved, so did the media's portrayal of him. While he remained a rock 'n' roll icon, he was increasingly depicted as a family man – an engaged father and devoted partner. This nuanced image resonated with fans, who appreciated his honesty and willingness to reveal a more vulnerable side. Still, he retained his outspoken and sometimes controversial nature, continuing to both delight and provoke the press.

In March 2024, Liam Gallagher took another step down his particular path and dropped a collaborative album with John Squire, guitarist of the Stone Roses. It was an unexpected lateral step. A magical mystery fan excursion. The fan in question being Liam.

For followers of indie rock it was a welcome surprise during a time when seemingly fewer and fewer indie bands were emerging. For fans, the collaboration of Oasis frontman and Roses lead guitarist was a dream team.

Liam, always happy to run open-armed towards a Beatles comparison, included 'Mother Nature's Song' (just one extra letter from being 'Mother Nature's Son' from *The Beatles*/'White Album') on the track list for *Liam Gallagher John Squire*. The new collaborators were clearly unbothered by outside opinions as many of the other songs drew directly from the signature sounds of Gallagher and Squire's former bands. 'I'm So Bored' channels the raw energy of *(What's the Story) Morning Glory?*, while 'One Day at a Time' could have been a *Definitely Maybe*-era B-side. Meanwhile, tracks like 'Mars to Liverpool' and 'Make It Up as You Go Along' carry a more delicate, melodic quality reminiscent of Stone Roses tracks like

'Mersey Paradise' or 'Going Down'. 'Love You Forever' echoes the heavy riffs and thundering drums of the Roses' 1994 comeback single 'Love Spreads'.

The duo supported the album with a short tour of intimate UK venues. It was a nice moment for Liam and his old mate John, as well as the fans who were treated to the fifty-minute long set, comprising the full album, but never rose above a moment in the developing story of Liam Gallagher.

19

Trying to Find a World That's Been and Gone – Noel, 2022–4

Having navigated the challenges of lockdown and celebrated a decade of his High Flying Birds, Noel ultimately emerged with a new album, *Council Skies*, in 2023, released a few days after he turned fifty-six. The title suggested that Noel was reflecting on his childhood days in Burnage, and the album marked a return to his roots as he adopted a more traditional approach to songwriting and production. The album artwork featured a black and white photograph of the band's gear set up on a patch of grass that marks the centre circle of Man City's former stadium, Maine Road.

However, things outside the studio had been going less smoothly for Noel, the rift between him and Liam a seemingly unbridgeable chasm. Their co-dependent toxicity had continued to corrode his happiness and that of those closest to him, most pressingly, his wife, Sara.

Noel had never been one to display his emotional

vulnerability openly. He tended to keep it tucked behind his sharp wit and blunt tone. But there was something about Sara MacDonald that had softened his edges, and it was already evident in an Oasis song he wrote and sang the lead vocal on back in 2002. 'Yeah, I'm in love with my girlfriend. I wrote a song, "She Is Love", about how lovely I think she is. I guess romantic is probably one of the words you could use to describe me. In the past, I've definitely shied away from using the word "love" in songs, but I'm an older gentleman now – so I really couldn't give a toss if people think it's soppy. That song's real, and it's how I feel about her. But I wouldn't like to dwell on that kind of stuff, because it would limit the appeal of the song.'

Sara had come into Noel's life at a time when he was ready for something different, specifically something different to Meg. The wild years of Oasis's peak had begun to wane and, with them, the reckless abandon of youth. He found in Sara someone who could hold her own against his sharp tongue, but who also understood him in a way few others did. His wife, he said, was his best friend, the only person he wanted by his side, the only person who truly made him laugh, and he respected her strength. 'Her bark is much worse than her bite, but her bark can be fucking brutal.'

But to the surprise of absolutely nobody, where Noel found solace, Liam found an enemy. Because in the Gallagher dynamic, the maxim that what feeds one starves the other has always remained true, and Liam exerts the jealous territorialism of a child over Noel.

Liam had never hidden his disdain for Sara MacDonald,

but in a series of ugly tweets in 2018, he took his hatred to a new level. 'Think it's time to address the witch,' he wrote. 'You want me to drop dead, you have a screw loose, and now the world knows.' He followed it with another tirade: 'She's the reason OASIS is no longer. Have to put it out there – she's DARK. We were about to go on tour to the USA, she robbed Noel's passport, fucked with his head for a week, and he came crying at my door. She's proper dark.'

Liam was relentless. In interviews, accusations flew like crescent-shaped tambourines, painting Noel as a man controlled by his wife. 'He's not allowed to, his missus won't let him now, 'cos she's another one.' In a textbook Gallagher passive–aggressive statement he put a fine point on his view of the problem: 'I know for a fact, deep down, he wants to be playing stadiums. You can only play stadiums when I'm there.' Liam had never adopted Michelle Obama's 'when they go low we go high' mantra. If Noel or Sara went low, Liam got out his shovel and went lower, equating his brother and sister-in-law to serial torturers and killers: 'Him and her are like Fred and Mary West, wishing people get AIDS and drop dead. As you fucking were – Oasis for life.' It was a fairly lame attempt to salvage some moral superiority over the couple. Noel had in the past wished AIDS on Alex James, for which he subsequently apologised to the Blur bassist and cheese enthusiast.

The sound of Twitter's bird-chirp notification is almost perverse when applied to Liam hitting 'tweet' as he continued, 'My mam's got your number darling, it's not hard to forget – 666.' When a follower compared Sara to Yoko Ono, Liam said, 'She ain't Yoko, she's a dick.'

Liam had been extra triggered by Sara's Instagram post in February 2018 wishing, 'Please God [you] have dropped dead by the time my kids are on social media.' When Liam expressed a lack of interest in how his tweets affected Anaïs, Sara followed up saying, 'You mean your gorgeous niece, you deplorable wanker.'

The half-life of Liam's Twitter meltdown included unflattering comparisons with world leaders: 'Coz I need to let the world know she's up there with Putin. And he's worse than Donald Trump. He's the biggest liar and biggest faker in the business, so yeah, him.'

Noel's response was absolute. He dismissed any lingering hope of reconciliation. 'Once you start texting my children – and his two sons have been going for her, too – and legitimise my wife being bullied on the internet, where she has to shut down Instagram accounts because of the vile shit being written about her and my daughter, then it ain't happening.' Liam has no boundaries and doesn't respect those of others. Noel has lots of boundaries and considered it a slight each time Liam crossed them. Liam thought it was funny. It was just a joke and not serious. But to Noel, it was very serious ... and personal. Every time Liam did it, it took another piece out of Noel.

At first, MacDonald claimed to like Liam but when she and Noel split briefly, early in their relationship, she saw the dark side of him. 'He rang me 11 times in one night. It was "fucking bitch" this, "fucking bitch" that.'

Witnessing a fight between Noel and Liam in her hotel room, 'They were rolling around like geckos. Noel's shirt was in ribbons. We left, but then I realised I'd left my bag in there. Noel knocked on the door and it was hurled down the corridor. It just became untenable, exhausting.'

For Sara, the whole friction with Liam was devastating, not just because of the abuse she endured, but because of what it revealed about Noel's past. She saw the same patterns repeating – the same isolation, the same relentless attack, the same deep-seated pain Noel had suffered as a child. 'I think Noel was singled out and bullied by his father. It's happening again. It's a lonely, unpleasant place for Noel to be,' she reflected, trying to make sense of the toxic Gallagher history that now plagued not just her husband, but their entire family.

Sara worried for her children, saying in 2020, when Donovan was twelve and Sonny nine, 'Donovan's new school friends can't understand why he's never met his uncle and he has started googling things. I've said, "You have to stop. You are going to read horrible things about us." I don't want my boys to think that's a normal relationship between brothers.'

She also worried for her stepdaughter Anaïs, who was then twenty years old. 'She had a relationship with Liam growing up ... and for your uncle to refer to you publicly as "his fucking kid" [as he did in the 2018 Twitter spat], I think to myself, how much longer before he goes for Sonny or Donovan?' She also revealed Liam had never met his nephews. Unfortunately this was an established pattern between Noel and Liam, their respective partners and children. The relationships between Noel and Liam's kids became stronger, and the older cousins started to socialise regularly. But at this point, Noel and Liam didn't really have a relationship with their nieces and nephews or with their in-laws or in-laws to be. Noel befriending Molly before her reconnection with Liam seems to have been the exception.

Sara also engaged Schillings, a law firm, who briefed the media on what she characterised as a campaign of harassment against her, asking that defamatory tweets not be printed. She had compiled evidence from social media measuring six inches thick.

At this point, Noel and Sara were based primarily in Petersfield in the South Downs, but they retained a home in London's Maida Vale. 'Noel is always noodling on his guitar, writing music. He never wants to move back to London,' she said, suggesting she was still heading into the city a couple of times a week. Sara was half right. Although Noel was enthusiastic about country life, and had owned a countryside property ever since the days of his marriage to Meg Mathews, he still panged for London. He enjoyed cycling through Hampshire's rural back roads and appreciated the peace and solitude, especially during a period of personal upheaval. But despite these moments of contentment, the isolation frustrated him. Unable to drive, he found the lack of spontaneity suffocating. Unlike the city, where he could make last-minute plans, country life required everything to be scheduled in advance. London offered the energy and excitement he craved. He yearned for the spontaneity and convenience, missing the ability to 'just go to the fucking pub' or pop into a shop on a whim. Being back amongst the people was something he longed for. The accessibility, the ease of socialising and the possibility of a random night out made city life irreplaceable.

Behind the drapes of their expansive country pile, the cracks in Noel and Sara's marriage deepened. Noel has suggested that the COVID pandemic played a part in the end of their relationship. The lockdowns placed an irrevocable strain on them, magnifying their differences. Sara felt that Noel had become increasingly difficult to live with during their stay in the countryside.

Noel loved having – and actually needed – a partner to share his life. Maintaining that became the overriding priority. Ultimately, it was Sara who ended it. Noel put a brave face on the split publicly, saying, 'I know a lot of people in the same boat as me and Sara. Particularly after the pandemic. It's not uncommon for people who have been in long-term relationships to go their separate ways in their fifties. When you get to your mid-fifties, you do come to some kind of crossroads in your life. The midlife crisis thing is true for men and women.' But privately, he was gutted. He really loved Sara and wanted to spend the rest of his life with her. He was completely blindsided by her decision to end their marriage.

Although she had wanted to split, Sara hadn't anticipated the social price it would come at. Her band of friends diminished hugely. Not as many of Sara's friends were as interested in her, rather than her famous husband, as she'd thought. Even during their marriage, many of them had hit on Noel.

It wasn't just Sara's friends who were disappearing. Noel had completely shut off to her, the way he'd done with Meg following his first divorce. Even Anaïs was shocked by the cold shoulder. She had struggled to bond with Noel at times, finding him shut down emotionally, but she'd never seen that degree of emotional isolation from him. But that's Noel. Just ask Liam . . . He just shuts off. He has the ability to act as if he doesn't need anyone or anything in his life.

As Noel's walls rose against Sara, they lowered for Meg and the two established a more cordial and constructive relationship following the January 2023 announcement that he would be getting divorced, with Meg offering conciliatory wishes when they spoke. Until this development, Anaïs had always had to shuttle between the two of them. Although Anaïs had struggled to reach her father at times, they continued to grow closer, especially following his divorce. She has developed into an unaffected and sweet young woman. Despite tedious shouts of 'nepo-baby' online, she has largely built a life independently as an influencer and occasional model. She is quietly confident in her own skin and regularly joins her dad at more social work events. Noel has started to include her more and more in his work life, even allowing Anaïs to shoot a behind-the-scenes documentary of the making of *Council Skies*. It's clear from the camera's gaze that she adores her dad.

Following the split, Sara immediately headed for Ibiza,

seeking an escape from the fallout. Noel, too, felt that partying was the best way to heal. He threw himself into the social scene, immersing himself in music, friends and nights out in an attempt to move forward. But deep down, the loss lingered, an echo of the love he had once believed would last for ever.

He moved into the luxurious Claridge's hotel four nights a week while his new Maida Vale bachelor pad was being renovated, Sara having received the couple's mansion down the road in the divorce settlement. 'I have builders in my house and uh, there's no heating or hot water and there's fucking plumbers in there, and I thought to myself, "Fuck this. I'm going to Claridge's. Bye-bye."'

Reminiscing about his time there, he said, 'I had some proper fucking good times there – it was a proper good time. I lived there for, let me see, most of last year. I had some fucking good times.' It was Alan Partridge at the Linton Travel Tavern on steroids. The reported £10,000 per week digs were at odds with his aversion to spending money, but his luxury accommodation became a form of therapy during the divorce. The weekly rate did make the three-figure monthly contribution he made to the rent on Anaïs's shared flat in Stoke Newington look a little tight in comparison.

As 2023 wore on, the late nights and drinking caught up with him, adversely affecting his health and appearance. 'I was fucked. I looked shit towards the end of last year. I've been drinking, I know ... before the lockdown, I never used to drink. Now I've been drinking every day for four years. I've been drinking kind of half a bottle of wine, but then going on tour and I was like, right, I'm going to move back into London over Christmas and then January.'

Noel decided to give up alcohol for Dry January and pencilled in the High Flying Birds show at the Royal Albert Hall in March 2024 as the end point, ready for the designated blowout.

As time began to heal Noel's broken heart, he became increasingly chipper. 'Things are fucking great in the present. Man City are great, my life is great. I'm happy and healthy. I'm about to go on tour around the world. It's happening now for me.'

In conversation with Matt Morgan, Noel spoke about his new life as a divorced man. Describing his daily bicycle commute from his new Maida Vale flat to his own new Lone Star recording studio in King's Cross, Noel joked: 'I can get on the bike and go down to the canal. And get on the canal path outside my wonderful ex-wife's house and give her a little wave, and go, "You didn't take this from me!"'

Like Liam, Noel's second divorce had strong parallels to his first. He was living in the country with a wife he adored, but the wife missed London's social scene and her drinking was becoming an issue. Only this time, he was the one who was dumped. Sara decided she'd had enough. And as with his first marriage, Noel wanted to keep his country sanctuary as part of the divorce deal.

*

Noel Gallagher's High Flying Birds' fourth album, *Council Skies*, was released in June 2023, having been largely recorded at Lone Star. The album was a blend of old and new. Tracks such as 'Open the Door, See What You Find', a song reportedly inspired by his move back to London after years in the countryside, and 'Dead to the World', a more sombre, introspective ballad, showcased Noel's ability to write songs that were both deeply personal and broadly relatable. 'Dead to the World', although one of the more mellow tracks, quickly became a fan favourite and a staple of his live shows. Noel would go on to describe it as one of the best songs he'd ever written.

Reviews of the *Council Skies* tour were overwhelmingly positive. Critics noted that he had lost none of his ability to connect with an audience, to create moments of collective euphoria. The *Council Skies* tour nonetheless didn't unfold quite as Noel had envisioned. Financial constraints meant that his band, the High Flying Birds, had to forgo certain destinations, including Australia – an omission that left a noticeable gap in the tour's reach. It was the experience of co-headlining a US tour with his old friends in Garbage, however, that left the deepest mark, and not in a positive way.

The reality of the arrangement soon became apparent. Sharing the bill meant that Noel's set was cut in half, diluted between High Flying Birds and Garbage's performance. It wasn't one thing or the other; neither fully Garbage nor High Flying Birds, it was something in between. For fans, it wasn't the immersive experience they had come to expect from his live performances. And for

Noel, it was a frustrating reminder that, sometimes, the road isn't as glamorous as it seems.

An uglier blemish on the tour's face came when Noel brought in Tom Meighan, the former Kasabian frontman, as the opening act for some of his *Council Skies* headline shows. It added another layer to the complicated workings of Noel's internal logic. Particularly when it comes to violence against women.

Meighan had been convicted in 2020 of assaulting his then fiancée Vikki Ager. The court heard how Meighan pushed his partner repeatedly, held her by the throat and threatened her with a wooden pallet. Ager also hit her head on a hamster cage after being thrown across a room. CCTV footage of the incident showed the singer dragging Ager by the ankles, and the attack left her with bruises to her knees, elbow and ankle, and 'a reddening around her neck'.

Meighan originally denied an assault had taken place, but when confronted with the video evidence, he said he couldn't watch it because it was 'horrible'. This ultimately led to his dismissal from Kasabian, who issued a strong statement condemning domestic violence and saying 'There is absolutely no way we can condone his assault conviction.' In contrast, Noel's decision to give Meighan a platform suggested either a disregard for the seriousness of the assault or an intentional choice to prioritise personal loyalty over ethical considerations.

This was particularly jarring given Noel's own experience with domestic abuse growing up and his past criticism of his brother Liam's treatment of women – most notably, allegations of a physical altercation with Debbie Gwyther in 2018 (which both Liam and Debbie said was blown out of all proportion by the media). While Noel has never publicly addressed Meighan's conviction, his continued association with individuals accused of harming women raises questions about his values and what behaviours he deems excusable within his circle. One of the people questioning this was Noel's daughter, Anaïs, who repeatedly asked her father to drop Meighan from the tour.

Loyalty to friends can be admirable, but in cases like this, it risks being seen as a tacit endorsement of inexcusable behaviour. Whether intentional or not, Noel's actions reinforce a troubling inconsistency: he condemned violent or misogynistic behaviour by Liam but appeared willing to overlook it in others such as Meighan and in some of his own statements on women.

Following *Council Skies*, Noel Gallagher initially planned to release an acoustic album – a gesture he described as a kind of fan service. However, midway through the process, he abandoned the project. Explaining his decision, he admitted to Matt Morgan: 'I got six tunes in, and I was so bored with the arrangement of it all and the slow pace of it. And actually, what made me think, right, fuck it, was that they were all songs about a bit of a broken heart, that kind of thing. And I started to sound like *Council Skies* without the strings.'

Not wanting to dwell in emotional territory longer than

necessary, Noel pivoted towards a new direction: a 'defiant rock record'.

This shift in focus led to a future album titled *Eastbound & Down*, after Danny McBride's cult comedy series about a washed-up baseball player. Noel described it as a 'proper rock and roll record' – guitar-driven, heavier, and with a rawer energy more reminiscent of his Oasis days. He emphasised that it wouldn't be 'pop rock' but rather a stripped-back, full-throttle rock album built around guitar and bass.

Gallagher outlined a timeline that included demoing tracks in 2024 and potentially beginning recording by the end of the year, with a projected release date in 2026. Conveniently, this schedule aligns with Oasis's soon-to-be-announced touring plans, stirring speculation that some of the songs originally intended for *Eastbound & Down* might be held back for a potential Oasis reunion album – should the initial tour dates go smoothly.

As Noel entered 2024, he joined Liam in the arthritis club. Noel told Matt Morgan: 'I've got bad knees actually. I've got to have an operation on my fucking knee.'

The Oasis question grew in prominence once Noel and Sara's separation became public. Noel's 'you should never say never' comment to BBC Manchester in January 2023 represented a softening of his previous always-say-never position. He caveated it with 'it would have to take an extraordinary set of circumstances' before leaving the door ajar. 'That's not to say that those circumstances would never come about.'

20

Hello – Noel and Liam, 2024

'The great wait is over. Come see. It will not be televised.' – Oasis

August 2024: This Is It. This Is Happening

The impossible and yet inevitable. The brothers who can't get along but can't escape each other. The Gallagher paradox had produced another chapter.

Liam and Noel Gallagher were back. Oasis was back. In all honesty, ever since Bonehead became the last original member not named Gallagher to leave the band in 1998, Oasis was only about two brothers. They were the centrifugal force at the centre of the Oasis storm and eventually everybody else had been spun out.

Despite the simplicity of the statement and accompanying black and white photograph of the two brothers, the path to reunification was intricate and often fraught.

It involved personal overtures, divorce, business alignment and a really big pot of cash. Noel once half-jokingly told concert promoter SJM that he'd prefer it if they sent him a photo of bins full of cash rather than a plaque to commemorate their joint successes. If he's to get his wish following this tour, SJM and their partner on this venture, Live Nation, are going to need a wide-angle lens.

Those in the music industry had heard that Oasis were holding dates at Wembley for 2023 and 2024 before finally turning the pencil into pen for the 2025 dates. This created a sense of boy-cries-wolf and insiders had begun to think it just wasn't going to happen.

The news that it really was happening, that Oasis were back, transcended nostalgia. The coming together of the two Gallagher brothers who, despite years of public feuding and divergent solo careers, found their way back to the music that had defined them sparked palpable excitement in fans around the world. The fans who were there first time around would revel in reliving the experience, but in the years of separation an entirely new generation of fans had also discovered the band and they would finally have the chance to get the Oasis hit in person.

In the lead-up to the August 2024 announcement there were subtle gestures, hints and a gradual thawing of the icy silence that had characterised Liam and Noel's relationship for fifteen years. Earlier in the year, at a concert in Sheffield, Liam dedicated a song to Noel. Shortly before the reunion, Noel discussed Liam's abilities during an interview with music writer, John Robb, as they thumbed through the vinyls at Mister Sifter's in Manchester. 'I can't sing "Slide Away" and "Cigarettes & Alcohol" and "Rock 'n' Roll Star" and "Columbia" and all that,' Noel explained. 'I mean I can do it but it's not the same. It's the delivery or the tone of his voice and the attitude. I don't have the same attitude as him.' Comparing the Gallagher brothers' voices to drinks, 'Mine's half a Guinness on a Tuesday. It's alright. Liam's is ten shots of tequila on a fucking Friday night.'

Noel also reflected on debut single, 'Supersonic': 'I sing "Supersonic" with the same melody, the same words, the same inflexions, but when he sings it, it's a bit more menacing.' Warming to his praise of Liam he added, 'When I would sing a song it would sound good, when he would sing it, it would sound great.' He also complimented Liam's solo career: 'What he did was inspire the kids at the front to do something, do you know what I mean? "If he can do it I can do it." And he's still doing that now.' This praise of Liam was positively glowing when compared to pretty much every other comment Noel had made about his brother (outside of official Oasis re-release promos) since they had split. He'd managed a few 'fair plays' but that was about it.

Behind the scenes, more substantive conversations were taking place. Paul Gallagher, the eldest of the three brothers, had helped mediate, as had Bonehead and, perhaps most impactfully, Debbie Gwyther. According to Liam, the boys' mother Peggy had wanted for years for him to sort things out with his brother.

Besides a very compelling business case for Noel, his position was softened after he and Sara MacDonald divorced. It was evident to the entire world that she and Liam did not get along and his loyalty to Sara bound Noel to his position. It's an interesting temporal quirk that the period of Oasis's separation aligns very closely with the duration of Noel and Sara's marriage (2009–24 and 2011–23 respectively).

Another significant factor was the maturing family dynamics. Liam's reconnection with his daughter Molly, and the growing bond between all of the Gallagher cousins, created a new context for the brothers' relationship. The friendships between the younger generation of Gallaghers offered a fresh perspective and a reason to reconsider the estrangement. Liam, in particular, spoke about the importance of setting a good example for his children, of showing them that even the most entrenched conflicts can be resolved.

These personal overtures were further seeded by a growing sense of nostalgia, both within Liam and Noel themselves and among their established and new fanbases, prompted by the making of the concert film that documented their career-defining appearance at Knebworth in 1996.

In the years spent apart, both brothers had helped the Oasis brand grow, participating (separately) in documentaries and promoting album re-releases. But Liam had actively pushed the agenda in the live arena most of all when he celebrated the thirtieth anniversary of *Definitely Maybe* in 2024. He'd made overtures for Noel to join him, but Noel didn't feel that was the right time. But that tour and Liam's very successful solo career, which saw him return to Knebworth, had moved the needle for Noel. Liam's success had not only boosted royalties and interest in Noel's publishing assets, it had made him view Liam as more of an equal. Somebody who could add an equal value to the business of Oasis.

In early 2023, Liam began to drop more explicit hints about a possible reunion. He tweeted about missing his brother and about the 'unfinished business' that Oasis still had. He also spoke more openly in interviews about the possibility of reforming the band, stating that he was ready whenever Noel was.

While personal factors had helped clear the path, the business considerations surrounding an Oasis reunion were growing. Their absence had made the hearts of music fans grow fonder. It was clear to promoters that a reunion would be a major global event with enormous financial benefits. Although Oasis profited hugely from the thriving record sales of the nineties and noughties, their live tours were relatively untapped in comparison to the modern touring behemoths on which artists such as Taylor Swift have built their wealth. Oasis toured in an era when the gigs served to promote a record. That has flipped entirely and the record now exists to promote the tour. The Gallaghers did well from their live exploits back in the day, but this would be a category above. A chance to build truly generational wealth. A tour at this moment in time could gross hundreds of millions of pounds, potentially making it one of the most lucrative tours in the history of British music.

With Liam and Noel now under separate management and with discrete recording and publishing agreements, there was a lot to address for their respective management teams, led by Debbie Gwyther for Liam and Marcus Russell for Noel. The thing about contracts in the music industry is they can really draw out the ego and friction between parties. Even the smallest clause can trigger a crack. Both creatively and financially there was a lot to navigate. They had to structure contracts that would be evenly beneficial for the two brothers, and a strategy for touring that reached the most people with the fewest dates.

Mitigating potential for a fallout was top of the planning agenda. Full-scale concerts across dozens of US cities were ruled out. Prolonged periods of sibling proximity combined with the physical toll of road life would simply invite too much risk. So it was decided their shows would take in key global cities and play multiple nights at vast stadiums. This had the additional effect of projecting top-tier status too. No 18,000 arenas in Kansas on this tour. Instead the NFL stadiums of New York, Chicago and Los Angeles – which had always eluded Oasis during their previous tours of the US – were decided on. It was another itch scratched.

The tour would need to be managed expertly. Besides the impressive logistical operation, the brothers themselves would have to be handled with care. The brothers had started travelling separately to gigs in the mid-2000s but this tour, with so much resting on it and heightened insurance and contractual commitments, needed more in terms of a guarantee against fratricide. They would effectively only see each other during the hours spent on stage. The travel, accommodation and media would all be arranged in a way that made Mick Jagger and Keith Richards appear hand in glove.

Another key issue was creative control. Noel had always been the primary songwriter and the driving force behind Oasis's sound. He had always been the one in control of Oasis. That would not work for Liam this time around. He needed equal say and veto on band members, support acts and all things related to performance. With former Oasis members split into the distinct camps of 'Liam', 'Noel' or 'gone for ever', it limited the choice of possible musicians. Although the latest iteration of Oasis wouldn't be an actual band in the true sense, it would seem strange to the fans if it was made up of anonymous session players or people not readily associated with the band's history. Additionally the personnel had to know how to navigate both brothers in a frictionless manner. Their habits – their personal predilections – couldn't be allowed to bring out the devil in Liam either, and the tour could not collapse because the wrong session bassist decided, at the wrong time, that he missed his girlfriend too much to continue. This had happened during Oasis's first proper crack at the States, when Scott McLeod, who was filling in for Guigsy's anxiety-induced absence, suddenly quit after a gig in Pittsburgh.

With all this in mind, the list of candidates for the rebooted Oasis included Bonehead, Gem Archer and Chris Sharrock.

Bonehead had enjoyed life as a touring guitarist in Liam's band and, having overcome throat cancer a few years earlier, was ready to do it all again with his mates from Burnage. He had always been Liam's closest mate in Oasis and Liam didn't feel it would be right for the band to regroup without him. Enough water had passed under enough bridges between Noel and Bonehead since he quit/was sacked in 1998. So Bonehead was in on rhythm guitar, for at least some of the setlist.

Gem Archer was the next to be included. He'd always managed to maintain his seat atop the fence when it came to the Gallagher brothers. If you were to cast Gem in an Oasis film, you'd probably go for a resurrected Richard Beckinsale of *Porridge* and *Rising Damp* fame. He'd played in Beady Eye with Liam, and Noel had brought him into the High Flying Birds after Gem fell on hard times in his personal and professional life following divorce from his first wife, Lou, and his traumatic head injury in 2013. Gem was also managing the art of ageing as a mod brilliantly. So Gem was in albeit with the question of whether he'd sub in and out with Bonehead on guitar or pick up the bass.

That left the drummer. Zak Starkey was too expensive and perhaps not the right person for this particular house of cards. Chris Sharrock was decided on. As with Gem, he'd played with both Noel and Liam in their post-Oasis adventures. They just needed to complete the formality of signing him up. Unfortunately for Oasis, Sharrock felt the wages were derisory and as an upwardly mobile session drummer said 'no thanks'. Wages in Noel's High Flying Birds were pretty low by industry standards so it's hard to know quite how stingy they'd have to be for him to pass up the reunion.

So, at the time of writing, the drummer and possibly the bassist remain open questions. It's possible they'll return to Sharrock with improved terms but that isn't very 'Noel'. There have, of course, been rumours around the supposed lineup, with some reporting that Andy Bell and Joey Waronker will be joining the brothers. But the Oasis camp are playing things close to their chest and nothing has been confirmed.

By early 2024, an agreement was reached and Oasis would reunite. The drip-fed press leaks in the days leading up to the announcement, and the announcement itself, were a masterclass in marketing, designed to maximise impact and generate excitement worldwide. Less was more but it still required careful orchestration. First, they'd announce the UK dates before going on to repeat the feat overseas. Hype rippled through local markets around the world with similar messages, bespoke to fans in each country. LED billboards from Times Square in New York to Sydney illuminated the stony-faced Gallagher brothers looking down on passersby, with the date of when the venues would be announced.

The accompanying promotional photographs were

stark. No smiles at such joyous news for these two Mancunians. Liam, aged fifty-one, and Noel, fifty-seven, looked down the lens sternly. Liam, pulling focus in a shiny, plum-coloured CP Company cagoule (a perhaps unintended reference to the now infamous 'plumgate') and doing his best (sky) blue steel; Noel in Levi's denim trucker jacket looking unimpressed. For most bands, the management and PR would be asking for a bit more enthusiasm, especially given the acrimonious nature of their relationship, but Oasis know their audience. Due to the nature of the compositions, the brothers stood disengaged but overlapping, leading to speculation that the photo was a composite and that the brothers had never actually been in the same room.

However, those rumours were quickly dismissed when it was revealed that the portraits, published in black-and-white, were taken by renowned photographer Simon Emmett. Having previously worked with Liam for *El País Icon* in 2019 and Noel for *Esquire* in 2015, Emmett was the natural choice to document the occasion. Defying expectations, they stood together – a rare and powerful display of unity. 'I know it looks like it could be photoshopped, but they were both there – they met up,' a source told the *Mirror*. 'They were laughing and joking. It was great to see after all these years apart.'

The session was conducted under strict secrecy, with only a handful of people aware of its occurrence. For fans, the sight of the two Gallaghers together again was nothing short of astonishing. Emmett, known for his striking celebrity portraits, managed to capture the raw energy in the room – a charged atmosphere, electric with possibility. For a moment, the past was just a shadow, and the lens focused only on the present.

The 'why?' of the reunion is pretty straightforward, with the Occam's razor being: loadsamoney.

Oasis is more than a band; it is a brand, which is something Noel has always understood. Unlike artists who rely on fleeting chart success, Oasis has built an enduring legacy rooted in identity, authenticity and a deep emotional connection with fans. Rather than simply a collection of hits, their music is the soundtrack of a generation, an experience that transcends time.

Industry experts recognise the power of this approach. 'One of the things I discuss with my students a lot is the power of an artist's identity,' industry veteran manager and UCLA lecturer, Jeff Jampol of JAM Inc. explains. 'When I was managing artists, I used to tell them: I don't manage songs; I manage artists.' Oasis exemplify this principle. Their brand is a force of nature – fiercely independent, culturally significant and driven by a loyal fanbase rather than the whims of the charts.

Some artists thrive on continual hit making, but others, like Oasis, cement their influence through a combination of brand strength, an extensive catalogue and cultural significance. This is what industry insiders call the golden triangle – a rare synergy of elements that makes an artist almost untouchable. 'Sometimes you get this golden triangle where an artist has a solidified brand, is not dependent on hits, and possesses a massive collection of amazing songs. That's Oasis.'

This unique position has given the band an almost limitless commercial potential, akin to a high-performance engine idling, waiting to be unleashed. Jeffrey Jampol, manager of the Doors and other 'long legacy' bands, explains, 'Artists who've been around for 20, 30, 40 years – the power of their brands is like a 428 Cobra Jet engine just sitting in neutral. All you need to do is hook up a transmission, put rubber to the road, and watch what happens. The ratio of effort to reward is off the charts. And that's exactly what's happening with Oasis.' Oasis also embodies the essence of true rock stars – authentic, unapologetic and uninterested in corporate endorsements or trend chasing. 'When you think about rock stars, Oasis was one of the last great rock bands. True rock stars. Not posing for a Gap campaign or buying into becoming an owner of Vitamin Water. Just rock stars because – fuck you.'

This rebellious spirit has added to their allure, amplified by what has been termed the 'red velvet rope syndrome'. Fans are drawn to exclusivity, to the sense of being part of something rare and unpredictable. 'It's like when you walk into a club and see a red velvet rope separating the regular area from the VIP section. There's no real difference, except that rope – but everyone wants to be on the other side. Who wouldn't want to hear "Champagne Supernova", "Wonderwall" or "Cigarettes and Alcohol" performed live by musicians who don't care about anything except the music, who might implode at any moment? That fragility makes it even more exhilarating.'

The timing of the tour announcement was no coincidence. It was the thirtieth anniversary of *Definitely Maybe*, their groundbreaking debut album, and nostalgia was one of the most powerful commercial forces in 2024. Oasis's campaign tapped directly into that sentiment. By framing the reunion around an anniversary, the band capitalised on both emotional and financial incentives. It was a perfect storm: nostalgia meets scarcity, urgency and demand. The Oasis reunion was an expertly timed event designed to maximise its cultural and commercial impact, and fans who grew up with their music are now in their forties and fifties – older, wealthier and more willing than ever to pay for the chance to relive those precious moments from their youth.

In today's music world, artists are primarily in the tickets and T-shirts business, not the recording business. As Jampol explained, 'The income pie chart should look something like this: 60 to 70% tickets, 10 to 25% tour merch depending on genre (metal being the biggest), 10 to 15% publishing, 2 to 5% ancillary, and 2 to 4% records.' He elaborates, 'If you're going to be a successful artist in today's music world, you are in the tickets and T-shirts business. You are not a recording artist.'

For Oasis, a reunion tour would be highly lucrative because they would own 100 per cent of the tour income. Unlike traditional album sales, where profits are often split with labels and distributors, concert revenue flows directly to the band, making live performance one of the most financially rewarding avenues in the modern music landscape. It was just too much money to miss out on.

Noel, in particular, has good reason for doing this tour at this time. Like a retiring gangster who agrees to do one last job, Noel Gallagher has an exit masterplan. His long game has always been strategic, and the upcoming Oasis reunion tour is no exception. Over the years, he has been reducing the length of Sony/ATV's claim over his publishing rights. They revert to him in 2025. Doing an Oasis tour right on top of his rights coming back under his control puts him in the optimal position to capitalise on a sale. So while both brothers could pocket £100 million each from the tour, Noel could bag a lovely 'Brucie Bonus' in the form of a £250 million buy-out of his song catalogue. One silver lining for Noel when it comes to his unwanted divorce from Sara is that she won't be entitled to any of the sale fee.

Noel has acknowledged a dilemma in interviews, weighing whether to leave his catalogue to his children or sell it while he's still alive to enjoy the windfall. 'What do you do? Do you leave it to your kids? They don't value music.' He joked about buying a massive superyacht. 'I've always wanted to buy an 88-metre superyacht and call it *Mega Mega White Thing*. You see them out at sea named things like *Ocean Breeze* – I want the biggest fucking yacht of all time.' Although given his tightfisted reputation, perhaps he wasn't joking about blowing it on a massive boat rather than leaving it to his kids.

Speaking on Matt Morgan's podcast in 2023, Noel stated he was working on a record with a stadium-rock sound. By then, he would have already been far down the process of confirming his return to Oasis. If those songs end up becoming a new Oasis album, it would serve as an immediate kicker to the eventual sale of his publishing rights.

In the short term, the announcement of the tour had already brought him a huge financial boost in terms of royalties, with three Oasis albums returning to the top ten, a raft of singles returning to the charts and a reported 690 per cent spike in Spotify streams globally. With the tour scheduled to run through the 2026 festival season, this surge in streaming numbers will have been sustained for nearly three years, coinciding with the financial evaluation period for any potential catalogue sale. As a result, Noel's publishing catalogue could command an even higher premium, making this tour not just a nostalgia-fuelled reunion but a meticulously planned financial manoeuvre to elevate the value of his intellectual property before a sale.

In the eyes of the fans, the only aspect that cast a shadow over the Oasis reunion was related to ticketing. Despite 2025's seventeen UK and Ireland dates selling out within hours, ticket pricing caused a stir among fans. Before the general sale on Saturday 31 August 2024, ticket prices were outlined as follows: standard standing tickets at approximately £150, standard seated tickets ranging from £73 to £205 (with Manchester being all-standing). Additionally, premium packages – including exclusive merchandise and access to both a pre-show party and a private Oasis exhibition – were available for both seating and standing, priced between £216 and £506.25, depending on the venue and ticket level. These were the official face value prices, but some fans ended up paying much more. Many who reached the Ticketmaster checkout on Saturday were shocked to see prices jump to £350. There were press reports of hundreds of thousands of Oasis fans facing long online queues and limited ticket availability, and then being stung by 'dynamic pricing' when they finally had a chance to buy a ticket. Dynamic pricing is based on supply and demand, allowing ticket prices to fluctuate accordingly. This system is not new and is an optional feature used by promoters and artists in collaboration with ticketing agencies like Ticketmaster. Artists including Taylor Swift and Robert Smith of the Cure have criticised dynamic pricing, and for a while the fallout threatened to overshadow the joy of the Oasis reunion, but not quite.

Oasis's legacy is immense – songs such as 'Don't Look Back in Anger' and 'Live Forever' became anthems of mid-nineties British optimism – but their impact extends beyond their music. The Gallagher brothers are not just estranged siblings; they represent an era, embodying Britpop and the cultural moment they helped define. They are more than musicians; they are icons of a generation's soundtrack.

Besides the inbound bounty, the prospect of earning multimillions, there is something bigger than themselves in the mighty O that has kept these two very different brothers in each other's orbits. Without the band they would have drifted away from each other much, much earlier.

The undulating fortunes of Liam and Noel have only ever matched up when they worked together. Oasis is bigger than them both. It is their universe. Like the big bang it expanded until they became separate planets, very far apart from each other, before gravity inevitably pulled them back together. In this case, the forces of physics are money, ego, personality and love.

It was 2024, thirty years after the release of *Definitely Maybe*, and yet, somehow, the same old story played out. For all the years, all the silence, all the barbed interviews and bitter social media jabs, they remained tethered to each other, bound not just by blood but by a history neither of them could outrun.

Noel, ever the architect, had built a life beyond Oasis – albums, tours, critical acclaim and a sense of control that had always eluded him when Liam was around. And Liam, the eternal frontman, had spent the last few years proving he didn't need his older brother to fill stadiums, to bring that fire to crowds who still chanted his name like a war cry. On paper, they had never needed each other less.

And yet, the cycle was hard to break.

As they prepare to take the stage once again, the old tensions will inevitably resurface. Essentially, for this tour to work, the brothers have to run a three-legged marathon without tripping each other up. In order to do that, they need to avoid the self-destructive Tom and Jerry routines that have defined their entire relationship.

Noel has managed to, if not forgive, at least accept his

brother's nature, for the moment, and has accepted his kid brother back into his life in a way that is interdependent. It's an emotional risk for Noel but one he feels has enough reward attached to it. His tendency to cut people off completely when he feels wronged stands in contrast to Liam's efforts to mend relationships – especially when he was the one who kicked the fences in after too many Guinnesses.

At the heart of the brothers' dynamic is the sibling archetypes they have both adopted since their traumatic days in their shared Burnage bedroom. Noel and Liam, although brothers, are diametrically opposite in behavioural type and characteristics. This shapes the way they see the world and their place in it. It also highlights the differences in how they interact with each other, others, and with the environment.

Noel displays characteristics often associated with what psychologists refer to as the 'responsible child' in dysfunctional families. He exhibits a strong need for control and order – he finds safety in control.

Liam, on the other hand, embodies the 'rebellious child'. He is impulsive, confrontational and seeks attention through acts of defiance and bravado. He needs to live in a vortex – no stability. There's always a sense of danger and unpredictability in his world. Liam frequently acts without considering the consequences, engaging in risky behaviour and making rash decisions. This impulsivity is evident in his personal life, his interactions with the media and his on-stage antics. He is prone to emotional outbursts and displays of anger, a volatility likely stemming from unresolved childhood trauma and difficulty regulating emotions. His anger often manifests in verbal and physical aggression, creating conflict in his relationships and public life.

Noel had spent a lifetime running – from Manchester, from his father, from anything that threatened his control. Liam had spent just as long fighting – against authority, against expectations, against the very idea of standing still. They had been shaped by the same childhood, the same wounds, yet had chosen opposite ways to survive. And despite all their years apart, they remained mirrors of each other, each carrying the burden of what the other refused to admit.

A former staff member who worked at Creation at the height of the Oasis juggernaut and has remained close to both brothers, describes their unique bond: 'Ultimately, you do still really love each other.' She acknowledges that 'they're both very stubborn in their opinions, and their opinions are very different', but their connection runs deep. 'It doesn't matter what the wives or the girlfriends say or what anyone else says. You will never understand the dynamic of those two boys.' And although Liam 'did say stupid things just to be horrible and awful', he would eventually apologise. 'He's a great one for making, you know, peace. He's the one that will make the peace and bring things back together with people.'

If 2024 had proven anything, it was that time had made the Gallaghers more aware of their patterns, even if they hadn't yet figured out how to escape them. And maybe – just maybe – that was the first step towards something neither of them had ever quite managed before.

Forgiveness.

The summer of 2025 will see Liam and Noel Gallagher take to the stage for the first time in sixteen years. Two brothers, reunited if not reconciled. They're a little older and hopefully a lot wiser than the last time. Noel has gracefully eased into the elder statesman of rock vibe. His famous mod cut is now entirely grey. Liam has yet to concede the dark tones of his trademark locks and continues to fight back against the waistband. Divorces, legal fights, family fallouts and replacement hips have all drifted in the water under the Gallagher bridge. But even the eroding sands of time will be no contest for the spirit of rock 'n' roll that strikes when Noel counts in to the opening tune at Cardiff's Principality Stadium on 4 July 2025. The world's most public family reunion will be electrifying.

If the initial run of tour dates goes smoothly, and the boys can resist the urge to unpick old scars, chances are the brothers will announce more dates for the venues they have holds on for 2026 and round the reunion tour off with a lap of honour at the major festivals.

Should they release new music – and Noel is regularly working at his King's Cross studio – to support those additional dates it will be fascinating to see whether Liam's unscratched creative itch results in the first ever Gallagher & Gallagher co-writing credit. It would provide a fitting end to their journey. Live Forever, Oasis.

Acknowledgements

Lesley McEvoy, Ros Urwin, Andrew Loog Oldham, Jeff Jampol, Jezabel, Kat, everybody who was kind enough to speak to me.

Thank you: my family, none of the good things in life would ever have been visible without them. Baby. Andrew. Jon and Safae at RCW. Kelly, Serena, Lucie, Jessica, Kirsteen, Frances and all at Hachette. Simon Astaire for pointing the compass towards true north. ET for their relentless encouragement. The friends and strangers who spread encouragement as they go.

Endnotes

Chapter 1

Page 28, 'Liam's disdain for Gordon ...', Jonathan Heaf, 'Liam Gallagher: "My thing was the whole cliché: the sex, the drugs, the rock'n'roll"', *GQ*, 30 July 2017

Page 29, 'Liam has a lot of buttons ...' quoted in Mat Whitecross, *Supersonic*, 26 October 2016

Page 29, 'I've kind of learnt ...' quoted in NME, 'Noel Gallagher: "Liam is frightened to death of me"', *NME*, 5 October 2005

Chapter 2

Page 37, 'I didn't feel ...' quoted in Nick Reilly, 'Noel Gallagher on the "shitstorm" sparked by Oasis split: "All fucking hell broke loose"', *NME*, 9 June 2021

Page 37, 'It's with some sadness ...' originally posted on oasisinet.com. Accessed via Tim Jonze and Rosie Swash, 'Noel Gallagher to leave Oasis', *Guardian*, 28 August 2009

Page 38, 'The details are not important ...' originally posted on oasisinet.com. Accessed via 'Noel reveals reason for Oasis split', *Express*, 29 August 2009

Page 38, 'I didn't write it. I was in such a fury ...' quoted in jomatami, 'Noel Gallagher Reveals Truth About His Oasis Breakup Statement, Recalls Massive 'Fury, Stress' the Night It Happened', *Ultimate Guitar*, 14 June 2021

Page 42, 'It wasn't a decision I took lightly ...' quoted in Reilly,

'Noel Gallagher on the "shitstorm" sparked by Oasis split: "All fucking hell broke loose"'

Page 43, 'The sudden impact ...' quoted in Tim Jonze, 'Noel Gallagher: "I'll never recover from Oasis fan attack"', *Guardian*, 24 March 2010

Page 45, 'Couldn't go back to England ...' quoted in Reilly, 'Noel Gallagher on the "shitstorm" sparked by Oasis split: "All fucking hell broke loose"'

Chapter 3

Page 49, 'In fact, Liam went on ...', Nick Reilly, 'Liam Gallagher says his life "caved in" when Oasis split up', *Rolling Stone*, 12 January 2024

Page 52, 'I fancied Nicole ...' originally published in *Q*, access via 'Noel & Liam Gallagher - Q - May 2002', oasisinterviews.blogspot.com, May 2002

Page 54, 'Gallagher looked as if ...' quoted in Liza Ghorbani, 'A Night Out With Liam Gallagher', *New York Times*, 2010

Page 54, 'They continued the affair ...' quoted in Emily Smith, 'Exxxclusive!', *New York Post*, 18 July 2013

Page 55, 'We're all writing ...' quoted in Lynn Barber, 'Liam Unleashed', *Sunday Times* magazine, 18 July 2010

Page 62, 'Noel, during the grandiose ...', Neil Crossley, Rob Laing, '"Even before we got to the day of the show, there was a 'concern' ... a concern with Liam" – the story behind the farce and the glory of Oasis's infamous 1996 MTV Unplugged performance', *Music Radar*, 21 November 2023

Chapter 4

Page 66, 'Although he refuted ...', 'NOEL – I DIDN'T CHEAT ON MEG', *NME*, 18 January 2001

Page 67, 'The card like ...' quoted in Vassi Chamberlain, 'Sara MacDonald On The Triumphs, Turbulences And Twitter Wars Of Oasis, *British Vogue*, 5 April 2020

Page 73, 'I almost called ...' originally published in MOJO, accessed via 'Noel Gallagher Almost Abandoned New Album', stopcryingyourheartout.co.uk, 27 July 2011

Chapter 5

Page 84, 'Perhaps Liam's angst ...', David Pilditch, 'I am Liam and Noel Gallagher's secret sister ... but here is the real reason why my multi-millionaire Oasis star brothers will NEVER meet me', *Daily Mail*, 15 September 2024

Page 86, 'Pennies they'd throw ...' quoted in Jason O'Toole, 'Liam Gallagher Opens Up About Needing Help To Pen "Big Songs" For Solo Album', *Hot Press*, 25 May 2017

Page 86, 'Drinking too much ...' quoted in Adam White, "Liam Gallagher slams brother Noel, divorce lawyers and his career in interview: 'Am I a has-been?'", *Telegraph*, 25 May 2017

Page 88, 'Why do you want ...' originally on XFM, accessed via Tom Goodwyn, 'Noel Gallagher: "Beady Eye had to ask permission to play 'Wonderwall'"', *NME*, 15 August 2012

Page 95, 'Beady Eye regret to announce ...' originally posted to beadyeyemusic.com, accessed via David Renshaw, 'Beady Eye cancel V Festival appearance following injury to Gem Archer', *NME*, 8 August 2013

Chapter 6

Page 103, 'Playing bass ...' quoted in 'Noel Gallagher's High Flying Birds' new album: everything we know so far about "Chasing Yesterday"', *NME*, 15 January 2015

Chapter 7

Page 113, 'I'm a cunt' posted to X/Twitter, https://x.com/liamgallagher/status/768776765028331520, 25 August 2016

Page 114, 'Do I really ...' quoted in Cian Traynor, 'Liam Gallagher at his unapologetic, audacious best', *Huck*, 1 September 2017

Page 114, 'I was gonna ...' quoted in Alistair Foster, 'Liam Gallagher: I thought I was a has-been but new love helped me roll with it', *Standard*, 24 May 2017

Page 114, 'I got this ...' originally published in *Mirror*, accessed via 'Liam Gallagher On Being Depressed And Bored', stopcryingyourheartout.co.uk, 1 August 2017

Page 115, 'He's making a ...' quoted in David Renshaw, 'Noel Gallagher says "Liam's making a fucking mess of things at the moment"', *NME*, 14 January 2015

Page 116, 'Debbie saved ...' originally published in *Q*, accessed via '"It's Boring Without Me": The Best Quotes From Liam Gallagher's Hilarious New Interview', *NME*, 23 August 2016

Page 117, 'I think I've ...' quoted in Miranda Sawyer, 'Liam Gallagher: 'Rock'n'roll saved my life'', *Guardian*, 4 June 2017

Page 118, 'I go for ...' ibid.

Page 119, 'Well yeah ...' originally published in *Vice*, accessed via Luke Morgan Britton, 'Liam Gallagher: "The majority of solo stars are c*nts"', *NME*, 9 August 2017

Page 120, 'Very excited to ...' quoted in 'Warner Records UK Signs Iconic Frontman Liam Gallagher', wmg.com, 25 August 2016

Page 120, 'Flair, attitude ...' originally published in *Q*, accessed via Elias Leight, 'Liam Gallagher Plans New Solo "Chin-Out" Album', *Rolling Stone*, 25 August 2016

Page 121, 'I'd like it ...' quoted in Sawyer, 'Liam Gallagher: 'Rock'n'roll saved my life''

Page 121, 'Not even if ...' originally published in *Q*, accessed via 'Some More Bits From Liam Gallagher's Interview With Q Magazine That's On Sale Now', stopcryingyourheartout.co.uk, 23 August 2016

Page 121, 'But he set ...' quoted in Heaf, 2017

Page 122, 'Noel lives in ...' originally published in *Q*, accessed via Jazz Monroe, 'Liam Gallagher's First Interview in 3 Years Is Everything You Want It to Be', pitchfork.com, 23 August 2016

Page 124, '"When I met him ...' quoted in 'My Heroes, My History, My Life in Music', *NME Gold*, 26 October 2017

Page 124, Tweets accessed via 'Why did Oasis break up? The story of Liam and Noel Gallagher's feud... and reunion', Radio X, 4 September 2024

Page 125, Tweets accessed via Jennifer Ruby, 'Lisa Moorish says Noel Gallagher was with Liam's daughter "who he has never met" during One Love Manchester concert', *Standard*, 5 June 2017

Page 126, 'I've just never ...' quoted in Gavin Martin and Frances Kindon, 'Liam Gallagher has NEVER met his two daughters because he 'hasn't got round to it'', *Mirror*, 17 February 2018

Page 126, 'Weed's all right ...' quoted in Sawyer, 'Liam Gallagher: 'Rock'n'roll saved my life''

ENDNOTES

Chapter 8

Page 131, "People who've made ..." quoted in Pat Gilbert, *MOJO*, November 2018

Page 132, 'I suggested making ...' originally published in *Uncut*, accessed via 'David Holmes says Noel Gallagher is incredibly creative when he wants to be', oasismania.co.uk, 17 November 2017

Page 134, 'Split his ...' originally published in *Q*, accessed via Robin Murray, 'Noel Gallagher Wants To Shake Off The "Parka Monkeys"', *Clash*, 9 November 2017

Page 135, 'She's French and ...' quoted in Matthew Whitehouse, '"i'm over here doing my thing, you're over there doing my thing" – noel gallagher on liam, scissors and his most joyful record yet', *i-D*, 10 November 2017

Page 136, 'I'm not a fan ...' originally published in *Q*, accessed via Andrew Trendell, 'Noel Gallagher discusses "common pigeon" Liam's new album and "Donald Trump" Twitter antics', *NME*, 24 October 2017

Page 136, 'I've been very consistent ...' originally published in *Q* magazine, accessed via '"I could never forgive him" - All the times Noel and Liam Gallagher addressed a potential Oasis reunion over the last 15 years', Fionnula Hainey, *Manchester Evening News*, 27 August 2024

Page 138, 'It's only now ...' quoted in Laura Craik, 'Anaïs Gallagher on life as rock n' roll royalty, her 'second mum' Kate Moss and those Brooklyn Beckham rumours', *Standard*, 23 February 2017

Page 139, 'U look like ...' originally posted on Twitter, accessed via Olivia Waring, 'WONDERBRAWL Liam Gallagher's son Gene lashes out at cousin Anais – saying she looks like Noel "in a wig"', *Sun*, 20 September 2017

Page 139, 'Anaïs had always loved her dad ...', Craik, 'Anaïs Gallagher on life as rock n' roll royalty'

Chapter 9

Page 143, 'One of the ...' posted to X/Twitter, https://x.com/liamgallagher/status/1154645622043160576, 26 July 2019

Page 145, 'While I wasn't ...' quoted in Sawyer, 'Liam Gallagher: 'Rock'n'roll saved my life''

Page 146, 'I had enough ...' quoted in 'Why did Oasis break up? The story of Liam and Noel Gallagher's feud... and reunion', Radio X, 4 September 2024

Chapter 10

Page 150, 'I'm genuinely not competitive ...' quoted in Gilbert 2018
Page 150, 'Good luck ...' ibid.
Page 152, 'I might have ...' quoted in 'WATCH: Noel Gallagher returns to the 70s in Black Star Dancing video', Radio X, 11 May 2019
Page 152, 'I'm not trying ...' quoted in Emily Zemler, 'Noel Gallagher's High Flying Birds Preview EP With "Black Star Dancing"', *Rolling Stone*, 2 May 2019
Page 153, 'Noel then accused ...' originally posted to Twitter, accessed via Issy Sampson, 'NO-ASIS Noel Gallagher accuses Liam of sending threatening messages about his wife to his teenage daughter – and puts it all on Twitter', *Sun*, 3 July 2019 and Jacob Stolworthy, 'Liam Gallagher apologises after 'sending threats' to Noel's teenage daughter Anais', *Independent*, 4 July 2019
Page 154, 'Shaking ...' quoted in Rachel Dale, 'LIAM RAGE Oasis star Liam Gallagher "grabbed girlfriend Debbie Gwyther by throat in vicious row on night out and calls her a f***ing witch"', *Sun*, 24 August 2018
Page 155, 'Because I've got ...' quoted in Tim Jonze, 'Noel Gallagher: "I liked my mum until she gave birth to Liam"', *Guardian*, 5 August 2019
Page 156, 'A fuckwit of ...' originally published in *Now*, accessed via 'Noel on ...', oasisinterviews.blogspot.com, 1 May 2002
Page 156, 'People keep asking ...' quoted in Gilbert 2018

Chapter 11

Page 161, 'It's fucking raining ...' quoted in Olive Pometsey, 'Exclusive: Liam Gallagher combats the elements in a behind-the-scenes clip of his One Of Us music video', *GQ*, 10 September 2019

Chapter 12

Page 168, 'My father was a labourer ...' quoted in Paul Gallagher & Terry Christian, *Brothers from Childhood to Oasis: The Real Story* (London: Virgin Books, 1996)
Page 170, 'Ah, Dad wasn't ...' ibid.
Page 170, 'Peggy Gallagher reflected ...', ibid.
Page 172, 'With Noel and Peggy ...', Liam McInerney, 'Inside Oasis' family life – "forgotten" older brother who shunned fame and "abusive dad"', *Daily Star*, 20 August 2024
Page 173, 'God, I don't ...' quoted in Sawyer, 'Liam Gallagher: 'Rock'n'roll saved my life"'
Page 175, 'Everything I needed ...' quoted in Whitecross, *Supersonic*
Page 175, 'Somebody knocked the ...' ibid.
Page 175, 'I was 14 ...' quoted in The Howard Stern Show, 'How a Head Injury Led Liam Gallagher Into Music', 2017
Page 176, 'Not a big ...' quoted in Rich Pelley, 'Liam Gallagher: "Would I give Noel a kidney? Without a doubt"', *Guardian*, 26 May 2022
Page 176, 'His mother said ...' quoted in Gallagher & Christian, *Brothers from Childhood to Oasis*
Page 179, 'It was the best ...' quoted in Whitecross, *Supersonic*
Page 180, 'I thought ...' ibid.
Page 181, 'I'll join your band ...' quoted in Paolo Hewitt, *Getting High: The Adventures of Oasis* (London: Boxtree Ltd., 1997)
Page 184, 'They were so volatile ...' quoted in Alan McGee, *Creation Stories: Riots, Raves and Running a Label* (London: Pan Macmillan, 2014)

Chapter 13

Page 189, 'We were a live band ...' quoted in Whitecross, *Supersonic*
Page 189, 'Liam was a live wire ...' originally published in *Q* in 2010, accessed via 'Owen Morrison On Mixing Definitely Maybe' on recordingyourmusic.blogspot.com 14 July 2016
Page 191, 'It was a serious ...' quoted in Peter Shuttleworth, 'Oasis: "I thought I split the band in Morning Glory recording sessions"', *BBC News*, 2 October 2020
Page 191, 'Now, I realise ...' quoted in Heaf, 2017

Page 199, 'Life affirming ...' quoted in Jake Scott, *Oasis Knebworth 1996*, 24 September 2021

Page 200, 'The referee ...' quoted in Gallagher & Christian, *Brothers from Childhood to Oasis*

Chapter 14

Page 202, 'Acid house and ...', Beth Neil, 'ROCK STEADY Britpop party queen Meg Mathews on drugs, divorce and why she's determined to break the taboo surrounding menopause', *Sun*, 24 November 2019 and Alice Hinds, '"I thought my wild '90s life had finally caught up with me. Then I learned I wasn't alone": Meg Mathews on the impact of menopause', *Sunday Post*, 14 October 2020

Page 208, 'Just fifteen minutes ...', 'Liam gives Oasis a scare', *BBC News*, 29 November 1999

Page 209, 'He particularly disliked ...', 'Noel Gallagher says Liam was 'weak' for not standing up to Patsy Kensit', www.femalefirst.co.uk, 4 May 2020

Chapter 15

Page 212, 'After he married ...' quoted in Carlos Megia, "An idiot with kids' and a compulsive cheater: Why Liam Gallagher is the worst husband in the world according to his ex-wives', *El País*, 8 August 2024

Page 212, 'Patsy lost it ...', Olivia Buxton, "I've had enough passion to last me a lifetime': Patsy Kensit on why she'll never marry again', *Mirror*, 21 April 2012

Page 212, 'I cried every ...' quoted in Laura Carreno, 'Patsy Kensit "cried every day" she was with Liam Gallagher as she lifts lid on nightmare marriage', *Mirror*, 28 August 2024

Page 213, 'We just clicked ...' ibid.

Page 213, 'In many ways ...' quoted in Francesca Cookney, 'Exclusive: Patsy Kensit on life with Liam Gallagher: I knew about his womanising but I regretted leaving him', *Mirror*, 7 October 2013

Page 214, 'I'm a father now ...' originally published in *Q*, accessed via 'Liam gives Oasis a scare', *BBC News*, 29 November 1999

Page 214, 'She later revealed ...', Cookney, 'Patsy Kensit on life with Liam Gallagher'
Page 215, 'I don't have to ...' originally published in *Now*, accessed via 'Noel on ...', oasisinterviews.blogspot.com, 1 May 2002
Page 216, 'Liam's better off ...' ibid.
Page 216, 'Liam used to ...' originally published in *Daily Telegraph*, accessed via 'Noel Gallagher – Daily Telegraph – 19th June 2001', oasisinterviews.blogspot.com, June 2001
Page 217, 'The Oasis Knebworth ...' quoted in Michael Odell, 'Meg Mathews', *Guardian*, 6 January 2008
Page 219, 'Meg estimated ...', Jack Newman, 'Meg Mathews reveals she would regularly spend £4,000 a night on drink and drugs during her marriage to Noel Gallagher', *Mail*, 5 June 2020
Page 219, 'We met through drugs ...' quoted in Janine Gibson, 'Gallaghers "lived for drink and drugs"', *Guardian*, 29 January 2000
Page 220, 'I had the baby ...' originally published in *News of the World*, accessed via 'I'm Sick of Noel's Lies', https://members.tripod.com/oasis_5/art19.html, 4 February 2001
Page 222, 'That woman has ...' originally published in *Daily Telegraph*, accessed via 'Noel Gallagher – Daily Telegraph – 19th June 2001', https://oasisinterviews.blogspot.com, 19 June 2001
Page 222, 'I never got ...' quoted in Odell, 'Meg Mathews'
Page 222, 'Grow up ...' quoted in Alison Maloney, 'SAD SONG Inside troubled life of Noel Gallagher's party queen ex Meg Mathews ... £4K benders with Kate Moss to "hitting rock bottom"', *Sun*, 11 July 2023
Page 223, 'The party girls ...' quoted in 'NOEL – SOUR AND NOT SO PROUD', *NME*, 19 June 2001
Page 224, 'After I had ...' originally published in *Daily Telegraph*, accessed via 'Noel Gallagher – Daily Telegraph – 19th June 2001', https://oasisinterviews.blogspot.com, 19 June 2001
Page 224, 'Me and Noel ...' quoted in Odell, 'Meg Mathews'
Page 226, 'The sound of ...' quoted in Dorian Lynskey, '"Flattened by the cocaine panzers" – the toxic legacy of Oasis's Be Here Now', *Guardian*, 6 October 2016

Chapter 16

Page 237, 'Touching festive ballad' quoted in Will Richards, 'Liam Gallagher's new song "All You're Dreaming Of" is a touching festive ballad', *NME*, 27 November 2020

Page 239, 'Silence is golden ...' originally posted to Twitter, accessed via 'Noel Gallagher slams brother Liam and mocks his Once track on Twitter', radiox.co.uk, 17 February 2020

Page 241, 'He should call ...' quoted in 'White & Jordan LIVE with Noel Gallagher', talkSPORT, 23 May 2020

Chapter 17

Page 247, 'The whole thing ...' quoted in Nick Reilly, 'Noel Gallagher refuses to wear face masks: "There's too many fucking liberties being taken away"', *NME*, 15 September 2020

Chapter 18

Page 251, 'Very fucking soon ...' quoted in Nick Reilly, 'Liam Gallagher says "greedy" Noel won't be able to turn down Oasis reunion offer', *NME*, 29 February 2020

Page 252, 'It's all happened ...' quoted in Andrew Trendell, 'Liam Gallagher's formerly estranged daughter Molly Moorish speaks out on their relationship', *NME*, 17 June 2019

Page 253, 'Entitled ...' quoted in Tristan Kirk, 'Liam Gallagher's son and Ringo Starr's grandson blasted by judge for "out of order" brawl in Hampstead Tesco', *Standard*, 1 April 2022

Page 255, 'Oh, I turned it ...' quoted in Nick Reilly, '"Go fuck yourself": Noel Gallagher explains why he wouldn't let Liam use Oasis songs in "As It Was"', *NME*, 11 July 2019

Page 256, 'I've met my soulmate' quoted in Maria Chiorando and Eleanor Dye, 'Who is Liam Gallagher's fiancée? How Debbie Gwyther has transformed his lifestyle and is even credited with the Oasis reunion - despite 11-year age gap', *Daily Mail*, 28 September 2024

Page 256, 'The Liam I know ...' quoted in Gavin Fitzgerald, Charlie Lightening, *Liam Gallagher: As It Was*, 6 June 2019

Page 256, 'Morning Rastas ...' originally posted to Twitter, accessed via 'Liam Gallagher says he's "getting there" following hip surgery', radiox.co.uk, 13 April 2023

Chapter 19

Page 260, 'Yeah, I'm in ...' originally published in *Now*, accessed via 'Noel on ...', oasisinterviews.blogspot.com, 1 May 2002

Page 260, 'Her bark is ...' quoted in Chamberlain, 'Sara MacDonald On The Triumphs, Turbulences And Twitter Wars'

Page 261, 'Think it's time ...' originally posted to Twitter, accessed via Tom Connick, 'Liam Gallagher says Noel's wife "is the reason Oasis is no longer"', *NME*, 28 February 2018

Page 261, 'I know for a fact ...' originally posted to Twitter, accessed via Rebecca Taylor, 'Liam Gallagher: Noel wants Oasis reunion but his wife "won't let him"', *Sky News*, 12 January 2018

Page 261, 'Him and her ...' originally posted to Twitter, accessed via Mel Evans, 'Liam Gallagher blames Noel's wife for breaking up Oasis in expletive-ridden rant', *Metro*, 28 February 2018

Page 262, 'Please God ...' originally posted to Twitter, accessed via Mike P Williams, 'Liam Gallagher told to "drop dead" by Noel's wife after comments about daughter', *Yahoo News*, 20 February 2018

Page 262, 'Coz I need ...' originally posted to Twitter, accessed via Eve Buckland, '"She's up there with Putin!": Liam Gallagher SLAMS estranged brother Noel's wife Sara MacDonald in ANOTHER bizarre Twitter rant.... after likening the pair to "SERIAL KILLERS"', *Daily Mail*, 16 March 2018

Page 262, 'Once you start ...' Jonze, 'Noel Gallagher: "I liked my mum until she gave birth to Liam"'

Page 262, 'He rang me 11 ...' quoted in Chamberlain, 'Sara MacDonald On The Triumphs, Turbulences And Twitter Wars'

Page 263, 'Donovan's new school ...' ibid.

Page 265, 'I know a lot ...' quoted in Simon Boyle, 'OAS-PLIT Noel Gallagher breaks silence on shock 20 year marriage split after being spotted on dates with models', *Sun*, 15 May 2023

Page 267, 'I have builders ...' quoted in Matt Morgan Patreon Podcast, July 2023

Page 267, 'I had some ...' quoted in Charlotte McIntyre, 'Oasis' Noel Gallagher's surprise divorce from wife Sara and Liam's scathing digs', *Mirror*, 27 August 2024

Page 268, 'Things are ...' quoted in 'Noel Gallagher on his divorce: "A lot of people are in the same boat after COVID"', radiox.co.uk, 16 May 2023

Page 268, 'I can get on ...' quoted in Charlotte McIntyre, 'Oasis' Noel Gallagher's surprise divorce from wife Sara and Liam's scathing digs', *Mirror*, 27 August 2024

Page 270, 'A reddening ...' quoted in Mark Savage, 'Kasabian confirm they ordered Tom Meighan to leave after his assault charge', *BBC News*, 8 July 2020

Page 271, 'I got six ...' quoted in Damian Jones, 'Noel Gallagher says he has scrapped acoustic album and wants to do a "defiant rock record"', *NME*, 5 April 2024

Page 271, 'Proper rock ...' quoted in Matt Morgan Patreon Podcast, April 2024

Page 272, 'I've got bad ...' quoted in 'Noel Gallagher frustrated over "bad knees" as he reveals he'll need operation', radiox.co.uk, 9 July 2024

Page 272, 'You should never ...' quoted in 'Noel Gallagher says he will never say never to Oasis reunion', *BBC News*, 17 January 2023

Chapter 20

Page 273, 'The great wait ...' posted to Instagram, www.instagram.com/oasis/p/C_KnmhWNhji, 27 August 2024

Page 275, 'I can't sing ...' quoted in Nick Reilly, 'Noel Gallagher praises Liam: "I don't have the same attitude as him"', *Rolling Stone*, 23 August 2024

Page 277, 'Unfinished business' originally posted to Twitter, accessed via 'Liam Gallagher says "Oasis have unfinished business"', radiox.co.uk, 8 June 2020

Page 282, 'I know it looks ...' quoted in Mark Jefferies, 'New Liam and Noel Gallagher Oasis photo sparks concern as fans spot major problem', *Mirror*, 27 August 2024

Page 286, 'One silver lining ...', Lizzie Edmonds, 'Noel Gallagher opens up about "£20 million" divorce from Sara MacDonald', *Standard*, 23 January 2024

Page 286, 'What do you ...' originally on Funny How? podcast, accessed via Natasha Hooper, 'Noel Gallagher reveals he plans to sell Oasis back catalogue for £200M to splurge on a superyacht', *Daily Mail*, 18 June 2021